# THE PROBLEM OF GOD

# THE PROBLEM OF GOD

## THE CHALLENGES OF FAITH, RELIGION, AND SPIRITUALITY TODAY

**Erin M. Cline**

GEORGETOWN UNIVERSITY PRESS / WASHINGTON, DC

Library of Congress Cataloging-in-Publication Data

Names: Cline, Erin M. author
Title: The problem of God : the challenges of faith, religion, and spirituality today / Erin M. Cline.
Description: Washington, DC : Georgetown University Press, [2026] | Includes bibliographical references and index.
Identifiers: LCCN 2025020049 (print) | LCCN 2025020050 (ebook) | ISBN 9781647126841 hardcover | ISBN 9781647126858 paperback | ISBN 9781647126865 ebook
Subjects: LCSH: God—Proof | Theodicy | Religious pluralism
Classification: LCC BT103 .C595 2026 (print) | LCC BT103 (ebook) | DDC 231—dc23/eng/20251128
LC record available at https://lccn.loc.gov/2025020049
LC ebook record available at https://lccn.loc.gov/2025020050

∞ This paper meets the requirements of ANSI/NISO Z39.48-1992 (Permanence of Paper).

EU GPSR Authorized Representative
LOGOS EUROPE, 9 rue Nicolas Poussin, 17000, LA ROCHELLE, France
Email: Contact@logoseurope.eu

27 26 9 8 7 6 5 4 3 2 First printing

Printed in the United States of America

Cover design by Brad Norr
Interior design by Paul Hotvedt

*To my friends from Lake Shore Baptist Church in Waco, Texas,*
*who explored the problem of God with me*
*while showing me God's kind of love.*

Lest we think the blessing is not in the mire, the grime, the muck.
Lest we think God cannot reach deep into the things of earth,
cannot bring forth the blessing that shimmers within the sludge,
cannot anoint us with a tender and grimy grace.
—Jan Richardson, "Blessing of the Mud"

# Contents

# Acknowledgments

Although "The Problem of God" is a signature course at Georgetown University, I owe much of my approach to my training in graduate school in the Department of Philosophy at Baylor University, from which I received my PhD. Although I did not realize it at the time, my particular education (especially Baylor's commitment to exploring the relationship between faith and reason) uniquely prepared me for the interdisciplinary teaching and research I do today on the boundaries of philosophy, theology, and religious studies. I thank Bill Cooper, C. Stephen Evans, and Robert C. Roberts for many thought-provoking classes and conversations. The late Carl Vaught and Stuart Rosenbaum also played key roles in my development as a teacher and scholar, and as a person of faith. But the influence of Bob Baird left the deepest imprint on me, and I was honored that he read the entire manuscript of this book and gave me detailed feedback, which improved it immeasurably. It was a joy to work with him—and to continue to learn from him—and I am profoundly grateful.

I thank my dear friend and colleague Otto Hentz, SJ, for his incredibly generous foreword and for all he has done to bring "The Problem of God" course to so many people around the world. I am honored to follow in his footsteps in teaching the course. I also thank Georgetown's Office of Mission and Ministry for the Jesuit Mission Grant that made this book possible. I am especially grateful for the support of Mark Bosco, SJ, vice president for mission and ministry.

I thank my colleagues and fellow teachers of "The Problem of God" at Georgetown for numerous conversations about its topics over the years, including Ariel Glucklich; Elizabeth Antus; Min-Ah Cho; Stephen Fields, SJ; Peter Folan, SJ; Julia Lamm; Leo Lefebure; Dan Madigan, SJ; Joe Murphy; Andrew Prevot; Jonathan Ray; Bud Ruf; Theresa Sanders; Salih Sayilgan; Michael Slater; Chris Steck, SJ; Lauve Steenhuisen; Julia Watts Belser; Bill Werpehowski; Stephen Wilson; and Lisa Zaina. I also thank all the students I have taught over the years in "The Problem of God" and related courses, whose questions guided my exploration of these issues.

I was honored to have two of my former students, Rebecca Friedman and Juan Connelly, read the entire manuscript and give me detailed feedback. I thank them both for their remarkably keen insights, suggestions, and encouragement. I also thank Juan Connelly for helping to create digital versions of the diagrams.

I am grateful to my editor at Georgetown University Press, Al Bertrand, who approached me with the original idea for this book, persisted until I had the time to write it, and then provided invaluable feedback on the manuscript. He was truly an outstanding editor and a joy to work with, and although his untimely death meant that he was unable to see this book in print, I hope it honors him in a way that is fitting and meaningful. I thank Don Jacobs, Hope LeGro, and Rachel McCarthy for seeing the book through to the finish line, and Tony Arend for his support and encouragement. I am also grateful to three anonymous referees for the Press, who provided excellent suggestions on the book's proposal and its final text; their recommendations resulted in a much better book. My thanks also go to Alfred Imhoff for excellent copyediting and the entire team at the Press for bringing the book to fruition.

Two of my closest friends were pivotal in writing the book, so much that it might not have seen the light of day—and certainly would not have been as good—if not for them. I am grateful to my friend and colleague Peter Folan, SJ, for his unfailing friendship and support in everything I do (including generously sharing his office with me when mine flooded while I was finishing the book). He teaches one of the best "Problem of God" courses at Georgetown, and our conversations enrich my teaching and writing in too many ways to name. My deepest thanks also go to my dear friend the Reverend Lisa Zaina, who leads the Forget-Me-Not House Church, an Episcopal congregation in the Diocese of Washington that serves families with neurodivergent children and anyone looking for a church home that is welcoming in different ways. Lisa presides each week at our church, which meets in my home, works full time, and also teaches theology part time at Georgetown, and I owe her a huge debt of gratitude for endless conversations and collaborations on faith, prayer, Christianity, and the problem of God, and especially for all her love and support in all my endeavors.

As always, I thank my family for their support. My mom, Dorothy Cline, is always a source of love and encouragement, and I know she is looking forward to this book in particular. My children, Patrick, Bridget, and Siobhan, ask the best theological questions, and they are constantly leading me to think in new ways about God. One day, I hope they will read this book for themselves and see how they have taught me to find God in all things.

This book touches on some of the wonderful religious communities of which I have been a part over the years. I thank the Reverend Ed Stanton and Blythe Stanton, the Reverend David Kidd and Pam Kidd, the Reverend Charles Martindell, the Reverend Dan Lush, the Reverend Lisa Talbott, and the Right Reverend Chilton Knudsen for nurturing my faith and showing me deep friendship over the course of my life. Special thanks to my friends Bill

Werpehowski and Kevin O'Brien, SJ, for their words of wisdom that found their way into these pages.

This work is dedicated to the faith community I joined during graduate school—a time when my faith was tested and formed in deep and challenging ways. My friends at Lake Shore Baptist Church actively encouraged difficult questions and wrestled with them just as I did, while living out the Gospel in a way that set the bar for every subsequent religious community I would encounter. My relationship with Lake Shore has turned out to be a lifelong one, as I have remained connected to my church family there across the miles and years. I especially thank Bob and Alice Baird, the Reverend Sharlande Sledge, the Reverend Dorisanne Cooper, Bruce and Terri Evans, Preston and Genie Dyer, and the Reverend Nick Mumejian—as well as the many other wonderful friends I made there—for showing me what a church family should be.

# Foreword

Erin Cline has been an exceptionally gifted professor of "The Problem of God" course for sixteen years, deeply esteemed by her students. I am honored by her invitation to offer this foreword.

Why me? The obvious reason: seniority. I have been a member of Georgetown's Department of Theology and Religious Studies for forty-nine years, and for forty-six of these years I have taught "The Problem of God," as well as courses in Roman Catholic theology.

Undergraduate education at schools in the Catholic and Jesuit traditions like Georgetown require coursework in theology and religious studies. Although pluralist in the student body and pluralist academically, Jesuit universities consider addressing faith in God, or not, to be fundamental to a liberal arts education. The reasoning is clear: a liberal arts education seeks to provide the formation for freedom—that is, intelligent life choices based on a serious effort to understand what it means to be human. This understanding requires inquiry about the reality of God, for the reality of God touches the meaning of everything.

"The Problem of God" course was introduced at Georgetown in the late 1960s as part of the revision of a curriculum that was thought to be outdated. The course title was borrowed from a book by John Courtney Murray, SJ, which is composed of three lectures delivered at Yale University, the third devoted to the existence of God in the face of modern forms of atheism.

The title of the course puzzles people. Why state the subject of God as a problem, especially at a university that understands itself as standing in the Roman Catholic and Jesuit traditions? However, I think the title is pedagogically effective. As a question, it frames the matter as a subject for inquiry, not simply a doctrine to be absorbed. As one Jesuit noted, students should enjoy the freedom to ask questions about God, for they are the ones ultimately responsible for their faith. Further, the question implies that the subject is not only a matter of curiosity but is also existentially significant, for it summons a mature decision about religious faith.

At Georgetown, students are required to take two courses in the Department of Theology and Religious Studies, one of which is "Biblical Literature" or "The Problem of God." The vast majority choose "The Problem of God," though they are welcome to take "Biblical Literature" as well as one of an array of varied electives. In fact, because for well over fifty years most Hoyas have taken "The Problem of God" course, it has been a bonding experience in their formation.

For me, teaching "The Problem of God" has been a joy, for it engages bright young people in a conversation about a matter fundamental to the human story. Most of the course's students are in their first year and are so fresh. For most of them, the material is unfamiliar. They are curious, perhaps hesitant, about the subject, and in some cases are a touch annoyed by the requirement. As a professor, one gets a first shot at engaging their interest.

Part of my appreciation of the opportunity to teach this course is the challenge. The students have grown up in a culture where the dominant mode of knowing is empiricism—that is, sense experience or science, engaging realities that by their nature are thing-like, figurable objects out there to be dealt with. But God is not a being one can get one's head around. So the teacher needs to invite students to consider the possibility of different kinds of knowing for different kinds of reality.

More specifically, what people mean by "God" is not a being among beings, nor a player on the field of human life, but a reality above, beneath, and around, embracing the whole game. To be aware of, or "know," such a reality, one needs to somehow experience it or be connected to it. Inquiry about God involves reflection to discover or strengthen the connection between the person and God. This requires a turn toward interiority, a look at one's looking, one's knowing, one's reaching to know. Otherwise, God cannot be found. This interiority is challenging for students who think of knowing as looking for something, so to speak, out there, to be spotted. This process can cause students to wonder, "Where did this professor come from—what planet?"

Professor Cline describes her particular treatment of the course as a "revisiting." And so it is. She brings to it her expertise in Eastern religions—such as Hinduism, Confucianism, and Daoism—as well as Western Christianity, weaving consideration of them into the various dimensions of the Problem of God. In her revisitation, pluralism is not just an issue added to the problem's regular elements but is also integral to their exposition.

I appreciate this opportunity to congratulate Professor Cline, my colleague and friend, for her wonderfully rich revisitation of "The Problem of God."

Otto Hentz, SJ
September 10, 2024

# INTRODUCTION

On a frozen night in 1914, at the height of World War I, the unimaginable happened. A young soldier fell to his knees and laid down his weapon on the battlefield, unable to bring himself to fire his weapon on Christmas Eve. All across the entire Western Front, British and German soldiers followed suit, laying down their weapons in an unofficial ceasefire, to celebrate Christmas Eve together. In the coming days, they spoke through broken words, used whatever they had as gifts for each other, and stood shoulder to shoulder with candles lit, praying and singing together, dreaming that the war was over. The peace lasted for two whole days, until they were ordered back to battle.

Yet this was not the first time a young soldier had fallen to his knees on a battlefield, bringing a war to an unthinkable halt. Halfway around the world, some two thousand years earlier, a young Hindu warrior stood on a South Asian battlefield and performed exactly the same action as that young soldier standing on the Western Front in 1914. Dropping to his knees in his chariot, he laid down his bow and arrows, his eyes brimming with tears as he looked out onto the field and saw members of his family lined up on opposing sides. His chariot driver stared at him in disbelief, but he was unmoved. To him, it seemed as if the world had stopped turning.

It is a stunning picture: two young men separated in every possible way—time, place, culture, ethnicity, race, religion—both performing exactly the same action, and bringing a war to a standstill. Even more stunning is the fact that they both were motivated to do so by their deepest religious convictions. In 1914, the soldiers shared the belief that to fire their weapons on Christmas Eve would be to abandon their Christian beliefs and values. On the South Asian battlefield that is the setting of the influential Hindu text, the *Bhagavad Gita*, the warrior Arjuna believed that to fight would be to abandon his moral and religious duties as a Hindu. Two young men, separated in every possible way but united by their courageous action and by the religious motivation for that action. These stories underscore how understanding different religious beliefs enables us to understand human actions and motivations throughout history, right up to the present. And they are stories that should never be forgotten.

"The Problem of God" is the first of two required courses on theology and religious studies that most Georgetown students take, and it takes its name from a book by John Courtney Murray, SJ.[1] The book contains a series of lectures Murray gave at Yale in 1962, concerning Biblical views of God and how they relate to the challenges of religious belief in his time. The course has been taught at Georgetown since the fall of 1968, designed by then–Theology Department chairman Bill McFadden, SJ, and his colleagues. The course seeks to foster an understanding of the religious dimension of human existence and the role of religion in human history, and to offer students the opportunity to explore the possibility of the infinite. As Otto Hentz, SJ, points out, when we explore the problem of God, we are exploring "basement issues"—issues that force us to dig down into the very foundation of who we are, why we are who we are, and why we believe what we believe.

I first began teaching "The Problem of God" in 2009, and this book is based on my course. It explores the challenges of religious belief and spirituality through the lens of both historical and contemporary sources from a diversity of global religious traditions. It explores fundamental issues concerning belief in God or another "religious ultimate," including the existence of God, the nature of God, different forms of theism and alternatives to theism, rational grounds for religious belief, and the challenges posed by the problem of evil, pain and suffering, modern science, atheism, and religious pluralism. It is divided into three main parts: I. Does God exist? II. What do we mean by "God" and what are the alternatives to God? III. Why believe?

Religious pluralism highlights the limitations of the course title: there is not one problem of God but many, partly because there are different conceptions of God, and God is not the only religious ultimate to which large numbers of people have devoted their lives. Exploring the problem of God is important because the spiritual dimension of human life (including religious practices and traditions) is an important source of human meaning, fulfillment, and happiness. It is also important because religious literacy often holds the key to understanding other members of our society *and* other societies and cultures, and our respective histories. It is often central to understanding domestic and global conflicts, and it is likely to be central to their solutions, as well.[2]

If we think about "The Problem(s) of God," the problems on our minds are likely to include religious violence and wars. Yet despite our awareness that religion has influenced the course of history in a variety of ways, many remain skeptical about its value and application to their lives and know relatively little about the particular religious commitments that contextualize current events. I hope that, having read this book, you will be convinced of the importance of thinking through the problem of God, as you will have experienced how a deep understanding of different religious beliefs and traditions usually leads us to respond to members of those traditions very differently. This kind of reflection also leads us to question our own assumptions and beliefs in ways that tend to make us kinder, gentler, more charitable, and more aware of our own limitations. I invite you to join me in exploring this question: What does "The Problem of God" have to teach us today?

## Notes

1. John Courtney Murray, SJ, *The Problem of God: Yesterday and Today (The Saint Thomas More Lectures Series)* (New Haven, CT: Yale University Press, 1965).

2. The clear and direct influence of religious traditions on cultures and societies around the globe is also why I (a specialist in East Asian and comparative philosophy and religion) am sometimes asked to give lectures at such places as the US Department of State and at the Pentagon. The relationship between understanding religious traditions and cross-cultural understanding, as well as its application to international relations, is one of the things that drew me to the study of East Asian and comparative religion in the first place.

# Part I

# DOES GOD EXIST?

# 1

# CLASSICAL ARGUMENTS FOR GOD'S EXISTENCE

## The Teleological Argument

Maybe the desire to make something beautiful is the piece of God
that is inside each of us.
—Mary Oliver

Even something as small as an apple, it's simple yet somehow complex. . . .
Are there blueprints or plans? Can I speak to the architect?
Is there an architect?
—Kacey Musgraves, "The Architect"

If you spend any time with young children, you will be struck by their sense of awe and wonder at the natural world. As toddlers, my children spent hours examining nature up close, running their hands over tree bark and touching the tips of their fingers to the dew drops on blades of grass. One day, while we were walking to school, my son, who was lagging behind his sisters and me, suddenly shouted out, "Wait! Wait! Come back! I need you to come back here *right now*!" The sense of urgency in his voice made me turn immediately, thinking perhaps he was hurt.

"What's wrong? Are you OK?" I asked, running toward him. He pointed at the bushes beside the sidewalk, smiling at something. As my daughters joined us, our gazes fell on a large spider web stretched out before us, with dewdrops scattered like diamonds throughout the expertly woven gossamer threads, glittering in the morning sunlight. We gasped, transfixed by the beautiful sight before us, until my son broke the silence by exclaiming, "There's our architect!" And indeed, there before us at the edge of the web was a tiny orb-weaver spider, resplendent in the beauty of its creation.

*There's our architect.* That phrase sums up the heart of the Teleological Argument for God's existence, also called the Argument from Design, which contends that nature evinces order, complexity, and design to such a degree that it proves there must be a designer. The most influential version of this argument is found in the work of the English theologian and philosopher William Paley (1743–1805). Paley was fascinated by the natural world, and he stood in awe of its architecture—much as my children and I stood before that magnificent orb-weaver's web, and as you, too, likely have observed and savored the remarkable complexity and beauty in nature. But Paley comes to a particular set of conclusions based on what he observes in nature, and these conclusions go beyond the simple observation that there is beauty, order, patterns, and purpose in nature.

## The Teleological Argument: From Aquinas to Paley

Paley offered a detailed version of the Teleological Argument originated by one of the most influential theologians in Christian history: Thomas Aquinas (1225–74). In Aquinas's "five ways" to prove God's existence, the Teleological Argument is the fifth argument he describes. (The first four, as we shall see in the next chapter, are different versions of the Cosmological Argument for God's existence). Drawing on Aristotle, he contends that a thing's form determines its function, activity, or behavior (e.g., a fish swims because of its fins, tail, and other features of its physical structure). Each thing, according to Aquinas, appears designed to fulfill a particular purpose. Things in nature cooperate and maintain an ordered world together, and this means, for Aquinas, that there must be an author or designer of it all. The historian of philosophy Fredrich Copleston argued that for Aquinas, "reflection on quite familiar features of the world affords complete evidence of God's existence."[1] The Teleological Argument—unlike other arguments for God's existence that we will explore in subsequent chapters—invites us to get up close and examine various features of this fragile planet we call home, and especially its plants, animals, and the human body.

In *Natural Theology or Evidences of the Existence and Attributes of the Deity* (1802), Paley presents an analogical argument in order to make the case for God's existence. He describes a walk in the woods so vividly and eloquently that it might have come from a Jane Austen novel: "In crossing a heath, suppose I pitched my foot against a stone and were asked how the stone came to be there, I might possibly answer that for anything I knew to the contrary it had lain there forever; nor would it, perhaps, be very easy to show the absurdity of this answer."[2] In these opening lines, we learn that Paley is not here to indoctrinate us or pretend as though we should all simply accept the view that God exists. Indeed, he acknowledges that much of the natural world does not, in fact, make us think there must be some brilliant architect behind it all. But, Paley continues, "suppose I had found a watch upon the ground, and it should be inquired how the watch happened to be in that place, I should hardly think of the answer which I had before given, that for anything I knew the watch might have always been there."[3] What would you think if you found a watch lying on a forest path when you were out for a walk? Perhaps you would wonder who had dropped it, and look around to see if anyone was ahead of you on the trail. You might pick it up to see if it were engraved, so that you could return it to the owner. You would not, Paley argues, assume that the watch had simply grown there amid the tree roots and wildflowers; nor would you pass it by without wondering about where it came from, and who it belonged to.

*Why* would we not simply assume the watch had always been there, as we might assume with a stone? Because, Paley writes,

> When we come to inspect the watch, we perceive—what we could not discover in the stone—that its several parts are framed and put together for a purpose, e.g., that they are so formed and adjusted as to produce motion, and that motion so regulated as to point out the hour of the day; that if the different parts had been differently shaped from what they are, or placed after any other manner or in any other order than that in which they are placed, either no motion at all would have been carried on in the machine, or none which would have answered the use that is now served by it.[4]

He goes on to describe the complexity of what the inside of an analog watch looks like, from the cylindrical box containing a coiled elastic spring to the flexible chain, to the wheels and teeth that catch in them, all designed to work together for a central and complex purpose. This leads us to infer "that the watch must have had a maker—that there must have existed, at some time and at some place or other, an artificer or artificers . . . who completely comprehended its construction and designed its use."[5]

The point, for Paley, is that we would never simply assume that an object as complex as a watch had just appeared or grown by chance on a forest path or that it had been there forever, and not just because we *know* that watches are made by humans. Rather, the complex ordering of its parts in order to serve a particular purpose leads us to correctly assume that it has a designer, and Paley believes we would come to that conclusion even if we were altogether unfamiliar with watches and watchmakers. It is the *design* of the watch that leads us to that conclusion, in contrast with the stone. For Paley, "design" means complex parts that are ordered in a way that allows them to achieve a particular purpose, goal, end, or *telos* (to use the Greek term, from which the Teleological Argument gets its name).[6]

Paley argues that the kind of complexity seen in a watch is found throughout the natural world, from trees and flowers to the human body itself, and he uses examples such as the human eye. He details its complexity, describing how it consists

> first, of a series of transparent lenses—very different, . . . even in their substance, from the opaque materials of which the rest of the body is, in general at least, composed, and with which the whole of its surface, this single portion of it excepted, is covered; secondly, of a black cloth or canvas—the only membrane in the body which is black—spread out behind these lenses, so as to receive the image formed by pencils of light transmitted through them, and at which alone a distinct image could be formed, namely, at the concourse of the refracted rays; thirdly, of a large nerve communicating between this membrane and the brain, without which the action of light upon the membrane, however modified by the organ, would be lost to the purposes of sensation.[7]

The more we learn about the world, Paley argues, the more we discover the remarkable organization and complexity of things that are *designed*: ordered to achieve certain ends or purposes. This, Paley contends, means that there must be a designer who has so ordered them.

Paley anticipates a number of objections to his view along the way. For instance, the fact that we have not ever *seen* a watch being made, or seen the *particular* maker of *this* watch, would not undermine our belief that a watch we found in the woods *has* a maker—someone who designed and made it, with tremendous care and skill, all oriented toward a particular purpose. So, our belief in a designer (God) should not be undermined by not having *seen* the designer. Additionally, it would not "invalidate our conclusion, that the watch sometimes went wrong or that it seldom went exactly right."[8] The purpose of the machinery, the design, and the designer still would be evident, whether we could account for its imperfections or not. This is one of the most important points Paley makes, because he is responding to an objection based on "the problem of evil"—something that we will explore at length later in this book. The problem of evil is rooted in the question of how a world that is so imperfect and so full of pain and suffering could have been designed and created by a loving and omnipotent God. Some form of the problem of evil is the most common reason why people leave or reject monotheistic religions such as Christianity, Judaism, and Islam. This makes Paley's response very important: he contends that simply because the world is imperfect or flawed does not mean that it still does not evince design. Here, Paley is crucially separating the question of whether God exists from questions about God's nature.

Paley is keen to remind us of our finitude and the limits of our knowledge, particularly as it pertains to the designer. He writes that even if we could not discover or had not *yet* discovered the way in which particular parts of a watch contributed to its functioning (i.e., its purpose), this would not mean that the watch does not evidence design. In other words, Paley believes we still have good reason to believe God (a designer) exists, even if it seems as though much of the pain and suffering in the world seems gratuitous, and without meaning or purpose. The matter of why God designed things *as they are* is a separate question from God's existence, and one that, as I noted, we shall explore at length in later chapters.

Paley anticipates and offers responses to another well-known objection made by atheists in his time and today: that the appearance of design is simply the result of chance. Paley's response is that we would never accept "chance" as an explanation for "a watch, a telescope, an organized body of any kind, answering a valuable purpose by a complicated mechanism."[9] Here Paley's approach aligns with modern scientific approaches, which seek to explain why things are the way they are, as opposed to simply attributing them to mystery or chance. He maintains, then, that nature is arbitrarily being treated differently than complex things designed by humans, even though it has all the same features as those things. But atheists today most often do not simply say that the appearance of design is a result of chance; they say that what Paley calls design—organized complexity designed to achieve particular purposes or ends in nature—can be explained by the theory of evolution.

Here, it will be helpful to pause and consider Paley's place in history. Paley is a naturalist. He believes that science helps us to understand God's creation. He believes, like Aquinas, and also like Galileo and Newton, that faith and reason are in harmony. But Paley is also writing before the advent of modern evolutionary theory. Darwin's *Origin of Species* was not published until 1859—more than fifty years after Paley published *Natural Theology*. (Darwin actually read Paley's work as an undergraduate at Cambridge University, and he was originally convinced by Paley's argument!)

When we examine an argument of any kind, we typically begin by examining its premises: the propositions or claims on which the argument is based. One begins an argument with particular claims, hoping that others will accept them, and then one moves to a conclusion based on those premises. Paley's argument takes this form: First premise: If there is evidence of design in nature, the only sufficient explanation for it is an intelligent designer. Second premise: There is evidence of design in nature. Conclusion: Therefore, there must be an intelligent designer.

Now there are different reasons why any given argument might fail to be convincing. One is an argument's form: an argument's premises must lead us to or support the conclusion. Paley's argument is what we call *logically valid*: its conclusion follows from its premises. (Put another way: if its premises are true, then its conclusion must also be true.) The Teleological Argument is valid because it follows the valid, simple argument form known as *modus ponens*: If P, then Q. P. Therefore, Q. The second way in which an argument might fail to be convincing is that its premises might be problematic. We must always ask ourselves, are the premises of the argument true? Indeed, since there is nothing wrong with the *form* of Paley's Teleological Argument (i.e., since it is logically valid), then the question is whether the *premises* of the argument are true. If Paley's argument is both logically valid *and* has no false premises, then Paley has what we call *a sound argument*. The conclusion of a sound argument is guaranteed to be true. If Paley has a sound argument, he will have succeeded in rationally demonstrating the existence of a designer. But are Paley's premises true?

We should note that Paley's argument entails a very strong claim: the first premise states that you *cannot* sufficiently explain design, order, or complexity in nature without an intelligent designer. This premise rules out any other explanation for design, order, or complexity; an intelligent designer is the *only* sufficient explanation for it. And Paley *must* make the first premise of the argument strong if he is to *prove* that God exists. The premise that an intelligent designer is *one of* the sufficient explanations for design, order, or complexity in nature fails to rationally demonstrate why God *must* exist. After all, there are other sufficient explanations of design and order. Nothing about this argument shows that it is necessary for God to exist.

Ultimately, Paley's first premise is problematic because the theory of evolution provides an explanation for the fact of design, order, pattern, and complexity in nature that by every reasonable standard is a sufficient explanation, most notably because it has a robust evidentiary basis. As a result, the Teleological Argument is incompatible with modern mainstream biology, because it rests on the claim that a designer is the only way to explain the complexity and purpose that we find in nature. The tension between the Teleological Argument and modern science is somewhat unique; as we shall see in the next two chapters, the other two classical arguments for God's existence in the Christian tradition are not in tension with modern science at all. This helps to show that the conflict between religion and science is not an inevitability.

Additionally, although the Teleological Argument fails to rationally *prove* God's existence, this does not mean there are not good rational *grounds* for belief in God—or good *reasons* to believe that God exists. Note, however, that this is different from offering a proof that rationally demonstrates the necessity of God's existence. Today, most of the leading contemporary proponents of natural theology have moved away from offering conclusive proofs for God's existence. Rather, they aim to show that there is strong rational support for belief in God.[10] In this view, even though we cannot rationally *prove* that God exists, there are nevertheless good reasons for believing that God exists. We shall explore some of these reasons in the next few chapters.

### Contemporary Responses to the Teleological Argument

There have been recent efforts to defend contemporary versions of the Teleological Argument. The Intelligent Design (ID) Movement is a family of views that contend that many features of living organisms are too complex to have evolved entirely through evolution, and some aspects of those organisms must have been created, fully formed, by an intelligent designer. Interestingly, proponents of this view have used analogies like Paley's watchmaker analogy in presenting the contemporary ID position, asking us to imagine, for instance, that we were walking on a beach and found the words "John loves Mary" written in the sand. ID proponents contend that we would not assume that the words had appeared there by chance, but that we would, of course, assume that those words were written by an intelligent person. This, of course, is precisely what Paley argues, and here we can see how ID proponents are offering a version of the Teleological Argument. But they further argue that ID is an alternative to evolutionary theory; they claim it is a competing theory with the power to overthrow evolutionary theory, underscoring the fact that one cannot accept both mainstream biology and the Teleological Argument. ID proponents explicitly deny the truth of evolutionary theory, arguing that it is inadequate, at least to some degree. Their empirical claims (e.g., the claim that many creatures are too complex to have evolved entirely through the process of evolution) are incompatible with those of mainstream biology (and the evidence that supports evolutionary theory). This is important to understand, because it highlights the fact that the conflict between ID and evolutionary theory is rooted in their incompatible empirical claims; it is not just because one is a religious view and one is a scientific view. Many people believe that religion and science inevitably conflict, but in fact, there are plenty of religious and scientific views that are fully compatible. One such view, embraced by biologists such as Kenneth Miller (who is also a Roman Catholic), is guided evolution or theistic evolution: the view that God created the world through evolutionary processes.[11]

Indeed, it is helpful to consider the full spectrum of *theological views* on the theory of evolution, with creationists (who accept a certain literal account of particular creation narratives in religious texts, most notably Genesis 1 in the Bible) clustered at one end of the spectrum, ID proponents a bit further down the line, and in the middle, proponents of guided evolution and various kinds of theistic evolution (including those who believe God created a self-sufficient world). One might place agnostics and "indifferent" atheists (who do not believe in God but do not have particularly strong views on what others should believe) a bit further down the spectrum. But at the far opposite end of the spectrum are atheists who contend that evolutionary theory demonstrates that God does *not* exist. Interestingly, creationists and atheists of this sort—though they occupy opposite ends of the spectrum—agree on one very important issue: they both claim that we *cannot* bracket religious issues when discussing evolution. While creationists contend that the correct view of God (and the correct reading of religious texts such as the Bible) ought to lead us to reject evolutionary theory, atheists of the sort described here contend that an understanding of evolutionary theory ought to lead us to reject belief in God.

One prominent atheist who defends this type of view shows how Paley's work has continued to inspire not just proponents of the Teleological Argument but also its critics. The prominent public intellectual and atheist Richard Dawkins describes himself as a "Neo-Paleyan" in his book, *The Blind Watchmaker: Why the Evidence of Evolution Reveals a Universe without Design* (1986), in which he describes evolutionary processes as analogous to a blind watchmaker. The Neo-Paleyan tradition in British evolutionary theory begins with Darwin and conceives of adaptation in terms of design, viewing natural selection as the designer. While this obviously underscores the rejection of Paley's argument (i.e., they are not Paleyans but Neo-Paleyans because they reject Paley's contention that God is the designer), it also underscores the enduring influence of Paley's work. Neo-Paleyans focus on design, like Paley, but they argue that evolutionary processes are the designer. For Dawkins, evolution ought to lead us to reject belief in God, because God is not *necessary* to explain the design and complexity of the world. Note how much of a Neo-*Paleyan* Dawkins is, here, with an emphasis on the "Paleyan": his view rests on the assumption that people believe in God because God explains how the world came into being and why it appears designed. As we shall see throughout this book, this view does not capture why most people believe in God.

The fact that Paley's Teleological Argument remains central to debates about the compatibility of belief in God with modern science highlights the contemporary relevance of Paley's argument for God's existence. To be sure, it is not just a relic of the past. The ID movement has found favor among the 30 to 40 percent of Americans who do not accept evolutionary theory, and who also tend to believe that religion and science are fundamentally incompatible.[12] It is helpful to look at American culture and history to understand why so many people in the United States do not believe in evolution. There is a long-standing anti-intellectualist strand in American culture—practical people who understand themselves as "do-ers" who are skeptical of formal education and the elitism they associate with it. In addition, the nineteenth-century reception of evolutionary theory in America involved widespread rejection by Christian leaders at the time—a legacy that endures.[13] While the Supreme Court ruled in 1987 that creationism cannot be taught in science classrooms in public schools, debates concerning religion in the public square continue to be live ones. In 2005, a school district in Pennsylvania that approved giving ID "equal time" with evolutionary theory in public science classrooms led to the federal trial of *Kitzmiller v. Dover School District*, which found that ID is not a scientific view but a religious one, and that members of the school board had violated the establishment clause (because they were motivated by religion or had the effect of promoting religion). Meanwhile, Dawkins, the philosopher Daniel Dennett, the neuroscientist Sam Harris, and the writer Christopher Hitchens, were dubbed the "four horsemen of new atheism," and all four dedicated a substantial part of their careers to arguing that religious faith is irrational. Those occupying opposite ends of the spectrum of views discussed above have little respect or regard for each other. Wherever one stands on these issues, though, one of the things that Paley's work (and the work of Aquinas before him) exemplifies is the idea that we can learn from science as well as faith, not seeing them as necessarily opposed. Paley and Aquinas both saw nature as an invitation to reflect and study not only the world around us but also the grounds for our religious faith.

What might such reflection look like if we do not view the design and complexity in nature as proof of either God's existence or nonexistence? There are many possibilities. Even if we believe that the Teleological Argument fails as a rational proof for God's existence, we need not reject Paley's conviction that the extraordinary complexity and beauty of nature in some way constitutes a signpost that points toward something greater than ourselves, or something infinite. Simply because God is not the *only* way to explain what we see does not mean that what we see does not evince a Creator. For perhaps one way that the Creator reaches out to us is *through* creation, evoking in us a sense—an intuition, a feeling—that there is more. And this—the "more"—is what religious belief is all about, as we shall see throughout this book.

### Our Creator and Our Creativity

In conclusion, I would like to note a final way that studying the Teleological Argument can be enriching: It draws attention to the way in which design and creativity are embedded in our world and in us. A central focus of this book is how religious and spiritual life informs our daily lives, as it informed the choices of those two young men standing on the battlefields discussed in the introduction. There are profound ethical implications of religious and spiritual life. So I especially want to linger for a moment over the sense of awe that the beauty of nature elicits. This chapter began with a quotation from the American poet Mary Oliver. In suggesting that "the desire to make something beautiful is the piece of God that is inside each of us," Oliver highlights Paley's conviction that whatever else God is, God is a *Creator*. And she points out the deep impulse that we, as humans, have to create. Perhaps the creature resembles the Creator in this respect; indeed, perhaps we are created with the inclination to create. Creating in various ways is undoubtedly one of the things that leads to our overall flourishing, happiness, and fulfillment.

And this raises a variety of interesting ethical questions, particularly because we live in a time when technology can increasingly replicate the results of our creative activities.

There are many kinds of beauty, and many kinds of creative endeavors. Among those (and dear to this author's heart) is writing. Yet writing is one of the endeavors that artificial intelligence (AI) actively undermines. Why write a paper, book, or song yourself, if AI can generate it for you? I think the most compelling argument for limiting our use of AI is that *it is good for creatures like us* to *create*. Additionally, one of the reasons why creative works bring us joy is that they were created by other human beings. The goal of writing is not simply a *product*: a paper, a book, a poem, or a song (and we can extend this argument to visual arts like painting and photography). Thanks to the advent of technology, we can generate these works without creating them ourselves. (Of course, it is worth noting that one reason why we are fascinated by AI-generated products is that *we designed and created* the technology that synthesizes the works of human beings in order to generate a new product. This is one reason why we call them "AI-generated" rather than "AI-created." In this sense, the products of AI are very much the products of humans.)

What makes literature, music, and art different from—or more than—products or commodities? My argument is that it is not simply the existence of the end product (e.g., an essay, poem, or song) but the *process* of creating, of seeing other people create, or of reading, looking at, or listening to something that a person created—that brings us joy, meaning, and purpose. It is easy to take the creative activities that contribute to our overall happiness and well-being for granted when we have no choice other than to engage in them in order to have beautiful end results such as literature and art. But why is writing important? Why is art important? Why are any creative endeavors important? With AI generating things for us, perhaps we can more easily appreciate that the human creative process is one of the reasons why we value these things. There are many goods that creativity (both creating and appreciating the creativity of other people) actively nurtures in us. We often develop virtues like persistence and gratitude. We develop relationships with those who teach us how to write and create art, as well as with those who enjoy what we write and create. We often become healthier, emotionally, as a result of expressing ourselves through writing and other forms of creativity. We become smarter and more reflective and deepen our understanding of ourselves and the world around us by thinking long and hard about difficult problems and experiences when we write or create. I tell my students that writing is a process of actively reflecting on what you have learned, of wrestling with ideas and experiences on paper. To use AI to write a paper, then, is to miss (or diminish) the opportunity to learn and reflect through writing. It is also to miss the opportunity to experience joy in developing and refining your own ideas (and in the case of poetry or songs, your own verses, meters, rhymes, and melodies). Perhaps even more importantly, it is to miss (or diminish) the opportunity to learn directly from other people about their own experiences.

The creative process actively contributes to our individual flourishing and to our ability to flourish as a wider community or society. Aristotle, Aquinas, and Paley all argued that just as fish were meant to swim, we as humans have large brains because we were meant to think, reflect, and to engage in wide-ranging creative endeavors. Creating is one of the things that we were created to do; it is part of our purpose, and thus one of the ways we find happiness and fulfillment. This idea of an end or telos is at the very heart of everything that Paley argues for in the Teleological Argument, and even if we do not find the argument compelling as a proof for God's existence, we should appreciate how it can help us to understand the key role of creativity in our own overall happiness and flourishing.

There is one final way in which the Teleological Argument can contribute to our lives, even if it does not convince us of God's existence. This argument focuses on the stunning complexity, organization, beauty, and design of the natural world. The kinds of patterns and purposes that Paley describes ought to inspire in us a certain reverence for nature—an appreciation of its beauty, of the marvelous and fascinating things we find in nature, and of the remarkably diverse purposes of different features and processes. If it awakens in us a sense that this world is beautiful, valuable, and worth preserving, then even if we do not agree with Paley that the only explanation for design is a designer-God, we will be more motivated to care for the fragile planet on which we live.

A final note: when we encounter something vast and wondrous such as the beauty and design of nature, or the beauty and insight of the creative works of other people, we experience something called awe. It evokes a sense of mystery and wonder in us, and scientists are increasingly exploring whether it is our most overlooked, undervalued emotion.[14] Later in this book, we shall see that awe contributes actively to our physical, mental, and emotional well-being, as well as its connection with a sense of the sacred, and with spiritual or religious experiences. For now, however, I simply want to note that savoring the design, order, and complexity of nature, as the Teleological Argument urges us to, has been shown to improve our lives in a variety of clear and visible ways—and in ways we will continue to explore throughout this book.

## Notes

Epigraphs:

Mary Oliver, "Franz Marc's Blue Horses," in *Devotions: The Selected Poems of Mary Oliver* (New York: Penguin, 2020), 21.

Shane McAnally, Josh Osborne, and Kacey Musgraves, "The Architect," on *Deeper Well*, Kacey Musgraves, Interscope Records / MCA Nashville, 2024.

1. F. C. Copleston, "Aquinas' Five Proofs," in *Ten Essential Texts in the Philosophy of Religion*, ed. Steven M. Cahn (New York: Oxford University Press, 2004), 140.

2. William Paley, "The Teleological Argument," in *Ten Essential Texts*, ed. Cahn, 266.

3. Paley.

4. Paley.

5. Paley.

6. Paley understands that stones can have great complexity and purpose as well, but his point is that ordinary stones are common, simple objects that do not immediately show evidence of purpose, order, and design, in contrast with many other features of nature, which exhibit the kind of complexity that evinces a designer.

7. Paley, "Teleological Argument," 273–74.

8. Paley, 267.

9. Paley, 274.

10. Examples include Richard Swinburne, William Lane Craig, and C. Stephen Evans.

11. This is also the official position of the Catholic Church. For Miller's view, see Kenneth Miller, *Finding Darwin's God: A Scientist's Search for Common Ground Between God and Evolution* (New York: Harper Perennial, 2007). See also Michael Ruse, *Can a Darwinian Be a Christian? The Relationship Between Science and Religion* (New York: Cambridge University Press, 2000). For an introduction to the ID movement and its critics, see *Intelligent Design: Science or Religion? Critical Perspectives*, ed. Robert M. Baird and Stuart E. Rosenbaum (Amherst, NY: Prometheus Press, 2007). For an influential work by an ID proponent, see William Dembski, *Intelligent Design: The Bridge Between Science and Theology* (Lisle, IL: IVP Academic, 2002).

12. For some recent statistics from the Pew Research Center on "Public's Views on Human Evolution," see www.pewresearch.org/religion/2013/12/30/publics-views-on-human-evolution/. For recent data from Gallup on the percentage of Americans who believe in creationism, see https://news.gallup.com/poll/261680/americans-believe-creationism.aspx.

13. As the Princeton theologian Charles Hodge, one of the most influential American theologians of the nineteenth century, put it, "Darwinism is atheism." Hodge, one of the architects of a view known as Biblical inerrancy, shaped the rise of American fundamentalism a few decades later.

14. Summer Allen, PhD, "The Science of Awe: A White Paper Prepared for the John Templeton Foundation by the Greater Good Science Center at UC Berkley," September 2018, https://ggsc.berkeley.edu/images/uploads/GGSC-JTF_White_Paper-Awe_FINAL.pdf.

# 2

# CLASSICAL ARGUMENTS FOR GOD'S EXISTENCE

## The Cosmological Argument

Does the hummingbird think he himself invented his crimson throat?
He is wiser than that, I think.
—Mary Oliver

Nothing within the universe itself can exist to explain the fact that it exists.
—Guy Consolmagno, SJ

Where am I? Who am I? How did I come to be here? What is this thing called the world? Why was I not consulted? And if I am compelled to take part in it, where is the director? I want to see him.
—Søren Kierkegaard

In her 2013 speech at Georgetown University's Senior Convocation, the acclaimed screenwriter, actress, and Georgetown alumna Brit Marling said that one of the coolest things about Georgetown is that "Georgetown makes you take "The Problem of God." . . . At Georgetown you have been taught to think grand, elliptical thoughts that have no answers, alongside narrow, linear thoughts that result in right answers. You have been forced to contemplate infinity. You have gotten outside of yourself. If you can, stay there. Stay there and bring other people with you."[1]

*To contemplate infinity*. To be sure, this is precisely what is at the heart of "The Problem of God." Those grand, elliptical thoughts and questions are perhaps nowhere captured more profoundly than in the fundamental question posed by the Cosmological Argument: Why does anything exist? From the get-go, it is important to recognize that this argument seeks to answer a very different question than the Teleological Argument. Instead of asking *how* the world came into being (i.e., through the work of a designer), the Cosmological Argument asks *why* the world came into being. And unlike the former question, this question cannot be decided scientifically. Indeed, it is not a scientific question. Even if we grant that evolutionary theory and the Big Bang theory explain how the world came into being, the question of why it happened remains. Was our emergence simply an accident? Are we merely the products of blind chance, or is there a reason for our existence? These are not scientific questions but philosophical and religious questions. Unlike the Teleological Argument, which falls prey to the objection that evolutionary theory offers a sufficient explanation for how the world came into being, the question posed by the Cosmological Argument—the question of why—moves us into altogether different territory.

### The Cosmological Argument: From Aquinas to the Present

In the last chapter, we learned how William Paley developed Aquinas's view that attention and reflection are what is really required of us in order to understand why God exists. Both Aquinas and Paley were convinced that there are good, rational grounds for belief in God. They both rejected the view that we ought to simply believe in God "by faith alone." Rather, in their view, faith and reason can go hand in hand: if we look to the world, we will find reasons for believing in God, from a rational standpoint. Aquinas is known for synthesizing Christian theology and Aristotelian philosophy: in his best-known work, the *Summa Theologica*, he introduces the method and principles of Aristotle into the study of Christian theology in order to explain what our purpose is, as human beings, and how we can achieve it. Theologians regard this work as one of the most if not the most systematic and thorough explanations of Christian ethics, and philosophers regard it as a paradigm of rational analysis, for he bases his arguments on reason rather than Scripture or Church authority. He weds Christian theology to Aristotelian philosophy by arguing that we exist for the purpose of knowing God, and that, as Aristotle argued, this is done through the use of our reason. (Here we see him following Aristotle's view that everything has a nature that inclines it toward achieving specific purposes or ends. Humans have the power to understand and reason, and so the activity of critical reflection is central to our overall flourishing.)

Aquinas's *Five Ways to Prove the Existence of God* focuses on how it is not only reasonable but *good for us* to ask whether God exists, and to offer a rational justification for belief in God.[2] The different ways of proving God's existence that he outlines reflect his commitment to Christian theology and Aristotelian theology: the Cosmological Argument is traceable to the writings of Plato and Aristotle, but Aquinas is responsible for the first major presentation of it in Christianity.[3] Sophisticated forms of the Cosmological Argument are also given by Islamic philosophers such as Ibn Sina (980–1037, also known to Westerners as Avicenna) and al-Ghazali (1058–1111), who like Aquinas were influenced by Greek philosophy. The Islamic version of the Cosmological Argument, known as the Kalam Argument, revived in the work of William Lane Craig, has generated much discussion and debate.[4] This helps to show that the Cosmological Argument has had an abiding influence in multiple theistic traditions.

Of Aquinas's five arguments for God's existence, the first four are different versions of the Cosmological Argument, while the fifth is a version of the Teleological Argument. The Cosmological and Teleological arguments share the fact that they are both a posteriori arguments (they are *post*-experience, or "from what is later"): they ask us to draw upon our observations and experience in the world in deciding the question of whether God exists. (As we shall see in the next chapter, this is in contrast to the Ontological Argument, an a priori argument, based on knowledge gained "from what is earlier," i.e., from the power of reasoning, as opposed to investigation of the world.) But while the Teleological Argument asks us to look up close, observing the patterns and complexity in leaves and anthills, the Cosmological Argument departs from the Teleological Argument in asking us to step back and, as Marling puts it, "contemplate infinity."

The concept of infinity is an excellent place to begin when considering the Cosmological Argument, because it is an argument that takes the possibility of infinity seriously. Unlike the Teleological Argument, the Cosmological Argument is not fundamentally concerned with where and how things began or how they came into being. Rather, what the Cosmological Argument contends is this: Even if the entire sequence of beings in the world is eternal, stretching back infinitely, we would still need to answer the question, Why is there anything? Why is there a series or sequence of beings at all? Why do we (indeed, why does *anything*) exist? Why is there something rather than nothing?

Before examining the premises and conclusion of the Cosmological Argument, I want to note a common and widespread misunderstanding of it. Many have taken the central claim of the Cosmological Argument to be that there must have been a first being in the sequence of beings that emerged in the world. This grew in part from the fact that Aquinas frames one of his versions of the Cosmological Argument as an argument for a "first cause." But Aquinas did not mean that it is necessary to have a first being or thing that started the sequence of things we have in the world. This is important because *that* argument falls prey to the objection that the entire sequence could be infinite. Proponents of the Cosmological Argument have long known that there is no reason why the sequence of things in the universe *must* have had a beginning. Even if one takes the Big Bang as the starting point, we can still ask, what was there before the Big Bang? (Perhaps I am now reminding you of Marling's reference to "grand, elliptical thoughts that have no answers.")

The question of *why* there is something rather than nothing cannot be answered by giving some kind of explanation for the emergence of the physical universe, for this would be to explain *how* there came to be something rather than nothing. (Even if one says the universe emerges from quantum fields, one is still left with the question, why are there any quantum fields?) As the astronomer and physicist Guy Cosolmagno, SJ, director of the Vatican Observatory, puts it, "Nothing within the universe itself can exist to explain the fact that it exists."[5] Since the question here is fundamentally about *the purpose of the existence of things*, a different kind of explanation is needed, and this is what I mean by saying that the Cosmological Argument presents a philosophical and religious question, not a scientific one.

In the contemporary essay "The Cosmological Argument: A Defense," the philosopher Richard Taylor points out that the Cosmological Argument depends upon the commonly held belief that there is an explanation for the existence of things—or a reason why various things exist. This is the Principle of Sufficient Reason (PSR), and it contends that there must be an explanation for (1) the existence of any being (an existent thing), and (2) any positive fact. Indeed, this is something most of us commonly accept: we believe that there is an explanation not only for why other people and different things in the world exist but also for various features of or facts about them. My red-haired daughter's existence is not a mystery; she exists because of her parents (and a long line of ancestors before them). The fact that she has red hair is not unexplainable; she has red hair because her grandmother (and her great-grandfather, and another long line of ancestors) did. Likewise, the seven fox pups that live in a den with their mother beneath my shed exist because of their parents, they have reddish fur because their parents are red foxes and not arctic foxes, and they live beneath my shed because their mother chose it as her whelping den due to (among other things) its safe location. These examples illustrate how we do not normally assume that the existence of something—or a particular fact or feature of it—is unexplainable. We may not yet know the explanation, but we assume there is one. That is because PSR is a commonly held belief for most of us. It is worth adding that the history of science is an expression of PSR: a fundamental part of the scientific attitude is that we do not simply assume that something is a mystery and give up trying to explain it. Rather, we seek to understand the origins of things and the reasons why they are the way that they are. We naturally assume that there are reasons and explanations for things, and this is because in the vast majority of cases, throughout human history, we have found that this assumption is correct.

In addition to PSR, the Cosmological Argument also rests on the distinction between a dependent being and a self-existent being. Dependent beings are beings (or things) whose existence is accounted for by the causal activity of other things. For instance, we as human beings exist because of the causal activity of our parents, grandparents, and earlier ancestors. I exist because my parents both chose to live and work in rural Alaska, and that caused them to meet, fall in love, get married, and decide to raise a family together. The same is true of nonhuman animals, and of the rich diversity of plants and other organisms that we find in the world around us, and also of inanimate objects like tables or computers: they exist because other things behaved in ways that caused them to exist. Simply put: we can identify and explain the causes of dependent beings or things.

Now it is tempting to think that everything must fall into this category. But the Cosmological Argument invites us to consider two other possibilities: a being or thing that is explained by nothing (i.e., something that is unexplainable), and a being explained by itself (a "self-existent being"). The Cosmological Argument excludes the possibility of the former because it rests on PSR, so let us for a moment focus on the latter possibility. A self-existent being is one whose existence is accounted for by its own nature: it does not depend upon anything else for existence. Existence is necessary to the very fabric of its being and to the very definition of what it is. It is the Ground of Being or the foundation of existence itself; it is unchanging and cannot cease to exist. Rowe notes that this idea is an essential element of the theistic concept of God. I would go further and add that it is an essential element of what I call "Religious Ultimates" across different religious traditions—from the concept of the Dao in the Daoist tradition to Brahman in Hinduism to the Great Spirit of Indigenous North American traditions. A Religious Ultimate refers to the central concept in a religious tradition or outlook, typically associated with the infinite, the divine, or the sacred. When Taylor seeks to correct the widespread misconception of what is meant by "first cause" in the Cosmological Argument—namely, that "first cause" means the first being in a temporal sequence—he is getting at the concept of a self-existent being:

> First here does not mean first in time, and when God is spoken of as a first cause He is not being described as a being that, at some time in the remote past, started everything. To describe God as a first cause is only to say that He is literally a primary rather than a secondary cause, an ultimate rather than a derived cause, or a being upon which all other things, Heaven and Earth, ultimately depend for their existence.[6]

Now we are ready to consider the premises and conclusion of the modern form of the Cosmological Argument, as it is outlined by the contemporary philosopher William Rowe:

1. Every being (that exists or ever did exist) is either a dependent being or a self-existent being.

2. Not every being can be a dependent being, therefore
3. There exists a self-existent being.[7]

This argument—like the Teleological Argument—is deductively valid: if its premises are true, its conclusion has to be true. So let us consider each of the premises, and whether they are true. The first premise asserts that all existent beings are either dependent or self-existent. It rules out the possibility of a being explained by nothing. If the first part of PSR (the claim that there is an explanation for the existence of any being or thing) is true, then the first premise of the Cosmological Argument is true. Here we see clearly how the first premise of the Cosmological Argument rests on PSR. To reject the argument, you must reject PSR.

The second premise states that not every being can be a dependent being. Why not? Because, according to Clarke and Leibniz, there would be no explanation for the fact that there are and always have been dependent beings. The series itself lacks an explanation. The second premise, like the first, rests on PSR, and to find either premise untrue, you must reject PSR. Here it is important to remember that the Cosmological Argument does *not* contend that there must have been a first being in the series or sequence of things. Rather, the basic point is that if you accept PSR, you need to show why there are any beings at all; you must account for the existence of the series or collection of beings. The key question is why anything exists, and not how it came into being. Interestingly, this is a matter on which proponents of theistic evolution and creationists can agree, because the Cosmological Argument does not try to answer the question of how the world came into being. It asks why it exists at all.

A very important feature of the Cosmological Argument is that it insists we ought to reject the claim that the world exists because of a random accident, or that the existence of matter is just a *brute fact*. PSR tells us we should not be satisfied with those answers, for they involve declaring some things simply to be a mystery, or unexplainable. Perhaps there are truly unexplainable phenomena, but those who are proponents of modern science—something that almost always characterizes modern atheists—ought to be the very last individuals to commit to such views. After all, throughout history, one of the key criticisms that atheists tend to make of theists is that they accept some things on "blind faith," taking them as "mysteries of faith," or as unexplainable through the laws of physics. Many atheists have insisted that theists therefore hold unwarranted beliefs. If atheists reject the Cosmological Argument on the grounds that *there is not an explanation* for why there is something rather than nothing, they are taking a view that is startlingly similar to the view that because some things are unexplainable, they simply must be accepted as "mysteries of faith"—only their faith is not in God. Atheists such as Richard Dawkins and Daniel Dennett explicitly place their faith in science alone, and they argue that if science cannot explain something, it must be unexplainable; the question of why there is something rather than nothing is a pseudo-question with no answer. Note, however, that this response is driven by a metaphysical commitment to naturalism, where everything is understood as the product of natural processes. An important lesson here is that anyone's metaphysical view shapes what views they accept or reject. And even atheists have metaphysical views.

### Criticisms of the Cosmological Argument

In his essay "The Cosmological Argument: A Critique," William Rowe (an atheist, by the way) demonstrates that the only way to reject the Cosmological Argument is to deny PSR. One must simply claim that the existence of dependent beings is a brute fact with no explanation. "Why, after all, should we accept the idea that every being and every positive fact must have an explanation? Why, in short, should we believe in PSR?"[8] Indeed, if you believe in PSR, then you must accept the Cosmological Argument. Rowe argues, however, that

> since we do not know that PSR is true, we cannot reasonably claim to know that the premises of the Cosmological Argument are true. They might be true. But unless we do know them to be true, they cannot *establish* for us the conclusion that there exists a being that has the explanation of its existence within its own nature. If it were shown, however, that even though we do not *know* that PSR is true, we all, nevertheless, *presuppose* PSR to be true; then, whether PSR is true or not, to be consistent we should accept the Cosmological Argument. For, as we've seen, its premises imply its conclusion and its premises do seem to follow from PSR. But no one has succeeded in *showing* that PSR is an assumption that most or all of us share.[9]

For Rowe, then, even if we cannot *demonstrate* that PSR is true, we should still accept the premises of the argument if PSR is an assumption all or most of us share, because this means that all or most of us believe it is true. I would add that this presupposition is rooted in evidence: the history of science lends considerable support to the view that *there are explanations* for things.

I have always found Rowe's response to the Cosmological Argument fascinating, partly because I think he is one of the smartest and most fair-minded atheists I have ever encountered. After painstakingly considering (and rejecting) the full range of historical objections to the Cosmological Argument, he ultimately concludes that because no one has demonstrated that PSR is an assumption most of us share, the argument does not succeed. But I cannot help but wonder if Rowe ultimately rejects PSR because, as he has shown, it is the only way to avoid the conclusion of the argument. Rowe himself described his atheism as rooted in the absence of religious experiences, like a sense of the presence of God, that typically sustain religious life and belief.[10] It was his experience—as it is for many if not most of us—that was decisive in his beliefs. All of us must consider how far we will allow reason to take us, if an argument's conclusion does not align with (or undermines) our beliefs. In the case of the Cosmological Argument, I think it is particularly tempting for atheists to say that they reject PSR simply to avoid the conclusion of the argument (since they recognize that rejecting PSR is the only way to do so). But this, of course, is to do precisely what atheists often criticize people of faith for doing: it is to already have one's mind made up and not to be open to the logical conclusion of an argument, as a result. Since most atheists today connect their belief in modern science with their own religious outlook (their atheism), it is important to highlight the fact that PSR is a fundamental part of the scientific attitude. Scientists do not decide in advance that it is impossible to explain or understand certain things. And interestingly, the Cosmological Argument is not in tension with modern science; to the contrary, it is a model of how theological and scientific views are not always or necessarily in conflict. Religion and science ask different questions. The Cosmological Argument is also noteworthy because it demonstrates the existence of a self-existent being but does not tell us more about the nature of that being. It does not require a commitment to belief in a particular kind of self-existent being—whether it is personal or impersonal, omnipotent or limited, perfect or imperfect, distinct from creation or laboring within it.

Unlike Rowe, I believe that PSR *is* an assumption that most of us share, and I think there is ample evidence of this in the myriad ways we as humans, across cultures, approach the world—from the curiosity of young children to the development of the scientific method. I also think the very question itself—why there is something rather than nothing—draws on our best science, for the most recent research concerning the origins of our world shows that if things had been even a fraction different, life would not have emerged. This is what leads the philosopher William Lane Craig to argue that God is the best explanation for the "fine-tuning" of the universe. The existence of intelligent life in the universe, he argues, depends upon a complex and delicate balance of initial conditions given in the Big Bang itself; the universe appears to have been incredibly fine-tuned for the existence of intelligent life from the very moment of its inception, something that the odds were very much against and that is not required or necessitated by the laws of physics.[11] This type of view differs from the Teleological Argument or the Intelligent Design Movement in focusing not on how the details of our design require an intelligent designer but on *why* we came into being at all, given that the universe easily *might not* have come into being if things had been even a fraction different. The question is not how intelligent life came into being but why intelligent life exists at all.

Particularly because the Cosmological Argument asks less of us than many other arguments, both in not conflicting with modern science or requiring a commitment to any particular conception of a self-existent being, I think religious skeptics ought to seriously consider whether they would reject PSR under any other ordinary circumstance, or whether they are inclined to do so simply because it is the only way to avoid granting that the Cosmological Argument demonstrates the existence of a being in which they do not believe. In matters of faith, if there are no rational grounds on which we could be convinced to believe (or not to believe) in God, then we ought to be willing to say so. For some, matters of faith are simply not matters of reason (and this is an issue we will revisit later in this book). But we must not hold others to a different standard than we hold ourselves. Atheists who deny the truth of PSR to avoid the conclusion that there are good rational grounds for belief in God must recognize that they are practicing the same kind of dogmatic faith in atheism that the most prominent atheists have decried in theists. In response to a pastor who said that faith was stronger than reason, Daniel Dennett once said, "Right there, I submit, lies one of the greatest dangers to civilization. As I have said, religious faith gives people a gold-plated excuse to stop thinking."[12] In reality, all kinds of beliefs (including atheism), if they are held dogmatically, sometimes give people an excuse to stop thinking. And this is something we should all seek to avoid.

Arguments for and against God's existence—and we will, indeed, explore arguments against God's existence later in this book, when we examine challenges to faith—are not designed simply to convince us to believe or not to believe. (Aquinas originally wrote his *Five Ways* for seminary students, who already believed in God.) These arguments are designed in part to provide an opportunity to explore and evaluate the reasons why we believe or do not believe in God. If we do this honestly, then we may, in some cases, be led to amend our reasons for believing or not believing. We may even be led to amend our beliefs. If we are interested in truth, we ought to be open to the possibility of such amendments. But we also ought to view this as an opportunity to better understand those who hold different beliefs than we do. In this book, one of the reasons we examine arguments both for and against God's existence, along with objections to these arguments, is because this allows us to see that people who hold very different beliefs about God's existence can have rational grounds for holding them.

## Notes

Epigraphs:

Mary Oliver, *Devotions: The Selected Poems of Mary Oliver* (New York: Penguin, 2017), 38.

Guy Consolmagno, *God's Mechanics: How Scientists and Engineers Make Sense of Religion* (New York: Jossey-Bass, 2007).

Søren Kierkegaard, *Fear and Trembling/Repetition,* ed. and trans. Howard V. Hong and Edna H. Hong (Princeton, NJ: Princeton University Press, 1983), 200.

1. Brit Marling, Senior Convocation Speech, Georgetown University, May 2013, www.youtube.com/watch?v=K5izKTfctX4.

2. Thomas Aquinas, *Five Ways to Prove the Existence of God,* http://guava.phil.lehigh.edu/aquinas/fiveways.html.

3. The earliest versions of the Cosmological Argument are found in Plato's *Laws* and in Aristotle's *Physics* and *Metaphysics*.

4. See William Lane Craig, *The Kalam Cosmological Argument* (Eugene, OR: Wipf and Stock, 2000); and Paul Copan and William Lane Craig, *The Kalam Cosmological Argument, Volume 1: Philosophical Arguments for the Finitude of the Past* (New York: Bloomsbury, 2019).

5. Guy Consolmagno, SJ, *God's Mechanics: How Scientists and Engineers Make Sense of Religion* (New York: Jossey-Bass, 2007).

6. Richard Taylor, "The Cosmological Argument: A Defense," in *Ten Essential Texts in the Philosophy of Religion*, ed. Steven M. Cahn (New York: Oxford University Press, 2004), 155.

7. William Rowe, "The Cosmological Argument: A Critique," in *Ten Essential Texts,* 158. This version of the argument originates with the eighteenth-century English theologian and philosopher Samuel Clarke (1675–1729), who offered one of the most influential and sophisticated presentations of the argument. It was his version that the philosopher David Hume (1711–76) critiqued, and that subsequently influenced other critiques of the argument. The basic version of the argument that Clarke offers is helpfully sketched by Rowe.

8. Rowe, "Cosmological Argument," 167.

9. Rowe, 168.

10. "Purdue Philosophy Professor a Gentle Atheist." *Terre Haute Tribune-Star.* April 1, 2005.

11. Among his numerous other works, see William Lane Craig, *How Do We Know God Exists?* (Bellingham, WA: Lexham Press, 2022).

12. Daniel Dennett, *I've Been Thinking* (New York: W. W. Norton, 2023).

# 3

# CLASSICAL ARGUMENTS FOR GOD'S EXISTENCE

## The Ontological Argument

For ["God"] is the final word before we become silent, the word which allows all the individual things we can name to disappear into the background, the word in which we are dealing with the totality that grounds them all.
—Karl Rahner

If it is beauty you want, I am beauty. If you want goodness, I am goodness, for I am supremely good. I am wisdom. I am kind; I am compassionate; I am the just and merciful God. . . . I am that supreme providence who never betrays my servants' hope in me in soul or body.
—Catherine of Siena

His eye is on the sparrow, and I know He watches me.
—"His Eye Is on the Sparrow" (gospel hymn)

One sweltering day in a remote village in southeastern China, I was conducting fieldwork on contemporary Daoist rituals when a member of my research team told me that his aunt lived in a nearby village and that he was going to visit her the next day. He invited me to come along. I initially declined; but he insisted, telling me that his aunt does religious work and that he thought I would be interested in talking with her about it. When I asked him what kind of religious work she does, he explained that powerful deities (from both Buddhism and Daoism) come into her body and people can ask them questions and get information and advice from them, through her. "She's a spirit medium?" I asked him, as we discussed the different terms for "mediumship" in the local dialects, Mandarin, and English. He nodded, and I immediately accepted the invitation.

I was relatively new to fieldwork at the time and was not adept at "participant observation"—a research method used by anthropologists to investigate different cultures and practices by participating in activities and not just observing them. So the next day, when we arrived at the home of my friend's aunt and he told her that I was interested in her work, I was taken aback when she assumed that I had come as a client. And much to my surprise, I was soon no longer in the presence of my friend's aunt but of a trancing spirit medium. Her affect, posture, and voice changed; her eyes closed; and she began to rock back and forth in her chair. Her family informed me that *she* was no longer there, and that the god-in-the-medium was now addressing me: "You have come to ask a question! You may go ahead and ask it!" I was speechless. I turned to my friend and said I did not have a question. But the god-in-the-medium addressed me again, this time more loudly, insisting, "I know you have a question! Ask it!" My friend's family members were all gesticulating wildly, telling me to go ahead, because the god-in-the-medium was getting annoyed. So I blurted out the first thing that came to mind: "How are my parents doing? Are they in good health?" At this, the trancing medium fell silent, and remained silent. She continued to rock back and forth in her chair but said nothing. Fearing that I had done something wrong, I asked the medium's family what was happening. They looked at me incredulously and chuckled. "Well, of course, the god is traveling to America *to find out* about your parents' health! The gods can fly very fast, but it still takes time to get there!"

Again, I was stunned, but this time it was not because I was talking with a trancing spirit medium but because it had never occurred to me how central the idea of God's omniscience was to my religious outlook. When the god-in-the-medium returned from its trip to America a few minutes later, I was struck not by the report that my father was experiencing stomach problems but by my own assumption that the god-in-the-medium would offer an immediate report. I was raised in a culture in which the very concept of God includes omniscience and omnipresence: the quality of being all-knowing and present everywhere, which means that God does not have to go and find out various kinds of information because God *already* knows. Yet in this culture, it was literally laughable to think that a deity would already know what was happening with my parents in America.

The expansive conception of God as omniscient, omnipresent, omnipotent, and omnibenevolent is found in Christianity, Judaism, and Islam but is not shared by all traditions. Although many theologians and philosophers have shaped this view of God, few have been as important in Christianity as Saint Anselm (1033–1109), archbishop of Canterbury. In his work *Proslogion*, Anselm offers an argument for God's existence called the Ontological Argument that is based solely on the concept of God's unlimited greatness. At this point, readers may have noticed my reverse chronological presentation of the Teleological, Cosmological, and Ontological arguments. Although Anselm offered the Ontological Argument before Aquinas developed his versions of the Cosmological and Teleological arguments, it is also, I think, the most complex argument of the three. I think it is easier to understand the Ontological Argument after having "warmed up" by studying the Teleological and Cosmological arguments.

In the preface to *Proslogion*, Anselm writes that he offers this argument "from the point of view of one trying to raise his mind to contemplate God and seeking to understand what he believes," and that he originally titled it *Faith in Quest of Understanding*.[1] So Anselm is not offering this argument with the aim of convincing someone who does not believe in God but rather as an expression of *faith seeking understanding*. This method rests on the view that understanding does not just *lead* to belief; belief, too, is a starting point for understanding. For Anselm, understanding *depends on* belief, in certain ways: one must at least entertain the possibility of faith in God in order to gain an understanding of God. The Ontological Argument is not designed, then, to convince the nonbeliever but rather to deepen the understanding of someone who already has at least some degree of faith in God.

Anselm issues a rousing invitation to readers, asking them to turn away from the world—as opposed to examining it, as the Teleological and Cosmological arguments ask us to do—and enter into deep reflection on what and who God is. This is our first indication that he will offer a very different *kind* of argument for God's existence: one that begins internally, with our conception of God and our capacity to reflect on it:

> Come, now, insignificant man, fly for a moment from your affairs, escape for a little while from the tumult of your thoughts. Put aside now your weighty cares and leave your wearisome toils. Abandon yourself for a little to God and rest for a little in Him. Enter into the inner chamber of your soul, shut out everything save God and what can be of help in your quest for Him. . . . Come then, Lord my God, teach my heart where and how to seek You, where and how to find You. Lord, if You are not present here, where, since You are absent, shall I look for You? On the other hand, if You are everywhere why then, since You are present, do I not see You?[2]

Here, Anselm openly affirms the idea that questioning God's nature is a fundamental part of faith. He goes on to offer his version of the Ontological Argument in section two of *Proslogion*, and it is here we can see how aptly named the argument is. Ontology is the study of what is real, the nature of reality, and what really exists. At the heart of the Ontological Argument is the claim that God *necessarily* exists; that God, *by definition*, has to be real. Here is how the argument proceeds:

> Premise 1: God is that-than-which-none-greater-can-be-conceived.
>
> Premise 2: It is greater to exist in reality and in the mind rather than simply in the mind alone.
>
> Therefore, God must exist in reality and the mind, and not in the mind alone (because if God only existed in the mind, we could conceive of a greater being: one that existed in reality also).

For Anselm, if someone denies God's existence, it is because they do not understand what kind of being God is: a being who, by definition, must exist. The Ontological Argument rests on the conviction that whatever else God is, God is unsurpassable. This is what Anselm means when he defines God as "that-than-which-none-greater-can-be-conceived": with this phrase, Anselm encapsulates that the idea is that we cannot conceive of anything greater than God. He is deeply grounded in Christian Scripture here, conceiving of God as infinite in the face of our finitude, and as a being that is unsurpassable in every possible regard. That is the key, for Anselm, regardless of whatever else we say about God's nature. So, for example, we might argue about the nature of God's goodness (e.g., whether an unsurpassable being would condemn nonbelievers or save them, or whether such a being metes out punishments or forgives everyone or both, and under what conditions it does these things). But what is essential to Anselm's proof of God's existence is simply that we grant that God is *unsurpassable*, or the greatest conceivable thing.

Anselm's proof is followed by a dialogue with Gaunilo, a French monk. Gaunilo raises a series of objections to Anselm's argument, and Anselm then replies to him. Gaunilo speaks "on behalf of the Fool who said in his heart that there is no God"—an individual Anselm considers in his text, referencing Psalm 13:1 ("How long, O Lord? Will you forget me forever? How long will you hide your face from me?) and Psalm 52:1 ("Why do you boast, O mighty one, of mischief done against the godly? All day long you are plotting destruction. Your tongue is like a sharp razor, you worker of treachery.").[3] Both these scriptural passages express doubt; we hear the voice of those who are questioning God. Gaunilo takes up this position, despite the fact that he is a monk—apparently, like Anselm, speaking from the standpoint of faith seeking understanding—and offers a number of objections to the Ontological Argument. First, he contends that it does not follow from the fact that I understand what the term "God" means that God *must* exist. Understanding the meaning of a concept, Gaunilo argues, does not mean that thing actually exists in reality. Fans of the Harry Potter series of novels and movies understand what Hogwarts School of Witchcraft and Wizardry is and can describe it in detail, but that does not mean that it actually exists. (Indeed, it saddens us that it does not exist.) Gaunilo's famous example is the perfect island: even though we can imagine the perfect island, "blessed with all manner of priceless riches and delights in abundance, . . . superior everywhere in abundance of riches to all those other lands that men inhabit," this does not mean that said island exists. Here, Gaunilo assumes—problematically, it turns out—that Anselm's argument can be applied to things other than God. He goes on to challenge Anselm's claim that God cannot be thought *not* to exist, because a part of what it *means* to imagine or think about God is to imagine an existing being. Gaunilo poses the question: Why do we need an argument for God's existence if God cannot be thought *not* to exist? For Gaunilo, it is not at all foolish to doubt God's existence. Gaunilo also objects to Anselm's argument on the grounds that his definition of God, "that-than-which-none-greater-can-be-conceived," is just a verbal formula and does not, in fact, enable anyone to form a clear idea of (or to conceive of) God at all.

Anselm offers many replies to Gaunilo, but most important is his reiteration and clarification of his argument: that God, by definition, has to exist. If God does not exist, then "God" does not mean "that-than-which-none-greater-can-be-conceived." But, he argues, it does mean this. And today, Anselm's basic point holds: no orthodox Christian (including Gaunilo) would deny that God is an unsurpassable being—despite their disagreements over what God's specific attributes are. Given this conception of God, he argues, it necessarily follows that God exists. If God is unsurpassable, this means God is the best of all things, and in order to be the best of all things, God must not only be omnipotent, omniscient, and omnibenevolent; God must also exist.

In response to the "perfect island" objection, Anselm contends that his argument applies only to God, because there can only be one thing that is greater than all things. Here the "nothing greater" part of Anselm's definition of God is especially important. While a perfect island might be unsurpassable among islands, it is not unsurpassable among *all* things. So a perfect island is not "that-than-which-nothing-greater-can-be-conceived." God *is* such an unsurpassable thing. Finally, Anselm rejects Gaunilo's claim that this definition of God does not give us a clear idea of God's nature. We can do this by reflecting on things we know, by analogy. If a part of God's unsurpassability is, as Christians have traditionally believed, omnipotence (all-powerful), omniscience (all-knowing), and omnibenevolence (wholly good), then we can understand God analogically, because we know what it means to be powerful, to know a great deal, and we know what goodness is—even if we have never witnessed complete perfection or unsurpassability in these areas. Just because we cannot *completely* understand God's nature does not mean we cannot know *anything* about it. The same is true of the concept of infinity in mathematics: while we cannot fully conceive of what it is, we can discuss its properties and use it to produce real outcomes. (This applies to our understanding of other people as well. Just because we cannot understand *everything* about what it is like to be someone from a different culture or faith tradition does not mean we cannot understand *anything* about what it is like.)

Here, Anselm urges us to use our *reason* to inform our faith, just as Aquinas and Paley do. In the previous two chapters, we examined their a posteriori arguments for God's existence: they are *post*-experience, in that they ask us to build upon our experience in the world in deciding the question of whether God exists. The Teleological Argument asks us to begin by observing the order, patterns, and design found in the natural world, while the Cosmological Argument urges us to look at the vast series of causes in the universe. By contrast, Anselm gives us an a priori argument: one that is *prior* to experience, based on knowledge gained not from investigating the world but from our own reflection and reasoning. What we must do, Anselm argues, is reflect deeply on the definition of God as the greatest conceivable being. An analysis of this definition will lead us to recognize that God *must* exist—or else there would be a greater conceivable being. Unlike Paley, who has us stepping outside to observe the patterns in leaves and pine cones and the ends for which they are designed, Anselm invites us to fly from our cares, enter into the inner chamber, and shut out the world in order to find God.

When readers confront the Ontological Argument for the first time, they often sense that something is wrong with the argument but cannot quite put their finger on what it is. Anselm's argument is deductively valid, meaning that there is nothing wrong with its structure, from a logical standpoint; if its premises are true, its conclusion has to be true. To have a good objection to a valid argument, you must have an objection to one of its premises. What, then, if anything, is wrong with Anselm's premises? Does the first premise offer an acceptable definition of God? If not, what is wrong with it? And does the second premise erroneously claim that it is greater to exist in reality and the mind than in the mind alone? Where, exactly, does the error lie?

The Ontological Argument has generated a remarkable body of literature throughout history, both in the form of defenses and critiques. (Indeed, it has generated enough literature that in graduate school, I took a graduate seminar that focused *exclusively* on the Ontological Argument, for an entire semester. We never ran out of sources to read.) The best-known critique of the Ontological Argument was offered by the German philosopher Immanuel Kant (1724–1804), one of the most influential thinkers in the history of Western philosophy. In a section titled "The Impossibility of an Ontological Proof of the Existence of God" in the *Critique of Pure Reason*, Kant distinguishes between analytic and synthetic propositions. Analytic propositions do not give us information about, or enlarge, a subject. (For instance, "All bachelors are unmarried men" does not tell us that there are any bachelors; it simply defines the word. If there are any bachelors, they are unmarried males.) Synthetic propositions, conversely, give us information about a subject. (For instance,

"My house is white" gives you information about my house; it enlarges your concept of it.) One of the key distinctions between an analytic and synthetic proposition is that a synthetic proposition includes predicates or attributes of the subject. This is what "enlarges" our concept of something. So if I describe my house for you, with every predicate (e.g., white, two-story, green roof, wrap-around porch), I enlarge your concept of it, or make clearer the conception or picture of it in your mind. When it comes to the Ontological Argument, Kant argues that positing "X exists" adds nothing to the idea of X. It is an analytic proposition. If I add "exists" to the description of my house above, it will not enlarge your concept of it or enable you to more easily find it when you come to visit. This is because, Kant argues, "'*Being*' is obviously not a real predicate; that is, it is not a concept of something which could be added to the concept of a thing. It is merely the positing of a thing, or of certain determinations, as existing in themselves."[4]

Kant goes on to consider the example of $100. We can imagine a hundred dollar bill—the kind of paper on which it is printed, the color of the ink, the font and numbering on the bill—but if I say I have a hundred dollar bill that actually exists, it does not enlarge my concept of it. As Kant puts it, "We do not make the least addition to the thing when we further declare that this thing *is*."[5] Kant's basic critique, then, is that existence is not a real predicate, quality, attribute, or characteristic of a thing. Predicates *add* to the concept of the subject or enlarge it, and existence does not do that. For Kant, we *always* imagine something as an existing thing; this is what it *means* to imagine or envision something. If I ask you to imagine Hogwarts School of Witchcraft and Wizardry, my house, or a hundred dollar bill, the only way to form a concept or picture of it in your mind is to picture it as an existing thing.

Kant's objection to the Ontological Argument often reminds me of a segment I used to love watching as a child on the educational children's television show *Sesame Street*. It featured a song called "One of These Things (Just Doesn't Belong Here)," and the television screen was split into four boxes, showing four different items or activities, one of which did not belong with the others. For instance, there might be an apple, an ice cream cone, a hamburger, and a mitten. Or there might be someone dribbling a basketball, someone throwing footballs, someone hitting a baseball, and someone eating a sandwich. Before the song ended, you were supposed to guess which thing was not like the others. A Kantian version of "One of These Things" would feature three predicates, and the fourth thing would be existence. Existence is *not like the other things*, from Kant's perspective, because it is not a real predicate. A mitten is out of place alongside three different kinds of food, as is someone eating a sandwich alongside three people playing ball games, because they are different kinds of things. Similarly, if I told you that one of my students will meet you at Georgetown University's main gates and guide you to my office, and that she is wearing a red coat and a broad-brimmed hat, it would be odd to then add to the description, "and she exists." When I add that my student exists, it does not enable you to more easily pick her out of the crowd at the main gates; to use Kant's language, it does not enlarge your concept of her. If we were to describe Anselm's God, we would undoubtedly include omnipotence, omniscience, and omnibenevolence. These are the things that, for Anselm, help to make God unsurpassable. But according to Kant, we would not include "existence" in that list of God's predicates or attributes, because it is not a real predicate; it does not enlarge our concept of God.

All this is decisive for Kant's critique, because Anselm's argument fails if we grant that existence is not a real predicate. If Kant is correct, then we ought to reject the second premise of the argument—the claim that it is greater to exist in reality and the mind than in the mind alone—because existence in reality does not add anything to a concept, let alone make it greater.

In his study of the Ontological Argument, the philosopher William Rowe points out that the key idea of Anselm's argument is "great-making qualities" and more precisely, Anselm's belief that "*existence in reality is a great-making quality*."[6] For Anselm, anything that has great-making qualities is a better thing than it would be without them. "By 'greater than,' Anselm means 'better than,' 'superior to,' or 'more worthy than,' and he believes that some characteristics, like wisdom and moral goodness, are great-making characteristics in that anything which has them is a better thing than it would be (other characteristics of it remaining the same) were it to lack them."[7] Indeed, even cultures with very different conceptions of God or gods tend to share the basic idea that great-making qualities distinguish them. This is why, for example, in Chinese religious contexts, it is better to pray to the bodhisattva Guanyin (widely known in East Asia as the Goddess of Mercy and the Giver of Sons) if one wishes to have a child than to another deity: she is believed to have a greater capacity to grant children. She has, in other words, a great-making quality in this area; she is, for devotees, unsurpassable in this regard.

But Anselm is *not* saying that anything that actually exists is greater than anything that does not exist. He would not agree that my office is a better office than Professor Dumbledore's office, simply because my office actually exists. As Rowe points out, "He is not comparing two different things (one existing and one not existing) and saying that the first is therefore greater than the second. Rather, he is talking about *one* thing and pointing out that if it does not exist but might have existed, then *it* would have been a greater thing if it had existed." So, if Professor Dumbledore's office actually existed (with its qualities like the Pensieve, Fawkes the phoenix, and an entrance revealed upon delivery of a password) it would be a greater office than the imaginary Dumbledore's office.

Here, we can begin to see why one might accept Anselm's second premise as true. It does seem like an actually existing God is better than an imaginary God, just as it seems like an actually existing version of Dumbledore's office would be better than an imaginary one. (Of course, God is the only unsurpassable, completely perfect thing, and so the argument could only prove that God has to exist—not the perfect office.) Would it not be remarkable—better, greater—if such things were truly part of our world?

After considering various critiques and defending Anselm's argument against them, Rowe goes on to offer a different critique of Anselm's Ontological Argument than his predecessors. He argues that if we introduce "existing" into the definition of a concept, as Anselm suggests we should, then no nonexisting thing can exemplify this concept. Logically, the only thing that could exemplify Anselm's concept of God is something that exists. But as Rowe points out, "From the mere fact that nothing but an existing thing *could* exemplify Anselm's concept of God, it does not follow that some existing thing *actually does* exemplify his concept of God" (emphasis added).[8] Rowe contends that Anselm asks us to "grant as a premise a statement that is virtually equivalent to the conclusion that is to be proved"—that God exists. The argument, according to Rowe, *begs the question*: it assumes the point it is trying to prove. Unlike the common colloquial misuse of the phrase "begging the question" to mean raising or prompting a certain question, in classical rhetoric and logic, begging the question (Latin: *petitio principii*) is an informal fallacy that occurs when an argument's premises assume the truth of the conclusion. It is to assume the truth of the very claim we want to verify. It is also an example of circular reasoning. It begs the question in the sense of "begging off" of, avoiding, or failing to answer the question of whether God exists.

Rowe concludes his critique of the Ontological Argument with a fascinating set of remarks: "If the above critique is correct, Anselm's argument fails as a proof of the existence of God. This is not to say, however, that the argument is not a work of genius. Perhaps no other argument in the history of thought has raised so many basic philosophical questions and stimulated so much hard thought. Even if it fails as a proof of the existence of God, it will remain as one of the high achievements of the human intellect."[9] I believe Rowe is correct, and even if Anselm's Ontological Argument fails as an argument for God's existence, it nevertheless provides us with unparalleled opportunities to reflect upon the nature and possibility of God. And this, of course, is precisely what Anselm says he set out to do.

At the beginning of this chapter, I noted that the Ontological Argument was not designed to convince the nonbeliever but rather to deepen the understanding of someone who already has some degree of faith in God. How does it serve to do this, and why is it important? I would argue that there are at least two important goods here, one ethical and the other religious. First, like my experience observing the spirit medium, studying the Ontological Argument prompts us to consider our unexamined assumptions about God. This type of exercise usually helps us to recognize that *all* of us have unexamined assumptions and views, some of which we are not even fully aware. The ethical result of this is that it tends to lead us to be more patient with and charitable toward others, and more willing to engage with and learn from those who differ from us. Engaging with the trancing spirit medium, for instance, prompted me to realize that the idea of an omniscient God is just as foreign and strange to many people as the idea of deities who *lack* omniscience was to me. This is because we are all shaped by the assumptions and views that are part of our respective cultures and religions: what we are raised with and accustomed to tends to strike us as the most logical. But this does not mean that it is, in fact, the most logical view.

For Anselm, this process of discovery can deepen our faith, because a key part of what it means to be a person of faith is to recognize one's own finitude and limits in the face of something much greater. This is the second, religious good that comes from studying the Ontological Argument: it prompts us to reflect deeply on God and our experience, and this includes questioning ourselves and our reasons for understanding God as we do. For Anselm, this is not something we should fear, for spiritual growth is only possible if we are willing to wrestle with our questions and doubts. We saw this not only in Anselm but in Gaunilo as well.

Anselm moves us significantly closer to the question of what we mean by "God." He invites us to consider what it would mean to believe in God as a vastly superior and perfect being. The final proof for God's existence that we shall consider truly brings this question to the fore, as it offers an argument for God's existence from the Hindu tradition. And as we shall see, it is an argument for the existence of a God who is markedly different from Paley's intelligent designer, Aquinas's and Clarke's ultimate cause, and Anselm's greatest conceivable being.

## Notes

Epigraphs:

Karl Rahner, *Foundations of Christian Faith* (New York: PublishDrive, 1982).

Catherine of Siena, *Catherine of Siena: The Dialogue*, trans. Suzanne Noffke (Mahwah, NJ: Paulist Press, 1980), chap. 141, p. 290.

Civilla D. Martin and Charles H. Gabriel, "His Eye Is on the Sparrow," in *Revival Hymns* (Chicago: Bible Institute, 1905).

1. Anselm, *Proslogion*, in *Ten Essential Texts in the Philosophy of Religion*, ed. Steven M. Cahn (New York: Oxford University Press, 2004), 68–69.

2. Anselm, 69. Anselm's text here closely resembles, in a number of ways, the opening paragraph of Augustine's *Confessions*, which we will examine in chapter 8.

3. Here, too, we find an interesting connection with Augustine's *Confessions*, as Psalm

13:1 includes the lines that Augustine recited aloud in prayer right before his conversion in the garden in Milan.

4. Immanuel Kant, "The Impossibility of an Ontological Proof of the Existence of God," in *Ten Essential Texts*, 100–101.

5. Kant, 101.

6. William Rowe, "The Ontological Argument," in *Ten Essential Texts*, 106.

7. Rowe.

8. Rowe, 113.

9. Rowe, 116.

# 4

# A HINDU PROOF OF GOD'S EXISTENCE

> We understand God to possess intelligence, . . . and to be intelligent means to act with sensitivity to specific factors. . . . In acting, the Lord looks to the conditions sufficient to bring something about. This includes the creatures who have accumulated karmic merit, the right time for the ripening of the merit and demerit that belongs to individuals, and the absence of conditions that would block such manifestation.
>
> —Uddyotakara (Nyaya philosopher)

The author Mike McHargue's story is not unlike that of many Americans. He was raised in a faith tradition, attending church regularly with his family (Southern Baptist); but over time, as he studied the Bible more carefully, and as his education in the sciences progressed, his faith slowly fell apart, until he found that he did not believe in God anymore. But then, years later, something surprising happened. As he describes it, "I was in California for a conference, and God appeared to me one night while I was standing on the beach. I saw a bright light and felt God's love emanating through the very fabric of reality."[1] He was so bewildered by this experience that he requested a CAT scan when he got home, thinking a brain tumor might explain his miraculous vision. But his neurologist found nothing. He spent the next few years exploring cosmology, neuroscience, and the nature of religious experience. He learned that there is a name for the kind of moment he had: a mystical experience. He also learned that 44 percent of Americans will undergo a faith transition in their lives, many of us finding that the ideas about God we grew up with are too rigid to stay with us as we grow older. Yet, he points out, "the exodus out of faith in this country leads to more people saying they are 'spiritual, not religious' than saying they are atheist. I think one reason is that a lot of people have had their own moment on the beach, an experience so powerful that skeptical language can't describe it."[2]

Anselm and Aquinas both contend that their goal is not to convince skeptics that God exists. This is at least in part because they recognize the critical role that religious experience plays in religious belief. Most people do not believe in God simply because it is the most rational view to take. While Anselm and Aquinas were dedicated to showing that belief in God *is* rational, they were both aware that the firsthand experiences people have of God's presence are decisive. But what kind of entity or being is experienced when we talk about religious experience? Descriptions of mystical experiences like McHargue's experience of love emanating through the fabric of reality (which led him to write a book titled *Finding God in the Waves*) invite us to explore this question. So do arguments that seek to demonstrate the existence of a different kind of God than most of us have considered.

Thus far, we have examined arguments for God's existence that are grounded in the Christian tradition. But did other religions take an interest in trying to rationally prove that God exists? The answer is yes. The Islamic tradition, like the Christian tradition, was influenced by early versions of the Cosmological Argument in Greek philosophy, which led Muslims to develop versions of the argument within their own tradition. Most notably, the Kalam Cosmological Argument, which contends that the universe cannot be infinite and must have had a beginning and therefore a cause, has proponents in the Islamic tradition, including Al-Kindi (801–73 C.E.) and Al-Ghazali (1058–1111), though its origins are found in the work of the Christian theologian John Philoponous (490–570 CE). But what about traditions in other parts of the world? After Plato and Aristotle's arguments for a being who fashioned the universe, the earliest arguments for God's existence are found in ancient India, in the Hindu tradition.

## Hindu Proofs of God's Existence

The *Vedas*, which date as far back as 1500 BCE, are the earliest compositions in the Hindu tradition. These sacred hymns, which began as an oral tradition and were eventually written down in *Vedic* Sanskrit, take a deep interest in the origins of the universe and the divinity that creates, labors in, and guides the world. In fact, there are multiple Vedic creation hymns. Over time in India, the goals and methods of Hindu philosophy became increasingly focused on rational philosophical interpretation of the *Vedas*, including proofs for the existence of a God who makes the world. The Nyaya school of thought, which developed in the second century BCE, is one of six orthodox schools to emerge in Hinduism—all of which were dedicated to defending the infallibility of the *Vedas*. (In contrast, the heterodox schools, including Buddhism and Jainism, rejected the infallibility of the *Vedas* and would grow into altogether different religions in their own right.) The Sanskrit word *nyaya* literally means logic, or "that by which the mind is led to a conclusion"; and indeed, Nyaya philosophers were dedicated to the science of right reasoning. Motivated in part by the criticisms of Buddhists and other schools of thought, they aimed to show that there is no conflict between reason and orthodox *Vedic* teachings. (Here, it is worth noting the resemblance with Aquinas's desire to demonstrate that there is no conflict between reason and faith.)

Among their efforts were multiple arguments for the existence of God, one of which we will examine here. While Hinduism is often described as polytheistic, the Hindu tradition also affirms the view that different deities are different manifestations of one ultimate entity. This is why Hindu texts sometimes refer to God as a singular entity. In the early Nyaya school, arguments for God's existence develop from the "theistic sutras"; but beginning with the commentator Udayana (c. 1000), a large body of literature emerges, including dozens of arguments. As Matthew Dasti and Stephen Phillips point out, the classical tradition "takes the sutras to endorse a brand of theism, and our commentators use them to launch a rational theology centered on the notion of Isvara, a being who assembles the manifest world out of eternal, indivisible atoms and governs it according to the karmic merit of individual selves."[3] As we shall see, Isvara ("God" or the "Lord") refers to the being responsible for the material arrangement of the world but not for the creation of atoms or individual selves or souls, which are eternal. This makes Nyaya arguments for God's existence particularly interesting in comparison with the arguments for God's existence that we have examined thus far, since they demonstrate the existence of a different kind of God. But much like Anselm and Paley, the Nyaya approach seems to be to avoid theological pronouncements about God's nature, beyond what is necessary to demonstrate God's existence.[4] We focus on the Nyaya argument that receives the most attention, sometimes called the argument from production, which demonstrates God's existence through inference. I first sketch the premises of the argument, and then explain them:

Premise 1: There are three classes of things in the world:

1. eternal, uncaused things (most notably, atoms)
2. effects with visible causes (e.g., objects such as tables and chairs)
3. effects without visible causes (e.g., mountains and rivers).

Premise 2: Every effect has a cause or maker.

Conclusion: God is the unseen maker of effects without visible causes.

The Nyaya were atomists, much like the ancient Greek philosopher Democritus and the Epicureans. They believed (correctly, it turns out) that the entire world was composed of infinitesimal atomic parts. The atoms themselves were uncaused, according to the Nyaya tradition: they had always existed. But the things we perceive in the world, they argued, are not eternal. Some effects have visible causes—such as things made by humans, like tables and chairs. But other effects do not have visible causes, including mountains and rivers. The Nyaya knew that these things are not eternal, because they were aware that at one time they did not exist. Mountains, rivers, valleys, and glaciers were formed; they took shape over time, eventually coming to be as we see them today. As a result, the Nyaya argued, they must have an unseen cause.

But why? Why must there be a cause? The second premise of the Nyaya Argument offers a basic axiom that answers this question: that every effect has a cause or maker. This basic principle is a part of Nyaya atomism. Why not just say there is no maker, or no cause? The answer is, because Nyaya were atomists. They believed that atoms are inanimate: they cannot move by themselves. They do not naturally "join up." They require a conscious agent to pick them up, organize them in a certain way, and put them together—just as pieces of wood, screws, and glue require humans to pick them up and organize them into objects such as tables and chairs. Mountains and rivers are complex effects; therefore, they require a maker. And so, God must exist, as the unseen maker: "the only being fit to bring about the order that we know as the world is God, an all-pervasive, unembodied spirit or self."[5]

## Karma and the Nyaya View of God

What *kind* of cause is God, for the Nyaya? We know that God is not creating ex nihilo (from nothing); after all, the atoms—the parts of which things are made—are eternal and uncaused. No, God is not a *creator* or a *designer* for the Nyaya, but an organizer and an assembler. This makes the Nyaya Argument very different from the Teleological Argument, which hinges on the idea that nature is designed and God is the necessary designer and creator. In contrast, for the Nyaya, God is eternal (like atoms are eternal), but God is a conscious agent who picks up the atomic parts and puts them together. God does not bring the stuff of which things are made into existence or cause the atomic parts to exist. Nyaya theism is unconcerned with where the stuff-of-which-things-are-made came from or originated. Atoms are simply posited to be eternal and uncaused—unlike complex effects. Mountains and rivers, however, are complex effects, and they are not eternal and uncaused. Nyaya philosophers knew, from their historical records and their own experience, that mountains and rivers are not eternal. In addition, *Vedic* creation stories affirm the view that certain dimensions of the universe are eternal, and also express a certain comfort level with mystery. The *Vedic* creation hymn, *Nasadiya Sukta*, is an example:

> There was neither nonexistence nor existence then; Neither the realm of space, or the sky which is beyond; What stirred? Where? In whose protection? There was neither death nor immortality then; No distinguishing sign of night nor of day; That One breathed, windless, by its own impulse; Other than that there was nothing beyond. Darkness there was at first, by darkness hidden; Without distinc-

> tive marks, this all was water, That which, becoming, by the void was covered; That One by force of heat came into being. . . . Whether God's will created it, or whether He was mute; Perhaps it formed itself, or perhaps it did not; The Supreme Brahman of the world, all pervasive and all knowing, He indeed knows, if not, no one knows. (*Rigveda* 10.129, trans. Kramer/Christian)

These creation stories contrast readily with the creation story in Genesis 1:1—and yet they also bear interesting resemblances to it: "When God began to create the heavens and the earth, the earth was complete chaos, and darkness covered the face of the deep, while a wind from God swept over the waters." Here, God is affirmed as creator from the start, and there is no questioning "what stirred," as there is in the *Vedas*. In both accounts, breath or wind play a key role, but "the One" breathes "windless" in the *Vedas*, while in Genesis a wind from God sweeps over the waters. The creation account in Genesis 1 is much more sequential, with God clearly presented as the ultimate creator of all.

In contrast, for the Nyaya, God is restricted in two ways: (1) the atomic parts of which all things are made, which already exist and always have existed; and (2) the plan that God follows for making or assembling things. God is not, according to the Nyaya, the author of the blueprint, plan, or design according to which effects without visible causes are made. Rather, God follows a preordained plan when assembling the atomic parts. This has an important implication: God is not responsible for the pain and suffering in the world, for the ways in which things seem to have been assembled poorly or with flaws. We call this—the question of why an all-powerful, all-loving God would create a world filled with so much pain and suffering—"the Problem of Evil." And it is the "problem of God" that looms largest for those who believe in a God who is both omnipotent (all-powerful, and therefore capable of preventing pain and suffering) and omnibenevolent (wholly good, and who therefore desires to prevent pain and suffering). We shall spend considerable time on this problem later in this book, but for now, I want to emphasize that in the Nyaya view of God, we cannot ask why God did not create a better world—one free of (or at least with fewer) diseases, natural disasters, and other sources of pain and suffering. For the Nyaya, God did not put the atoms together according to his own design. Rather, God puts the atoms together, serving solely as an assembler following a preordained plan.

So, where does the plan for assembling the atomic parts come from? God does not write or create the plan. Rather, according to the Nyaya, the plan is written (so to speak) by karma: a blind, metaphysical, moral law that governs the universe. The Nyaya theistic sutras "are embedded within a long discussion of causation and the origins of the world as we experience it. The topic of causation is introduced through a concern with rebirth and the karma caused by action. Our sutras, 4.1.19–21, then take up the role of Isvara, God, in relation to factors that influence the unrolling of an individual's life."[6] This view rests on the fact that my body has a certain shape and size, and will be exposed to certain pleasures and pains over the course of my life. Likewise, I am born into a certain family with a certain background, and into a society in a certain place and time. The Nyaya accepted the fundamental Hindu belief in reincarnation, which entails the view that we each have an eternal soul (*atman*) that is linked up with our body. At death, our soul leaves the body and is reborn in another body. We live multiple lives, our souls moving from life to life until we reach spiritual liberation (*moksha*), and are finally freed from the cycle of death and rebirth. We will discuss this view in detail in the next chapter, but for now it suffices to say that the law of karma explains why my soul was linked up with my body in this life. For the Nyaya, and more broadly in the Hindu tradition, God does not dream up the shape of my body. Its design is generated by my conduct in my previous life. This is why it is accurate to call karma a *moral* law. All our actions (and attempts or failures to do the right or wrong thing) generate karmic power: an unseen potentiality in our actions that becomes a part of a karmic blueprint that will determine the body into which we will be reborn in our next life. A bad action generates bad karmic potential. God is aware of it; it is stored, and after we die, God looks it up in the karmic blueprint and arranges the atoms so that, at some point, we will suffer for the bad karmic potential that our actions generated. If I lead a life with a greater balance of good karmic potential, then my body in my next life will be one that experiences less suffering and more joy. But the reverse can also be true. As the Nyaya commentator Uddyotakara (c. 550) puts it, "When the time comes for what anyone has done to fructify karmically, the Lord accordingly apportions causal power at that moment. . . . God's creative action is in accord with karma."[7]

All creation is connected by the karmic law. Humans and nonhuman animals—all different forms of sentient life—live according to the karmic law. Mountains and rivers, though not sentient, are also connected with the lives of sentient beings, which is why God assembles them according to the karmic blueprint. My family may live next to a river that floods and destroys our crops regularly, or in a coastal area regularly devastated by destructive hurricanes. And we may not have the means to move. Or we might live next to a mountain that allows us to have a view of the surrounding area, allowing us to more easily hunt and to see potential threats coming. I may be born into economic privilege, or into a loving and supportive family that gives me advantages that outweigh economic privilege. In assembling all the atomic parts, God follows the karmic blueprint, as governor of the law of karma. The Nyaya commentator Uddyotakara puts it this way: "Primordial matter, atoms, and karma have to be directed by a conscious agent before they can function. . . .

As axes, due to insentience, cut only when directed by an axeman, so too do insentient things, such as primordial nature, atoms, and karma, come to function." He concludes, "Therefore, they too are directed by a conscious agent as a cause."[8] Karma is a blind, mechanical law by which the world operates and is ordered—similar in some respects to the laws of physics. But since the atomic parts of which things are made cannot move themselves, the law of karma needs a governor. This is God's role: to oversee the karmic law, look up karmic potential, and assemble the parts according to that karmic blueprint. And the karmic blueprint, remember, is written by our choices.

When it comes to the Problem of Evil, this has profound implications, because this problem is not a problem for the Nyaya tradition. We are not faced with the dilemma posed by God being *capable* of preventing (or lessening the extent of) evil and of *wanting* to do so, and yet evil still existing. As Dasti and Phillips point out, "Mainstream Hindu theodicy has it that God is never absolutely free to create a world without pain and suffering, as this would ignore selves' karma," which determine the blueprint that God follows as maker.[9] God is limited in certain ways, yet still notably different from us. The Nyaya commentator Vatsyayana (c. 450) writes that God is "different from other selves in that merit (*abharma*), mistaken cognition, and delusion are absent, while he is perfect in merit (*dharma*), knowledge, and yogic concentration and accomplishment (*samadhi*). . . . His merit (*dharma*), which conforms to his intention, activates the merit and demerit collected in each individual self as well as in gross elements such as earth. And so God's irresistible will in creating should be understood as enacting what individuals have themselves done."[10] While "God is a perceiver, a knower, and omniscient,"[11] the pain and suffering we and others experiences is the karmic result of our own choices. While God can accompany us in our suffering—something in which the Hindu tradition believes firmly, as we shall see in the next chapter—God *cannot* assemble the atomic parts differently than the karmic blueprint specifies. The universe operates according to certain laws, one of which is the law of karma. This law is viewed as eternal, just like the atoms, and also like God. Therefore, God is not responsible for the pain and suffering that plague this world. Human freedom, and human responsibility, have a key role to play here.

In the last chapter, we saw that in some religious traditions deities are not omniscient or omnipresent—a view that is very different from the God of Anselm and Aquinas. Here, we see another view of God that completely contrasts with their conception of God, and especially with the view of Aquinas and Paley that God is a designer. The Nyaya contend that God is indeed powerful, as an unseen maker of mountains, rivers, and other things without visible causes. But God is not a designer, because God is limited by the blueprint that he must follow in assembling the parts he has to work with. God cannot put them together in a different way. God is also not a creator, because God cannot create more parts. God is bound by the karmic law and the eternal atoms. To offer an illustration, consider the task of someone who puts together a LEGO set. They are conscious and intelligent, capable of following the instruction manual to put together all the LEGO bricks in the box, to make the item that is pictured. But they are limited by the LEGO bricks that are in the box, and they must follow the instructions to create the item in question. (As anyone who has assembled a LEGO set knows, putting things together in the right order, according to the instructions, is essential.) According to the Nyaya argument for God's existence, God cannot create more atomic parts or dream up a different blueprint, any more than someone assembling a LEGO set can create more LEGO bricks or a new instruction manual on the spot. Both are preexisting. God is the assembler (or maker), but not the designer or the creator. Another way to think about God's role is as an infinite jigsaw puzzle-solver: God has to put the pieces in *the place* where they fit because they cannot go anywhere else.[12]

One might object that the Nyaya God does not seem very "godly." Why would one conceive of a God who is so limited? Is the idea of being all-powerful not a fundamental part of the concept of God? If we look at the history of religious beliefs around the world, the answer is no. There is incredible diversity in understandings of God, deities, theistic concepts, and the divine. Why is this the case? For one thing, Hindu conceptions of karma are very old, dating back to the earliest *Vedic* texts, and so Nyaya views of God developed in relation to the law of karma. Simply put: the Nyaya would have been unlikely to conceive of God as independent from, or in the absence of, the law of karma. Indeed, it would have been just as unlikely for the Nyaya to conceive of a God who designs and creates everything from nothing as it would have been for Anselm to conceive of a God who is limited by a blind, metaphysical law that generates a blueprint according to which God assembles things in the world. Yet God is necessary, for the Nyaya, because atoms are inanimate and cannot move by themselves; they require a conscious agent to pick them up and put them together according to the karmic plan.

Our understanding of the world is strongly influenced—though not fully determined—by our cultural and religious contexts. But we often only recognize that when we encounter a very different view from our own. This is one of the things that drew me to the study of comparative philosophy and religion. The more I immersed myself in and learned deeply about other cultures, the more I learned about my own views and the traditions that influenced them. (Indeed, I remember returning from studying abroad in China for the first time and thinking, *I learned a lot about Chinese culture, but I learned even more about American culture!*) Encountering views that are very different from our own leads us to notice and examine aspects of our own views to which we might never have given a second thought. It is quite natural to think that one's own conception of God is the one that makes the most sense. For those who accept (or have been culturally influenced by) the expansive, omnipredicate conception of God associated with the major monotheistic religions, omnipotence seems like an essential feature of what "God" is. Anselm argues precisely this, and his view continues to influence us today.

If we turn the tables, a Nyaya philosopher might ask Anselm: Why do you think God is omnipotent, omniscient, and omnibenevolent, particularly in light of all the evil we see in the world? Indeed, the Problem of Evil poses such a daunting challenge to belief in such a deity that it is the primary reason why people choose to leave monotheistic faiths. Here, the question would be, why would you believe in a God who is unlimited in every way, when the world suggests something very different to us?

Studying the Nyaya proof for God's existence unveils our unexamined assumptions about what God must be like. But what makes something God, a deity, or divine? What is basic (or essential) to the concept of God? As we have seen, a helpful place to begin is with some of the varieties of theism (the view that God exists) that we encounter in the world. We have examined monotheism (the view that there is one deity who is separate from the rest of creation). Most people are familiar with polytheism (the view that there are multiple deities who are separate from the rest of creation). But there are a wide range of other forms of theism as well. Henotheism, the view that there are multiple deities, only one of whom should be worshiped, is distinct from monotheism and other forms of polytheism, and an example of it is seen in the ancient Israelites. There is also pantheism: the view that God is everything; God is the one substance in the universe. This view is a theistic variety of monism (the view that everything in the world is one substance). As we shall see in the next chapter, pantheism characterizes a majority of theistic views found in the Hindu tradition. A position called panentheism, however, differs in maintaining that everything is in God. Some Christian and Islamic mystics embrace versions of panentheism, maintaining that God surrounds us, enveloping us, but we are nevertheless distinct from (and not one with) God. Alternatives to theism also exist, of course, such as deism, which arose as an intellectual movement in eighteenth-century Britain in response to modern science. Deists argued that God created a self-sufficient world but has not intervened since. All claims made by traditional religions concerning revelation, miracles, or incarnations of God, then, are rejected by deists.

Considering all this, let us revisit the question of what is basic to the concept of God. I would like to propose two characteristics that are fundamental to theism, and I will go on to illustrate these characteristics in our study of different traditions in the subsequent chapters. The first characteristic of theism is belief in a powerful spiritual being (or beings) of some sort. The second characteristic is belief in a spiritual being (or beings) that have personal attributes, or person-like qualities, such as desires, intentions, emotions, plans, and a will. (These are some of the things that distinguish God from the karmic law in the Nyaya tradition.) Theistic views involve a belief in a spiritual being who shares many of the same characteristics as humans. Indeed, this is one reason why we describe theism as a belief in a being, as opposed to an entity or force. Now, as we have already seen, there are many different kinds of beings, some that are more personal and some that are more impersonal. We will examine this range in the upcoming chapters. But we will also examine views that are not clearly or obviously theistic in nature. Such views present us with an even broader range of Religious Ultimates that may resemble God in some ways but that are not just different versions of theism, therefore highlighting the rich variety of religious views found in traditions around the globe.

## Notes

Epigraph:

Matthew Dasti and Stephen Phillips, trans., *The Nyaya-sutra: Selections with Early Commentaries* (Indianapolis: Hackett, 2017), 122–23.

1. Mike McHargue, "I Lost My Faith, Then I Found It; Now It's Complicated," *Washington Post*, September 18, 2016.
2. McHargue.
3. Dasti and Phillips, *Nyaya-sutra*, 116.
4. Dasti and Phillips, 116–17.
5. Dasti and Phillips, 117.
6. Dasti and Phillips.
7. Dasti and Phillips, 119.
8. Dasti and Phillips, 120–21.
9. Dasti and Phillips, 134.
10. Dasti and Phillips, 118.
11. Dasti and Phillips, 119.
12. I am indebted to my former student, Juan Connelly, for this helpful illustration.

# Part II

# WHAT DO WE MEAN BY "GOD"?

## Varieties of Theism and Other Religious Ultimates

# 5

# *THE BHAGAVAD GITA* AND HINDU VIEWS OF GOD

If the light of a thousand suns were to rise in the sky at once,
it would be like the light of that great spirit.
—*The Bhagavad Gita*

O grace abounding that had made me fit
to fix my eyes on the eternal light
until my vision was consumed in it!
I saw within its depth how it conceives
All things in a single volume bound by Love
Of which the universe is the scattered leaves.
—Dante Alighieri, *Paradiso*, Canto 33

In the last chapter, we were introduced to a mystical experience of God "emanating through the very fabric of reality." This experience, perhaps more than any other, speaks to the heart of Hindu conceptions of God, for the central contention of the Hindu tradition is that God is actually *in*—and *one with*—every fiber of the universe. As we explore conceptions of God in different religious traditions, we will focus on particular texts, and in the case of Hinduism, our focus will be on the *Bhagavad Gita*, due to the powerful way it presents how God is understood in Hinduism, and also due to its enduring influence. The influential anticolonial and nonviolent resistance activist Mahatma Gandhi (1869–1948) once said of the *Gita*, "When doubt haunts me, when disappointments stare me in the face, and when I see not one ray of light on the horizon, I turn to the *Bhagavad Gita*, and find a verse to comfort me, and I immediately begin to smile in the midst of overwhelming sorrow. My life has been full of external tragedies, and if they have not left any visible and indelible effect on me, I owe it to the teachings of the *Bhagavad Gita*."[1] That such a text would inspire such a person to say this in itself gives us a good reason to study it.

## God and Oneness in the *Bhagavad-Gita*

The *Gita* comes from the Epic Period of Indian literature, whose origins are in the sixth century BCE. It is a small part of a much larger text, one of the great Sanskrit epics, the *Mahabharata*, which is eighteen books and over 100,000 verses long—roughly eight times the size of the *Iliad* and the *Odyssey*. The *Gita* consists of just seven hundred verses from the *Mahabharata*. Its title, *Bhagavad Gita*, means "the Song of the Lord," and the text, set in the tenth century BCE, consists of a dialogue between Arjuna and Krishna—who is a human (or incarnate) form of the Hindu God Vishnu. (The reader may remember that we have already met Arjuna, the central character in the *Bhagavad Gita*, in the introduction to this book. He was the young Hindu warrior who stood frozen on the battlefield, unable to fight because it would violate his most deeply held moral and religious beliefs.) Krishna's teachings to Arjuna are like a song, eliciting from him different emotions, attitudes, and a different response to his situation, and showing how the *Gita* is an outgrowth of the ancient ritual hymns of the *Vedas*. Over the course of the text, Krishna offers an exposition of yoga—ethical action—which is very much bound up in Arjuna's relationship with and devotion to God. His aim? To bring Arjuna to his feet again and convince him that it is his moral duty to fight.

Ethics and faith, according to Krishna, must go hand in hand. And the opening lines of the *Gita* are themselves a study in ethics. It opens on "the fields of righteousness," variously translated as the fields of sacred duty, the fields of Truth, the fields of morality, and the battlefield of life. Arjuna, caught in the midst of a long-standing argument within a family that leads, eventually, to a battle, finds himself in the middle of the battlefield as the war is poised to begin. Yet he is unable to fight. Seeing family members on both sides, he cannot bring himself to fire his weapon. He sinks to the floor of his chariot, dejected, "his sad eyes blurred by tears."[2] And, the text tells us, "Krishna gave him counsel." Arjuna's charioteer is Krishna, an avatar (or human incarnation) of Vishnu. How did Arjuna come to have God incarnate as his chariot driver? As the two sides prepared for battle, they both petitioned Krishna for help. Although he refused to fight, Krishna offered the opposing sides a choice between his impressive army or his own personal counsel. Arjuna's opponents chose the army, thinking it would make them invincible. And so Krishna offered to be Arjuna's charioteer.

In Krishna, we encounter a God who comes to humans in their time of need to offer assistance. Hindu deities are as many in number as they are diverse, and they have been understood in a variety of ways throughout history and by different branches of Hinduism. They are often understood as aspects or expressions of one Ultimate Reality or Spirit called Brahman (which we will explore in a moment). Since the first millennium BCE, one popular representation of Hindu gods has been the Trimurti (the image of three), consisting of the Creator (Brahma), the Preserver (Vishnu), and the Destroyer (Shiva). The idea here, as in many representations of Hindu deities, is to show how different deities are manifestations of one God, who is one with and at work in every aspect of the world. As things are created, preserved, and destroyed, God labors in *all* those processes. The concept of an avatar has its origins in Hindu mythology (and not in modern video games). An avatar is an incarnation or manifestation of a deity on Earth. In Sanskrit, the term means "descent," and it is the descent to Earth of a deity; an avatar is their material appearance in human or animal form. The idea of an avatar is particularly developed in stories about Vishnu, the preserver-God who appears at different times and in different forms on Earth (i.e., different avatars) to accompany and assist humans who encounter difficulties during their lives. Hindus traditionally believe that Vishnu has appeared ten different times in history, and Krishna is one of the ten avatars of Vishnu. He is widely revered in Hinduism. (The historical Buddha is also regarded by Hindus as an avatar of Vishnu; that is, they view the Buddha as the deity Vishnu, in human form.)

In its understanding of God, the *Bhagavad Gita* builds on the ancient foundations of Hinduism. In the last chapter, we briefly touched on the *Vedas*—the ancient sacred hymns that are the oldest sources in Hinduism. These hymns were composed by *rishis* ("seers"), an elite group of priests who served as mediators between humans and the divine. Tradition holds that they "saw" the structure and nature of the universe and transformed it into a form that could be heard: the *Vedic* hymns. While the earliest parts of the *Vedas* come from about 1500–1000 BCE, the next most influential Hindu source, the *Upanishads*, dates to around 800–500 BCE. The *Upanishads* offer a much more detailed philosophical and religious view, sort of like flowers that blossom from the seeds of the *Vedas*.

At the heart of the *Upanishads* and subsequent Hindu texts like the *Bhagavad Gita*, is the concept of Brahman: the underlying reality of everything, the ultimate inner essence of everything, the fact of existence (pure existence itself), the root cause of everything (from the Sanskrit root "to grow," in the sense of the root of existence from which the world grows). Brahman is pure consciousness or Spirit (*purusha*) itself, and it is the One of which all deities are an expression or manifestation. It is also ineffable: we can never fully grasp or understand it. But we can experience it, and so religious experience has a key role to play.

The *Upanishads* and the *Gita* rest on (and develop) a robust metaphysical view. They maintain that we do not experience the world as it truly is. Rather, we experience the world of temporary, changing forms (*maya*). *Maya* is not reality; it is the *appearance* of many out of one. We perceive ourselves as being separate from other things, but this is an illusion (known as *avidya*). Each of us has an individual *atman*—a soul or conscious essence (from the Sanskrit root "to breathe," as in, *to breathe life into* something), which is the inner self or core of all sentient beings; but the ultimate truth for which the Hindu tradition argues is articulated by the Doctrine of Brahman-Atman: Atman *is* Brahman. We are not, in fact, distinct selves or souls. We mistakenly believe we are separate, but even though each of us has an *atman*, every *atman* is part of the same fabric or whole, which is Brahman. A helpful illustration of this is threads woven together into a single piece of fabric. Our souls are inextricably bound together. Every *atman* is joined with every other *atman*, forming one whole: Brahman. According to Hindu philosophers, we are destined to experience death and rebirth repeatedly (a cycle known as *samsara*), until we awaken to our Brahman identity and realize that we are not separate, but one with all creation. At this point, we are liberated from the cycle of death and rebirth, and we enter into an indescribable state called *moksha*, which represents complete liberation and awakening.

No tradition has a deeper interest in oneness than Hinduism. So when Krishna begins to give counsel to Arjuna, it is important to remember that the larger message of the *Gita*—concerning faith in God and how we live our lives ethically—hinges on our ability to recognize the deep oneness that characterizes who God is, and who we are, in relation to others. By opening on "the fields of righteousness" and "the battlefield of life," the *Gita* reminds us from the start that the story it tells represents each of our stories, told through a particular story. The entire text is a metaphor for the battle between good and evil, between awakening to reality (our Brahman identity) and being trapped in an illusion (of separateness).

As Krishna begins to talk with Arjuna, telling him to get on his feet again, Arjuna refuses, offering a series of arguments against fighting. First, he argues that there will be no good outcome or consequence of fighting, no matter who wins: "I see no good in killing my kinsmen in battle."[3] Second, he argues that he has a moral duty not to fight his family members. All along the battlefield, he sees "teachers, fathers, sons, and grandfathers, uncles, grandsons, fathers and brothers of wives, and other men of our family. I do not want to kill them even if I am killed, Krishna. . . . Honor forbids us to kill our cousins."[4] Third, and in turn, he argues that war disrupts the social order: "When the family is ruined, the timeless laws of family duty perish; and when duty is lost, chaos overwhelms the family. In overwhelming chaos, Krishna, women of the family are corrupted; and when women are corrupted, disorder is born in society."[5] Here, Arjuna expresses the concern that if his family goes to war, the men of a certain class will be killed, which will force women to do things they are not supposed to do—like marry outside their class or caste (a concept to which we will return in a moment). This creates tremendous social disruption, leading to chaos at the level of society. Arjuna insists that he is faced with a moral dilemma that has no solution, because he has conflicting moral and religious obligations: he has a moral duty not to fight his family, and there are more reasons why this would have bad results. But he is a member of the warrior class or caste, and so, like a member of the military, he has a moral obligation to fight. It seems to Arjuna that he must fight or not fight, but either way, he is doomed. So he remains on the floor of his chariot, in the middle of the battlefield. Laying down his bow and arrows, he opts for inaction.

## Caste and Society in the *Bhagavad Gita*

Before proceeding further, it will be helpful to discuss the institution of the Indian caste system—a rigid class system consisting of four castes, or *varnas*: *brahmins* (priests and scholars), *kshatriyas* (warriors and rulers), *vaishyas* (farmers, merchants, and artisans), and *shudras* (laborers). A final category emerges later: the casteless—*candalas* or *dalits* (untouchables). Ancient Hindu texts mention the four *varnas* as a framework for grouping people by profession, but they were not a part of the earliest Vedic texts, and scholars doubt that this framework was ever operational in early Indian society. (The closely associated but distinct term *jati*, meaning "birth," is mentioned less often than *varna* in ancient texts and refers to smaller social groups into which one is born, of which there are not just four but thousands.) In ancient India, there were tribal divisions, but kings from all four *varnas* had ruled India by the ninth century. The *Mahabharata*, which was complete by the end of the fourth century, mentions the four *varnas* but then says, "There is no distinction of *varnas*. The whole universe is Brahman. It was created formerly by Brahma, came to be classified by acts."[6] Here we see the characteristic emphasis on *oneness* in the Hindu tradition. The text goes on to specify that people who were inclined toward certain activities and their associated virtues attained those *varnas* (e.g., those inclined toward boldness attained the *kshatriya varna*). In such a view, it is at least in part on one's own merits that one "attains" or becomes part of a certain caste. Here we can see how differently *varna* was understood in these early texts, compared with the modern phenomenon of the caste system in India. Recent scholarship suggests that social organization was little touched by caste until relatively recent centuries. The anthropologist Susan Bayly argues that the caste system as we know it today as a "ritualized scheme of social stratification" developed in two stages in the eighteenth and early nineteenth centuries, and colonialism played a key role in this process.[7] When British rule arrived, East India Company officials adopted constitutional laws that segregated people by religion and caste. (In 1949, the caste system was repudiated in the Indian Constitution, and discrimination due to caste was outlawed. But caste still plays an important role in many aspects of life in India.)

What role does caste play in the *Gita*? We have already seen Arjuna refer to it, in presenting his view that he has a moral duty to fight as a *kshatriya* (warrior). We have also seen him refer to how "the sins of men who violate the family create disorder in society that undermines the constant laws of caste and family duty."[8] In any tradition where the law of karma and a belief in reincarnation play a key role, one's moral conduct in this life plays a central role in determining where one is reborn in the next life. Sources in both the Hindu and Buddhist traditions contend that the status of one's rebirth includes such things as one's parents' professions, socioeconomic status, and geographic location. In this view, Arjuna is a *kshatriya* at least in part because of his good moral conduct in a previous life. Much hangs in the balance, then, when it comes to fulfilling his moral duties in this life. There are cosmic consequences for all his actions. On one hand, one must fulfill one's caste-specific moral duties in order to have a good rebirth, and the belief is that those in higher positions in society have earned their status due to good karma generated by moral conduct in a previous life. On the other hand, one must never conduct oneself in a way that expresses entitlement to one's position in society, for the only way to progress to a good rebirth in the next life is to fulfill one's duties and live in a way that expresses oneness with (not separation from) others. The ultimate goal, as we have seen, is to be liberated from the cycle of death and rebirth, and the only way to do this is by fully realizing the Doctrine of Brahman-Atman: that we are not separate from others, but all things are one.

As I mentioned above, the *Gita* is more than just the story of Arjuna's moral dilemma on a battlefield sometime around the tenth century BCE. The text serves as a metaphor for Hindu teachings, where the real battle is waged in the human heart. Arjuna represents our ordinary state, trapped in the illusion that we are separate selves; he is bound up in his attachment to his desires, his position in his family and society, and his ego. Krishna, conversely, represents the true *atman* or innermost self, and the reality that we are one with everything.[9] Over the course of the text, Krishna urges Arjuna to fight, but this is not just because Arjuna's moral duty as a warrior is to fight. Krishna urges Arjuna to do battle against his desires and ego attachments and slay them. He reminds Arjuna that the *atman* is immortal: "Arjuna, when a man knows the self to be indestructible, enduring, unborn, unchanging, how does he kill or cause anyone to kill? . . . If you think of its birth and death as ever-recurring, then too, Great Warrior, you have no cause to grieve!"[10] After reminding him that the *atman* survives death, he responds to Arjuna's arguments for not fighting, as Arjuna sits dejected between the two armies, in the middle of the battlefield. Krishna tells him, "Be intent on action, not on the fruits of action; avoid attraction to the fruits and attachment to inaction! Perform actions, firm in discipline, relinquishing attachment; be impartial to failure and success—this equanimity is called discipline."[11] He insists that Arjuna must not focus on the consequences of his actions, but simply on doing what is right, without concern for the outcome. In response, Arjuna expresses doubt that it is really possible to act with this sort of discipline. He presses Krishna repeatedly on this matter, asking him, "What defines a man deep in contemplation whose insight and thought are sure? How would he speak? How would he sit? How would he move?"[12]

In the eighteen verses that close book two of the *Gita*, Krishna answers Arjuna's question, describing the characteristics of the perfect sage. (Gandhi called these verses "the essential wisdom" of the *Gita*.) Here, Krishna offers an account of how our *desires* are an expression of the illusion that we are separate from others. The only person who finds peace is one who conquers desires completely: "When he renounces all desires and acts without craving, possessiveness, or individuality, he finds peace. This is the place of the infinite spirit; achieving it, one is freed from delusion; abiding in it even at the time of death, one finds the pure calm of infinity."[13] Arjuna, in his tortured state, finds this prospect most appealing, but he continues to question Krishna about how and why he ought to fight. Krishna continues to insist that Arjuna must get up from the floor of his chariot and act: "A man cannot escape the force of action by abstaining from actions. . . . No one exists for even an instant without performing action."[14] Further, he emphasizes that Arjuna must act in accordance with his caste-specific duty, as a warrior, telling him: "Your own duty done imperfectly is better than another man's done well. It is better to die in one's own duty; another man's is perilous."[15] And Krishna goes on to remind us that he is not asking Arjuna simply to get up and fire his arrows; this is a cosmic battle that is waged inside us. Our desires are the true enemy, because they sustain the illusion that we are separate selves, when in fact the true self—the *atman*—is one with all things: "Knowing the self beyond understanding, sustain the self with the self. Great Warrior, kill the enemy menacing you in the form of desire!"[16]

Krishna insists that Arjuna can do this through ethical action (yoga), which consists of acting skillfully by doing the right thing (his moral duty) simply because it is the right thing to do, and not because it will bring about good consequences. Right actions are right no matter what their consequences, according to Krishna. (The Hindu tradition articulates right actions, including the moral duties, rights, laws, conduct, and virtues associated with different members of society, including different castes, in a number of early texts.) Additionally, when we do the right thing, we should not focus on the possible consequences of our actions, nor on fulfilling our desires or on the potential pleasure or pain that our actions might bring. Ethical action (yoga) consists of fulfilling your caste-specific moral duty (in Arjuna's case, his duty as a warrior to fight), solely because it is your duty. The only way to stop viewing yourself as separate from others is to let go of "your" desires and ego attachments. The importance of doing one's caste-specific moral duty is also cosmically enforced: in this ethical system, I cannot always generate good karma simply by doing exactly the same thing as you; some of our moral duties differ, depending on our position in our families and in society. In society, for instance, schoolteachers, doctors, and members of the military have different moral duties by virtue of their different vocations (even though they all have some of the same moral duties as citizens, e.g., to obey the law). Similarly, parents have different moral duties than those who do not have children. In the view presented in the *Gita*, Arjuna will face cosmic consequences if he does not fulfill his duties as a warrior, because when we fail to fulfill our moral obligations, bad karma is generated.

## Arjuna's Vision of Krishna's Totality

Arjuna goes on to press Krishna on the matter of how it is really possible to act in this way. In Krishna's response, we learn more about the nature of God and the role of faith in this tradition. Earlier in the text, Krishna articulates his true nature as an eternal and everlasting God (or to use the language of the Cosmological Argument: a self-existent being), as well as his ability to incarnate himself in human form when the need arises: "Though myself unborn, undying, the lord of creatures, I fashion nature, which is mine, and I come into being through my own magic. Whenever sacred duty decays and chaos prevails, then, I create myself, Arjuna. To protect men of virtue and destroy men who do evil, to set the standard of sacred duty, I appear in age after age."[17] When Krishna tells Arjuna that he must follow the Path of Devotion (*bhakti* yoga) to conquer his desires and act ethically, he tells Arjuna that following the Path of Devotion means making his actions an act of worship, devotion, and service to a personal savior, a loving God who has come to accompany him in his time of need. His actions must also be done out of love. Krishna says,

> Listen, Arjuna, as I recount for you in essence the divine powers of myself; endless is my extent. I am the self abiding in the heart of all creatures; I am their beginning, their middle, and their end. I am Vishnu striding among sun gods, the radiant sun among lights; I am lightning among wind gods, the moon among the stars. I am the song in sacred lore; I am Indra, king of the gods; I am the mind of the senses, the consciousness of creatures.[18]

He goes on to describe himself as everything imaginable in the universe, from deities to trees to syllables and vowels to death to the meter of sacred song and seasons.

Arjuna says, "I want to see your form in all its majesty, Krishna, Supreme among Men. If you think I can see it, reveal to me your immutable self, Krishna, Lord of Discipline." Krishna complies, saying "Arjuna, see my forms in hundreds and thousands; diverse, divine, of many colors and shapes; . . .

see all the universe, animate and inanimate, and whatever else you wish to see; all stands here as one in my body."[19] Book eleven of the *Gita* goes on to describe the Vision of Krishna's Totality: "It was a multiform, wonderous vision, with countless mouths and eyes and celestial ornaments, brandishing many divine weapons. Everywhere was boundless divinity containing all astonishing things. . . . If the light of a thousand suns were to rise in the sky at once, it would be like the light of that great spirit. Arjuna saw all the universe in its many ways and parts, standing as one in the body of the god of gods."[20]

Arjuna goes on to narrate his vision of Krishna's true form—his vision of God—which is a vision of everything in the universe. This means that the vision not only includes terrific and beautiful images but also terrifying images of destruction: "Rushing through your fangs into grim mouths, some are dangling from heads crushed between your teeth. . . . You lick at the worlds around you, devouring them with flaming mouths; and your terrible fires scorch the entire universe, filling it, Vishnu, with violent rays. Tell me—who are you in this terrible form? Homage to you, Best of Gods! Be gracious!"[21] Arjuna goes on to ask Krishna (whom he calls "Shelter of the World") to dispel his fear by returning to his human form, and Krishna "once more revealed his intimate form, resuming his gentle body."[22] From this point on in the dialogue, Krishna urges Arjuna, "Focus your mind on me, let your understanding enter me; then you will dwell in me without doubt."[23]

Krishna is the embodiment of a God who is a loving counselor and guide, and who seeks a relationship with humans. At the same time, God is one with all things: here we see a genuinely pantheistic view. And this view gives rise to the Hindu image of God as the Creator, Preserver, *and* Destroyer.

It is tempting to view Anselm's God—that-than-which-none-greater-can-be-conceived—as the most expansive conception of God that is possible. But the Hindu tradition offers us an even more expansive conception of God—or at least one that is expansive in a different way. For Anselm, God is unsurpassable when it comes to good qualities like power, knowledge, benevolence, and love. In the Hindu tradition, God is *everything*. And it is not just that God is at work *in* everything; rather, God is *identifiable with* everything. In addition to being the most comforting presence, God is also the most terrifying presence. Just as God is Creator, God is Destroyer.

This is why the diversity of Hindu images of God, or the diversity of gods in Hinduism, are diverse not just in number but also in character. This applies not only to images of God as the Creator (Brahma), Preserver (Vishnu), and Destroyer (Shiva), but also to such categories as male and female. In the denomination of Hinduism known as Shaktism, God is metaphorically envisioned as a woman. But even in images of Hindu goddesses, who are almost always conceived of and addressed as Divine Mothers, we find that Hindu images of God reflect all dimensions of reality. This makes them a contrast to Christian images of the Blessed Virgin Mary, the Mother of Jesus, in two ways. First, Mary is not divine; according to the Doctrine of the Trinity, which understands Jesus (the Son) as one with God (the Father), she is the Mother of God, and she is "Blessed"— worthy of reverence because she is the Mother of God but not because she is divine (or part of God) herself. Second, images of the Blessed Virgin Mary, though diverse, are consistently of a comforting, reassuring, merciful, and nurturing figure, very much like images of her son. Here we see Anselm's view of God expressed in Christian iconography: God is unsurpassable in all good qualities or virtues, and those who are chosen and blessed by God (most notably, Mary) or who are God (Jesus) mirror these qualities.

In contrast, as I noted above, God is *everything* in Hinduism. Among the more prominent Hindu goddesses is Kali, who is associated with power, destruction, and death. She destroys evil to defend the innocent, she protects her devotees from misfortune, and she grants *moksha* or liberation. Kali's skin is dark because she symbolizes Brahman—all things united as one, all colors mixed together. And she is both comforting (as one who grants liberation) and terrifying, but images of her bend toward the latter. Kali is the consort of Shiva (the Destroyer), and she embodies the power of destruction: she is often depicted standing with her right foot on his chest, or dancing on the corpses of the slain, sometimes wearing a garland of human heads. She is almost always holding a sword and a severed head and a bowl for its blood. This iconography symbolizes the same thing that Arjuna's story symbolizes in the *Gita*: slaying the human ego and the ignorance that leads us to believe that we are separate individuals. To shatter this illusion permanently requires a kind of violence done to the illusory self, much like slaying an enemy in battle. This is the only way to attain liberation (*moksha*), just as fighting is the only way for Arjuna to do what is right.

In this chapter, we have seen how much God can be, all at once, when one conceives of God as *everything*. We have seen just how differently God can be (and is) conceived of—even when one believes in just one God. Next, we will begin our exploration of alternatives to theism or belief in God, as we turn to the two most influential indigenous religious and philosophical traditions to China: Confucianism and Daoism. In these traditions, we find conceptions of powerful spiritual entities (or Religious Ultimates) that are not God but that give us interesting models of what alternatives to theism can and do look like.

## Notes

Epigraph:

Dante Alighieri, *Paradiso*, trans. John Ciardi (New York: Signet, 2009), xx.1.

1. Mahatma Gandhi, *The Bhagavad Gita According to Gandhi* (Berkeley, CA: North Atlantic Books, 2009; reprint).

2. *The Bhagavad-Gita: Krishna's Counsel in Time of War* (New York: Bantam Classic, 2004), trans. Barbara Stoler Miller, 31 (*Bhagavad-Gita*, 2:1).

3. *Bhagavad-Gita*, 27 (1:31).

4. *Bhagavad-Gita*, 28 (1:34–37).

5. *Bhagavad-Gita*, 28–29 (1:40–41).

6. Alfred Hiltebeitel, *Dharma: Its Early History in Law, Religion, and Narrative* (New York: Oxford University Press, 2011), 529–31.

7. See Susan Bayly, *Caste, Society and Politics in India from the Eighteenth Century to the Modern Age* (New York: Cambridge University Press, 2001).

8. *Bhagavad-Gita*, 29 (1:44).

9. For a detailed discussion of this metaphorical interpretation, see Patrick Bresnan, *Awakening: An Introduction to the History of Eastern Thought, Third Edition* (Upper Saddle River, NJ: Pearson, 2007), 65–67.

10. *Bhagavad-Gita*, 34–35 (2:21, 26).

11. *Bhagavad-Gita*, 38 (2:47–48).

12. *Bhagavad-Gita*, 39 (2:54).

13. *Bhagavad-Gita*, 42 (2:71–72).

14. *Bhagavad-Gita*, 43 (3:4–5).

15. *Bhagavad-Gita*, 48 (3:35).

16. *Bhagavad-Gita*, 49 (3:43).

17. *Bhagavad-Gita*, 52 (4:6–8).

18. *Bhagavad-Gita*, 93–94 (10:19–22).

19. *Bhagavad-Gita*, 97–98 (11:3–7).

20. *Bhagavad-Gita*, 98 (11:10–13).

21. *Bhagavad-Gita*, 102–3 (11:27, 30–31).

22. *Bhagavad-Gita*, 106, 108 (11:45, 50)

23. Bhagavad-Gita, 110 (12:8).

# 6

# CONFUCIAN VIEWS OF TIAN ("HEAVEN"), ANCESTOR SPIRITS, AND RITUALS

If I'm not fully present at a ritual, it's as though I haven't participated in it at all.
—Kongzi (Confucius)

The words of my great-grandmother May ring through my head each time I butter a piece of toast. Of her six daughters-in-law, who took turns caring for her as she died slowly and painfully from cancer, my grandmother was her favorite caregiver. Once, someone asked her why. In a weak voice, Great-Grandmother May replied, "She always butters the toast to the edges."

As a little girl, I remember sitting next to my grandmother at the kitchen table, eating my toast, thinking about this story, which my mother had told me the first time I tried to butter a piece of toast by myself. Now, it is one of the most vivid memories I have of my grandmother. Growing up, when I came home from school, the house would be filled with the smell of freshly baked bread when Grandpa and Grandma were visiting. She always waited to slice the bread until we were there, and then she would butter it for us, with the butter melting into every slice . . . right to the edges. When I was sick, Grandma would bring me toast and tea on a tray. She showed me how to dip the toast into my tea so that it would go down more easily when I had a sore throat. But in truth, Grandma's toast always went down easily, because it was buttered to the edges.

At my grandmother's memorial service, the minister described her as "Christianity in an apron." To be sure, my grandmother embodied Jesus's love, humility, compassion, and gentleness. But she also showed me that being a Christian—or being a part of *any* tradition—has more to do with the seemingly little ways in which we care for one another, than anything else. The truth is that it makes a *lot* of difference whether a pat of butter is slapped in the center of a piece of toast or spread carefully to the edges. Taking an extra 5 seconds to make sure a piece of toast is buttered to the edges may seem like a miniscule thing, but it made all the difference in the world to Great-Grandmother May and me. Even as a child, however, I understood that my grandmother was not just admired for being attentive to the food she prepared; she was known for going "to the edges" in all that she did for others. She exemplified Jesus's teaching about "going the extra mile" with people (Matthew 5:41).

What would the world be like if we all went "to the edges" for others, and what rituals can help us to do so? These questions are at the very core of the Confucian tradition, which defines the category of ritual very broadly, including wide-ranging social customs, practices passed on in families, and matters of etiquette, in addition to the religious and civic rituals that usually come to mind when we think of ritual (e.g., bat mitzvahs, baptisms, weddings, commencements, inaugurations). From a Confucian perspective, buttering toast to the edges is a ritual in my family. This simple action is done consistently with a sense of reverence, and it carries a greater sense of meaning, reminding us of who we are and what we are about. It expresses care and concern for others while simultaneously cultivating attentiveness, compassion, and love for others.

## Ritual, Ethics, and Religion

Indeed, the importance of ritual in Confucianism is one reason why Confucianism resembles other religious traditions like Hinduism, Judaism, and Christianity more than philosophical traditions like Platonism, Kantianism, or Continental Philosophy. Yet when people find out that I specialize in Confucianism and teach in Georgetown's Theology and Religious Studies Department, they frequently ask, "Is Confucianism a religion?" And the matter of how to categorize Confucianism—as religion or philosophy?—is a challenge in the Western academy. (So, too, is the question of how to define "religion"—something I return to below.) I believe Confucianism is *both* a religious and a philosophical tradition, and that it provides us with an opportunity to broaden our conception of religion beyond traditions that focus on God. (It also provides us with an opportunity to broaden our conception of philosophy.[1])

As we shall see, Confucians most definitely held religious beliefs and engaged in religious practices, including the rituals they believed were essential to following the Confucian Way (the Dao 道 or Kongzi zhi dao 孔子之道 "the Way of Kongzi," as they called it). The Way is a path or way of life that is defined by cultivating particular virtues and practicing rituals that help us to become better people. Many of the rituals that constitute it involve making regular offerings to different kinds of spirits, including the spirits of one's own deceased ancestors. Early Confucians also believed that the Way has a more ultimate source: a mysterious entity they called Tian 天 (often translated as

"Heaven"). They believed that Tian wants humans to flourish, and as a result has designated certain individuals, including Kongzi ("Confucius"), to teach about the Way and encourage people to follow it.

The Confucian emphasis on moral cultivation and human flourishing can sometimes make Confucianism seem more like an ethical tradition than a religious one. But this is another reason why I think Confucianism is worth studying in order to better understand the nature of religion: it highlights the fact that living a good life and becoming a good person are not distinct from religion but central to it. To be part of a religious tradition is to be part of an ethical tradition. One cannot make sense of the Ten Commandments, Jesus's teachings in the Gospels, the teachings of Islam (which means "surrender" or "submission" to God's will), or Krishna's counsel to Arjuna without talking about the ethical values that are central to being Jewish, Christian, Muslim, or Hindu. Additionally, like these traditions, Confucian virtues and rituals usually involve a sense of reverence for something greater than ourselves, and a sense of the sacred. We tend to use words like "religious" or "spiritual" when describing these sensibilities.

What is it, exactly, that makes something religious? What makes any tradition a religion? Today, one of the few things on which most scholars of religion agree is that it is difficult to offer a fully adequate definition of religion. A broadening of attempts to define religion occurred when theologians and scholars of religion came to appreciate religions that did not have a concept of God. The concept of religion was transformed in the process, as people came to see that religions consist of much more than beliefs about deities, spirits, other supernatural entities, or transcendent realms, and that not all religious practices relate to these things.

I will not offer a definition of religion here. Instead, I invite readers to consider the things that the different traditions we are exploring throughout this book have in common. We will see that traditions we call "religions" fulfill a similar range of functions for humans. This is one of the things that is emphasized by scholars such as Ninian Smart, who argues that religions possess certain recognizable elements that are usually, though not always, present to some degree. He discusses these seven dimensions of religion:

1. Doctrinal: They offer systematic formulations of religious teachings in a coherent form.
2. Mythological: They have stories that work on multiple levels, sometimes fitting into a fairly complete interpretation of the universe and our place in it.
3. Ethical: They articulate expectations for human behavior and character.
4. Ritual: They regard the practice of different sorts of rituals and ceremonies as central to being a part of the tradition.

5. Experiential: They place an emphasis on such experiences as awe, mystery, liberation, and inner peace.
6. Institutional: They articulate a belief system and attitudes shared by a group, often with rules for the community.
7. Material: They value ordinary objects or places that symbolize or manifest the sacred or the supernatural.[2]

Smart argues that although not all these dimensions are found in all religions, every religion shares in some or all of them to greater or lesser degrees. In other words, different religions bear a "family resemblance" to one another. This concept of family resemblance has its origins in the work of the influential Austrian philosopher of language Ludwig Wittgenstein (1889–1951). Wittgenstein argued that some concepts (like religion) do not have a single defining feature or essence but are more like the resemblances between family members.[3] While red hair, fair skin, blue eyes, a petite stature, and left-handedness are all common characteristics in my family, not all of us have all these characteristics. Yet we bear a resemblance to each other; you can recognize that we are related, partly because each of us possesses *some* of these characteristics. Religions resemble each other in a similar manner.

Another reason why people often question whether Confucianism is a religion is that Confucian values and practices permeate East Asian cultures to such a degree that even those who frequent places of worship associated with other religions (including Buddhism, Daoism, and Christianity) embrace many dimensions of Confucianism. Exclusive devotion to one tradition, however, is not a defining feature of all religions. Indeed, religious practice in general tends to be highly syncretic in East Asia, which means that it involves mixing together beliefs and practices from different traditions (including, e.g., Buddhist, Confucian, Daoist, Shinto, and other indigenous practices) and viewing them as complementary. This would be unthinkable in the case of monotheistic religions in the West. Even though they share some of the same sacred texts, members of these traditions usually do not attend regular services at a Jewish synagogue, a Christian church, *and* an Islamic mosque, as membership or full participation in these religions is typically regarded as precluding full participation in the others. But in many other parts of the world, syncretism is and has long been characteristic of religious practice. So, for example, many people in East Asia frequent some combination of Buddhist, Daoist, Confucian, and Shinto temples on a regular basis.

## The Origins of Confucianism

The *Analects* (*Lunyu* 論語) is the earliest and most influential record of the teachings of Kongzi ("Confucius"), who lived from 551–479 BCE. If we measure influence according to the number of people who have lived their lives according to a particular person's teachings (or teachings attributed to that person), there is a good argument to be made that Kongzi is the most influential thinker in human history, due to the remarkable influence of Confucianism on the cultures of East Asia and Southeast Asia. This influence is impressive not only in length (since Kongzi is passing along the teachings of an earlier tradition that dates at least to the twelfth century BCE) but also in breadth and depth. Confucian values saturate the cultures of China, Korea, Japan, and Taiwan, as well as Southeast Asian countries like Singapore, Thailand, and Vietnam. Confucian values have long defined people's values in these parts of the world, even if they practice different religious traditions.

Kongzi insists, "I am a transmitter, not an innovator. I trust in and love the ancient" (*Analects* 7.1).[4] Kongzi understands himself as passing along and working to preserve and revive a set of traditional rituals and virtues that he attributes to ancient sage-kings. But when we look at his teachings compared with earlier sources that document that tradition, we can see that he is both transmitting *and* innovating. Kongzi is putting it all together in a new way, and this is why the tradition comes to name itself after him, referring to the Way of Kongzi. Kongzi's understanding and interpretation of this tradition became the standard—the Way that others found compelling and that served to influence and inspire them for thousands of years.

Kongzi lived and taught during the latter part of the Zhou Period, also known as the "Eastern Zhou" (770–256 BCE). It was a time of great political turbulence characterized by violence and warfare both between and within different states. Kongzi, like many other thinkers and teachers in his time, proposed a potential solution to the crisis his society was facing. Partly because the earlier part of the Zhou Period (the "Western Zhou," 1045–771 BCE) had been a time of peace and stability, Kongzi argued that the root of the problem was moral and cultural change: he believed that the steady abandonment of traditional rituals and virtues such as filial piety was the source of the problem with his society. His view was particularly compelling to people, and as a result it became a catalyst for debate and discussion between different emerging schools of thought.

Kongzi spent much of his time discussing rituals. As we have seen, these include not only what we would call religious or civic rituals but also social customs, manners, matters of etiquette, and traditions within families. He maintained that we should regard all these things with reverence and prioritize them. Despite the fact that we—like many people in Kongzi's time—might think our ways of greeting each other or expressing gratitude (or buttering toast) are minor affairs, Kongzi insisted that rituals like these are in fact complex and act in powerful ways to create and sustain relationships within families, communities, and societies, and to express and cultivate virtues like kindness, humility, generosity, and gratitude. In his view, this is critical to our overall flourishing, because good relationships and virtues like these hold the key to a good life. Take the virtue of gratitude, for example. Grateful people are happy people. And so practices that not only express but also cultivate the virtue of gratitude in us contribute directly to our sense of meaning, fulfillment, and overall happiness and satisfaction in life. Practicing gratitude also strengthens our relationships with others. For instance, when we practice a ritual such as writing a thank-you note, we not only express our appreciation for what someone has done (which enriches *their* life); it also affirms and strengthens our connection to them. Additionally, if we do it not just as a perfunctory gesture but with a sense of reverence, and use it as an opportunity to stop and reflect on what others have done for us, it also serves to *deepen* our gratitude for them and for what we have been given.

Human relationships are absolutely central to our flourishing, from a Confucian point of view. Among the most important relationships are those within families, as well as friendships. But Kongzi reserves a special category for the relationship between parents and children. He prioritizes the virtue of filial piety, which in his view entails a deep-seated respect, reverence, and love for one's parents, as well as gratitude for the unique forms of support and nurture that good parents provide. For Kongzi, these relationships provide the foundation for our development, setting us up to have good relationships with others (or hampering our progress toward that goal). Today, we have plenty of evidence from modern psychology that supports the Confucian view. As *Analects* 1.2 puts it, "Filial piety and respect for your siblings—are these not the roots of Ren 仁?" Ren 仁, often translated as humaneness or complete goodness, represents the ultimate state of character we are striving for. A Ren person possesses *all* the Confucian virtues. This is the person who is truly flourishing and who has reached their full potential as a human being (hence the translation "humane")—much like a tree that is flourishing is one that has reached its full potential by having full, robust branches and thick, consistent bundles of leaves throughout its canopy. But it all begins with, and is enabled by, the "roots"—family relationships that are defined by filial piety and respect.

## Tian

Some of the most interesting and mysterious dimensions of Kongzi's life and thought are his religious beliefs and experiences. Tian 天 is often translated as "Heaven" because it is a force or entity associated with the sky. But unlike our modern English term "Heaven," Tian does not refer to a place. For Kongzi and his disciples, Tian is a quasi-personal entity or agent, meaning that it possesses *some* personal (or person-like) qualities but also some impersonal qualities. In *Analects* 3.24, Kongzi's disciples are told, "The world has been without the Way for a long time now, and Tian is going to use your Master like the wooden clapper in a bell." That is, Tian intends to use Kongzi to get people's attention or to wake up the world, as the clapper in a bell would, in order to help people return to following the Way. In two different passages from the *Analects*, Kongzi expresses the belief that Tian will protect him while he is doing this work. In 7.23, after a military minister named Huan Tui tried to assassinate Kongzi, he says, "Tian has implanted this moral power in me. What can the likes of Huan Tui do to me?" In 9.5, Kongzi, who was detained in Kuang because he was mistaken for someone who had led a revolt in the region, says, "Is this culture not alive here [inside me]? If Tian intended this culture to perish, then after [Sage-King Wen's] death it would not have given us this culture. Since Tian does not yet intend this culture to perish, what can the people of Kuang do to me?"

Although Tian clearly has intentions, plans, and sometimes offers protection, Kongzi says that it does not speak or issue commands (17.19). But it certainly communicates its will to people. It is also possible to incur its wrath: in 3.13, Kongzi says, "If you incur the wrath of *Tian*, you have nowhere to turn in prayer." He also suggests that it is impossible for us to deceive Tian, suggesting that it knows and understands quite a bit, including who is making appropriate ritual sacrifices to various spirits and who is failing to do so (9.12). He says, "If anyone understands me, it is Tian" (14.35), suggesting that Tian understands our (or at least his) thoughts and feelings. Although Tian is believed to have a plan that will help human beings flourish: the Way, which we can follow by practicing traditional rituals and cultivating Confucian virtues, certain dimensions of Tian's plan are beyond our control or understanding. Fate (*ming* 命) refers to difficult circumstances that we cannot influence or control but which are believed to be a part of Tian's plan. For instance, when Kongzi's student, Bo Niu, is suffering from a serious illness, Kongzi goes to visit him and says, "We are losing him. It has to be fate! For such a person to have such an illness! For such a person to have such an illness!" Fate describes events that are unexplainable—in this case, that such a good young person has such a devastating illness—but which are believed to be a part of Tian's plan, even though we cannot fathom what the purpose might be. The term for fate, *ming*, carries the sense of a mandate or command from Tian, and this is why the early Confucians believed it is not only futile but harmful to struggle against it.

Why did Kongzi believe that Tian existed, and how did he know that he was meant to teach about it? One possible answer to this question is that the concept of Tian was simply a part of the religious culture in which he lived. And it certainly is true that we uncritically absorb a variety of ideas and views from our respective cultures. But Kongzi is more critical than most; he amended and criticized several dimensions of his culture—critiquing, for instance, the haphazard and unreflective ritual practices of his time. In contrast, he insisted that people should know the purposes of rituals and be "fully present" when they participate in them. This is in part because he believed the most important dimension of rituals is how they transform us as people. So he was hardly someone who simply "went along with" prevailing religious views and practices. The more likely answer to the question of why Kongzi believed he was called to teach about Tian is that he discerned or experienced such a calling. We do not have a record of what he perceived or experienced, but we also do not have any writings of his own. We do, though, have records of his conversations, including his claim that Tian implanted a kind of moral power in him that gave him protection, and that the culture of the ancient sage-kings is alive inside of him, as well as his claim that if anyone understands him, it is Tian. He says these things with conviction. Indeed, he expresses faith in Tian's existence and purposes.

The only place where we find Kongzi questioning his faith in Tian is after the death of one of his most exceptional followers, Yan Hui. In what is perhaps the most poignant passage in the *Analects*, upon learning of Yan Hui's death, Kongzi cries out, "Tian has abandoned me! Tian has abandoned me!" (11.9) This response is a notable contrast to the impending death of Bo Niu (discussed above), where Kongzi expresses a kind of faith that this tragic turn of events must be due to fate. Those familiar with the Christian tradition may think of resonances here with Jesus weeping at his friend Lazarus's tomb, or crying out on the cross, "My God, my God, why have you forsaken me?" In all these cases, we see the *humanity* of the central figures in these religions, including their experiences of pain and anguish, and their feelings of being abandoned by Tian (in Kongzi's case) or God the Father (in Jesus's case).

Why is this significant? For one thing, it makes the central figures of both Confucianism and Christianity more *relatable*: their vulnerability helps us to see them as examples that we can follow, even though we lack their wisdom or divinity. (Indeed, the Confucian tradition eventually deifies Kongzi. Shortly after his death, temples were built to honor him, and he has been venerated throughout most of Confucian history, right up to the present.) This helped Confucianism and Christianity to become more effective contexts for people to bring about real change in themselves and their lives, which contributed to their growth as religions.

### Ancestor Veneration

In addition to Tian, during his life Kongzi also expresses an unwavering belief in and devotion to ancestral spirits—understood as more powerful, ethereal members of this realm. Confucians contend that we continue to exist in a spiritual form after death, but we do not go to another place or realm.

Rather, the spirits of the dead exist in an unseen dimension of this realm. As spirits, they are not completely self-sustaining: they have both physical needs (or needs relating to their *qi* 氣 "energy"), as well as emotional needs. So, our deceased family members depend on sacrificial offerings of food for sustenance, and they like to be remembered by loved ones. While people in Kongzi's time and throughout East Asian history have long been concerned with keeping these spirits happy so that they will not wreak havoc on the lives of their descendants, Kongzi and his followers were most interested in how ritual sacrifices to these spirits can help make us better people. They believed that ancestral sacrifices could facilitate moral cultivation by giving us regular opportunities to remember and honor those who have gone before, and to reflect on ourselves as part of a lineage that stretches back in time, as well as forward. At times, we might draw inspiration from those who have gone before; but we also might be motivated to become better versions of ourselves when we remember that one day we will be ancestors, with our descendants looking back on our lives.

The final assignment in my Chinese philosophy course is for students to research one of their great-grandparents, largely by conducting interviews with their parents, grandparents, and other family members, and then—based on their experience—discuss why they think ancestor veneration was such an important ethical practice for the Confucians. My students usually come away from this with a deep sense of gratitude for what they have and for the decisions and sacrifices that many people before them made, which led them to where they are today. It puts their problems into perspective and reminds them of the remarkable struggles that people in the past have faced. Students also regularly remark on how this experience led them to deepen their relationships with their living family members and helped them to better understand their family as a whole. In the interviews, families often talk about things they would never otherwise discuss, and the experience frequently leads family members (even my students' parents) to share details of their own lives and experiences that were previously unknown. Indeed, this is one of the important functions of ancestor veneration: the ritual of storytelling that is a part of it creates and sustains our relationships with each other, and reminds us of shared values, virtues, and vices that have been passed down in our families, defining and uniting (or separating) us. But my students are most affected by the fact that learning their ancestors' stories makes them *believe* that they can become better people (because they are literally *made of the same stuff* as their ancestors), while also nurturing their *desire* to become better. This is why the Confucians believed that ancestor veneration plays a special role in self-cultivation. Unlike other people we admire or look up to, our ancestors are literally a part of us—not just through our DNA but through the shared customs and values that have been handed down from them. As a result, when we hear that they overcame various kinds of challenges or possessed certain virtues, it is easier to believe that we, too, can do the same. Conversely, when we hear about their moral failings, it tends to make us want to do better, to right past wrongs, so to speak. This moral response stems from the sense that we are not fully distinct from them.

Kongzi's emphasis on the ethical dimension of ancestral sacrifices certainly does not mean that he did not also hold traditional beliefs about the spirits. He expresses the concern that improper sacrifices to both ancestral spirits and nature spirits (e.g., those associated with mountains and rivers) may incur the wrath of those spirits (e.g., *Analects* 2.24, 3.6, 6.6). He also maintains that these spirits know when the wrong person is performing a ritual sacrifice, and when someone is performing a ritual for the wrong reason (e.g., just to curry favor, to usurp the role of a ruler, or to display their wealth). Kongzi urges people to respect the spirits while maintaining an appropriate distance from them (6.22)—which means showing reverence for them, not behaving in an overly familiar manner toward them, and not becoming overly concerned with (or distracted by) the unseen dimension of this world. Kongzi does not dissuade people of the belief that unhappy spirits can wreak havoc on our lives, but he does think we should practice rituals out of genuine love, reverence, and appreciation for our ancestors, and not out of fear or the desire to pacify them. If we are fully present at rituals in these ways, we will honor and provide for the spirits *and* we will become better people in the process (which is another way of honoring them).

To be sure, the boundary between the living and the dead is not an impermeable one, and we navigate it through ritual. Among the most important Confucian rituals are those we practice when mourning the deaths of our parents and other loved ones. This large set of rituals are designed to guide people through the difficult process of grieving the loss of loved ones, and learning to live with them as a part of our lives in a different way. Mourning rituals in Confucianism provide a comprehensive outlet for our grief: they give us a way of expressing the pain we feel through the clothing we wear, the music we listen to, and the food we eat. They include weeping, sharing memories, and spending time with others who cared about our loved ones. Mourning garments signify the need to treat someone gently, since they are grieving a loss, and rituals such as bowing when one passes someone wearing mourning garments provide a way for all members of society to express care, concern, and sympathy for those in mourning. But even in a contemporary society without such rituals, clothing can serve an important therapeutic function. After my father died, I only wore black and blue for a long time, because the pain was so deep that I felt like I had been beaten up. It was therapeutic for me to express my grief in this way, even though it was a solitary action in a society bereft of rituals.

Rituals that are performed with the right feelings and motivations are not empty, transactional practices but are invested with meaning and have tremendous transformative power in our lives. We see this view at work in descriptions of Kongzi's own religious practices. *Analects* 10.11 tells us that he set aside a portion of every meal for his ancestral spirits, "and did so with reverence"—a traditional ritual designed not only to provide sustenance to the spirits but also to get us to pause and consider where we came from in relation to where we are. At one meal, you might remember your grandmother and her tremendous generosity. At another, you might consider the courage your great-grandparents must have had to board a boat to an unknown land, in hope of giving their children a better life. Doing this at every meal carves out dedicated space and time to reflect on why you are where you are and who you are, not simply as a result of your own choices. Practiced in the right way, rituals of this sort give us hope that we can rise above our challenges and problems by reminding us that we are made of the same stuff as people who embodied virtues such as perseverance and resilience in the face of tremendous adversity. They also inspire in us a sense of responsibility to make the most of what we have been given, and to consider how we can provide for those to come (not from a material perspective but an ethical one: through our values, traditions, and the example we provide). Here, we can see why Kongzi thinks rituals are so important: practiced in the right ways, they are the most effective tools for shaping us into better people. But they can only do this work if we are "fully present" in mind, body, and spirit when we perform rituals; as he puts it, "If I am not fully present at the ritual sacrifice, it's as though I haven't participated in the ritual at all" (3.12). In 17.11, Kongzi goes on to criticize those in his own time who neglected the importance of being fully present: "'Have rituals! Have rituals!' they say. But is it [only] having jade and silks?" His question is intended to help us to see that, no, it is not only about what we do; it is about developing feelings and virtues such as gratitude.

In its conception of Tian and ancestral spirits, the Confucian tradition offers us an interesting alternative to traditional forms of theism. Early Confucians did not believe in God, nor did they claim that Tian is omniscient, omnipotent, omnibenevolent, or a personal being. If we understand theism as a belief in a powerful religious being of some sort that has personal attributes, then it does not seem accurate to call Tian a theistic concept or deity, because it lacks some of the most important personal (or person-like) attributes that we typically associate with deities: it does not seem to have emotions; nor does it speak or issue commands. It is not understood as a Creator. I have argued that Tian is best understood as a quasi-personal entity or agent, since it has personal attributes such as intentions, plans, and desires but is much less personal than God or deities.[5] Additionally, ancestral spirits do not seem to serve or interact with Tian in any way. The Confucian belief in different kinds of spirits would suggest that we can characterize Confucianism as involving a belief in polytheism, but it is important to remember that these spirits are not all-powerful, and they depend upon humans for sustenance and happiness.

To be sure, Confucianism provides an example of what an *alternative* to belief in God looks like, in different religious traditions. Even if one does not believe in God, one might still believe in a quasi-personal entity such as Tian that wants us to flourish and guides us in various ways. Confucianism also highlights the ethical goods that come from being part of a religious tradition. One of the things that different religions have in common is their devotion to helping us to become better people. In the Confucian tradition, this occurs largely through ritual practice, which highlights another important dimension of religious traditions. In most religions, one's dedication to practicing particular rituals is a defining feature of being a part of that tradition.

Modern American culture is far less ritualistic than ancient Confucianism. This means that we must create or revive rituals if we wish to have more of them. I began this chapter with the story of how my grandmother's practice of buttering toast to the edges became a ritual in my family. Many years later, this ritual continued in an unexpected way after my father's death, as I traveled with my children from our home in Washington, DC, in the dead of winter, to my small hometown in Alaska for the funeral. We had an overnight layover in Seattle, and with a tired and cranky two-year-old, six-year-old, and eight-year-old in tow, I was exhausted. That is when our lifelong family friends, Ed and Blythe, who live in Seattle, offered to come meet us. He had been the minister at our church when I was growing up, and they had known me since I was a child. So when they offered to come to our hotel to visit us that evening, I said yes, knowing that seeing them would be a source of comfort.

What I did not know was that they remembered the story I had shared with them about my grandmother buttering toast to the edges. That evening, they showed up at our hotel carrying a large grocery bag. Inside was a toaster, a loaf of homemade bread, a stick of butter, a knife, and some jam and cheese. Amazed and overcome with gratitude, I watched as Blythe set up the toaster on our hotel room desk and began to make toast for us. My children perched on a chair observing her in fascination. And we all marveled at a pair of toast tongs she used, which enabled her to draw the hot pieces of toast out of the toaster easily, before she buttered them to the edges.

As I watched her, I thought of my grandmother's buttered toast, but I also remembered watching Ed break the communion loaves in the ritual of Holy Communion at the church where I grew up. I remembered my father's hand in mine as we walked down the aisle and kneeled together, side by side, to receive communion. I remembered the smiles on the faces of our church family members as we returned to our seats. In the coming days, these memories would anchor me, as those same church members crafted my father's casket from locally sourced wood, lined it with a quilt they had made, and accompanied us to the icy cemetery for the graveside service.

The bread that Jesus broke with his disciples the night before he died symbolizes many things for Christians, including the deep love and compassion that Jesus taught us to offer each other in the midst of the brokenness we experience in life. From a Confucian perspective, this is precisely how rituals work. Here we see what the Confucian tradition can contribute to our understanding of the problem of God, especially in the insight that rituals are essential to our flourishing. They weave our lives into the lives of others. They are overflowing with meaning, memories, and reminders of who we are. They show us the way forward in difficult times. They remind us that we are loved, and they show us how to love others. The next Christmas, a pair of toast tongs arrived in the mail from Ed and Blythe, as a gift to our family. Every time I use them, I am reminded of how love endures. All because of the ritual of buttering toast to the edges.

## Notes

1. For a compelling discussion of this issue, see Bryan W. Van Norden, *Taking Back Philosophy: A Multicultural Manifesto* (New York: Columbia University Press, 2017).

2. This is my summary. Smart originally outlined six dimensions of religion, and he adds the seventh in *The World's Religions: Old Traditions and Modern Transformations*, by Ninian Smart (Cambridge: Cambridge University Press, 1989).

3. Some of Wittgenstein's clearest remarks on family resemblance are found in his *Philosophical Investigations*, trans. G. E. M. Ancombe (Upper Saddle River, NJ: Prentice Hall, 1973), paras. 65–67.

4. All translations from the *Analects* are my own. See my *The Analects: A Contemporary Translation*, New York: Liveright, 2026.

5. For further discussion of these dimensions of Kongzi's view, see my *The Analects: A Guide* (New York: Oxford University Press, 2021).

# 7

# DAOIST VIEWS OF THE INFINITE DAO

## Theism, Deism, and Agnosticism

. . . a wren in the privet began to sing.
He was positively drenched in enthusiasm. . . .
But I thought, of the wren's singing, what could this be
if it isn't a prayer?
—Mary Oliver

The Dao is the altar of all the creatures in the world.
—the *Daodejing*

Without looking out of my window, I can know the ways of Heaven.
The farther one travels, the less one knows.
—The Beatles, "The Inner Light"

In the middle of morning rush hour, he positioned himself against a wall beside a trash can in the L'Enfant Plaza Metro Station—the nucleus of federal Washington. Dressed in jeans and a T-shirt, he opened his violin case, removed his violin, swiveled the case to face pedestrian traffic, and began to play. Each passerby then had a quick choice to make, "one familiar to commuters in any urban area where the occasional street performer is part of the cityscape: Do you stop and listen? Do you hurry past with a blend of guilt and irritation, aware of your cupidity but annoyed by the unbidden demand on your time and your wallet? Do you throw in a buck, just to be polite? Does your decision change if he is really bad? What if he is really good? Do you have time for beauty? Should you? What are the moral mathematics of the moment?"[1]

That morning, those questions were answered in a very public way, since the musician standing against the wall at the top of the escalators was one of the finest classical musicians in the world, playing some of the most elegant music ever written, on one of the most valuable violins ever made. Two weeks later, he would play to a standing-room-only audience in the Washington area that was "so respectful of his artistry that they stifled their coughs until the silence between movements."[2] The *Washington Post* had convinced this violinist, Joshua Bell, to participate in an experiment "in context, perception and priorities—as well as an unblinking assessment of public taste: In a banal setting at an inconvenient time, would beauty transcend?"[3] The staff of the *Post* had discussed how to handle the possible mob scene that might result when people recognized Bell. But they never anticipated the scenario that actually unfolded that morning.

Over the course of 43 minutes, as Bell performed six classical pieces, 1,097 people passed by. Only 7 people stopped to listen the performance, at least for a minute. Twenty-seven gave money, most of them on the run—for a total of $32.17. ("Yes, some people gave pennies," the *Post* noted.) Only one person recognized him and stood there taking in the remainder of his performance, appalled that her fellow commuters were throwing small change into his case. A total of 1,070 people hurried by, oblivious, many only a few feet away, with very few of them even turning to look.

When interviewed by the *Post* a few hours later, some people explained that "they were busy, had other things on their mind." Some had earbuds in and could not hear him. Some, using cell phones, spoke more loudly as they passed by. Many did not remember there having been a musician in the subway at all. The *Post* noted that there was no ethnic or demographic pattern to distinguish those who stopped to watch Bell or gave money, with one very important exception: "Every single time a child walked past, he or she tried to stop and watch. And every single time, a parent scooted the kid away."

Ancient Daoist philosophers would absolutely love this story.[4] And it is a great illustration of why ancient Daoist philosophers believed we are born good but are corrupted by the world. Unlike their Confucian adversaries, the early Daoists believed that the forces of socialization and education are in fact insidious influences; they erode our natural goodness. Indeed, Daoists would be keen to point out that not a single child in the subway station that day needed to be taught that the music was worth stopping for; their natural curiosity led them to stop. It was the adults who rushed past, even though many of them know a great deal about classical music.

This is a larger metaphor, in the Daoist view: we fail to even notice many (most?) of the things worth savoring because we are busy pursuing the goods society values: a successful career, wealth, prestige, and power. As the *Post* points out, if "the surge of modern life so overpowers us that we are deaf and blind to something like that—then what else are we missing?"[5] And so the Daoists argue against the Confucian view that we ought to engage in moral self-cultivation. Instead, we should resist this process, which destroys our naturally good tendencies—among them our natural curiosity for all things, and the way in which our unsocialized minds are more perceptive of what they would call the manifestations of the Dao (e.g., music).

### The Daoist Critique of Confucian Self-Cultivation

The most influential Daoist text in the world, the *Daodejing*, is the second-most-translated text in English; only the Bible has more translations. It has had an extraordinary influence in East Asia and became of particular interest to the English-speaking world during the countercultural movement of the 1960s. It dates to the third century BCE, and although it is attributed to a mythical Daoist sage referred to as Laozi ("Old Master"), it was in fact written by multiple people, in a beautiful poetic style. The form of the text is important: written in verse, it is designed to put readers at ease, helping them to settle down and begin to undo the damage that socialization and education have done. This dimension of the text stands the test of time: I often have students tell me that they enjoy reading the *Daodejing* because it has a therapeutic effect on them, leaving them feeling less anxious and more at peace than when they began.

Like the *Daodejing*, many religious texts do not just aim to articulate a particular view of the world but also to elicit a therapeutic result in readers. Think, for example, of the Psalms in the Bible: for thousands of years, Jews and Christians have read, recited, and sung the Psalms to express gratitude, anger, despair, and hope within the context of their faith in God. But at the same time, the Psalms are presenting a view of what it means to lead a good life by bringing ourselves into relationship with our Creator, acknowledging our own finitude in the face of an infinite God. The *Daodejing* contends that we stand in relation to an entity known as the Dao that nurtures and guides us and that we can live immeasurably better lives by acknowledging our own finitude in the face of the Infinite Dao.

Additionally, the Daoist tradition contends that we are born in harmony with the Dao, aware of its presence and dancing in time to its rhythms. That is, we naturally respond to the world as the children in the subway responded to the music: we are alert and curious, inclined to stop and savor beauty and interactions with anyone who passes by (human and nonhuman animals alike)—all of which brings us joy and satisfaction. But we are also born into a world full of Confucian self-cultivationists who are convinced that we need to work hard to become good. The early Confucians were fond of metaphors that illustrated this process through carving and polishing jade, bone, or ivory until it becomes beautiful. The *Analects* quote the ancient classic, the *Book of Odes*: "As if cut, as if ground, as if carved, as if polished" (1.15), and Kongzi emphasizes the importance of early upbringing as pivotal for later moral cultivation, saying that "rotten wood cannot be carved" (5.10). The third-century-BCE Confucian Xunzi takes this even further, describing how moral cultivation resembles artisans working in a difficult medium. While some wood must be straightened on a shaping frame, other wood must be steamed and slowly bent to make a wheel. These images illustrate how we must be reshaped by rituals in order to become good.

The authors of the *Daodejing* respond critically, with their own set of metaphors. They contend that we are like beautiful pieces of unhewn or uncarved wood, and that "the greatest carving cuts nothing off" (chap. 28). From a Daoist perspective, we come into the world already resembling the choicest wood, with colors, patterns, and combinations of textures that are a work of art in themselves. Then the world does violence to us, insisting that the wood must be carved to become beautiful, and using the sharp edges of its knives and tools to cut into our originally good nature. Things we naturally do, such as responding with love to those who love us, and with compassion to those in need, are warped as we seek to cultivate rigid Confucian virtues such as filial piety and benevolence. And so the *Daodejing* tells us we must cease and desist the process of Confucian cultivation. Using the Confucian terms for sageliness, and enumerating the Confucian virtues, they write, "Cut off sageliness, abandon wisdom, and the people will benefit one-hundred-fold. Cut off benevolence, abandon righteousness, and the people will return to being filial and kind" (chap. 19).

Of particular note is that people will *return* to being filial and kind if they stop practicing Confucian self-cultivation, because we are *all* born naturally and originally good. The authors of the *Daodejing* are aware that "this might leave the people lacking in culture, so give them something with which to identify: Manifest plainness. Embrace simplicity. Do not think just of yourself. Make few your desires" (chap. 19). They value a simple life, not one that is filled with complex rituals and the pursuit of lofty goals. Think back to the image of the children naturally stopping to listen to the music, but being hurried along by parents because of the day's agenda. We are taught to name and label things, carving up the world as we are carved by the world. We are also made to desire things that we do not desire naturally, and so they write, "Nameless unhewn wood is but freedom from desire" (chap. 37). Think of very young children, who do not (yet) care what toys everyone else has and are content to play with (or in) an empty cardboard box—which they do not view as a mere container that holds something desirable.

This is why the *Daodejing* repeatedly appeals to infants and young children as models of our original goodness: "I alone am still and inactive, . . . like a child who has not yet learned to smile. . . . I seem to have nowhere to go" (chap. 20). It is not that the authors of the text want us to act like babies; rather, they want us to take inspiration from the untarnished nature of children to live in a way that is closer to our original, good nature. So they recall our earliest stages of development with explicit references to *newborn* children and infants who have not yet learned to smile, because they know that the forces of socialization and education act on us very soon after our birth. A newborn infant's capacity to "wail all day without growing hoarse," their firm, fisted grip that exceeds ours in strength, and their unparalleled physical flexibility (chap. 55) are all forms of strength that we lose as we grow. Additionally, infants cry when they are hungry, eat until they are full, and sleep when they are tired. As we grow, we learn to hide our true feelings and needs. We resist eating in order to conform to artificial standards of beauty (and we sometimes overeat, losing our awareness of when we are full, largely as a result of the social pressures of this world). We resist sleeping when we are tired because there is work to be done. All these things represent departures from our original tendencies that guide us toward our own well-being, and they are driven by societal and cultural expectations. In addition, all these things actively undermine our well-being, carving us like knives cutting into a piece of wood.

Early Daoists contended that this process of corruption continues as we grow. The world encourages complexity and materialism, when in fact the simplest things in life bring us the greatest joy and fulfillment. While we tend to think that infants and young children are not worthy of our admiration because they do not do much—they are not "high achievers" by the world's goals and standards—the authors of the *Daodejing* contend that this inactivity is precisely why they are so much happier than the rest of us. We do not care for the fact that they lack autonomy, having to be literally carried everywhere and not being capable of making their own decisions, but the *Daodejing* points out that they have few worries because they are cared for, and they are not competitive, aggressive, or self-conscious as a result. Infants and young children are unrefined, uncultured, and spontaneous—often embarrassing or inconveniencing us—but from the perspective of the *Daodejing*, they are at home in the world and genuinely happy. This is why we should seek to "return home to be a child" (chap. 28). (This idea can be compared with Jesus's words in the Gospel of Matthew, when he urges us to "become like children" in order to enter the Kingdom of Heaven.[6]) If you have ever longed for the happy, carefree moments of your childhood—something we call "nostalgia"—then you can begin to understand where the authors of this text are coming from. Our lives are too complex, and this breeds anxiety and unhappiness. It is not *just* that children are being taken care of (by adults) that leaves them with fewer worries; it is also that their goals and agendas are simpler: they do not care about (or worry about) as many things as we do, and the things they do care about are inherently simpler, which leaves them with fewer worries.

## What Is the Dao?

One of the keys to retaining or recovering our original goodness is inherently religious, because it involves being filled with the infinite: "If you are a canyon for all the world, constant virtue will never leave you, and you can return home to be a child" (chap. 28). Emptiness is held up as a good because if we empty ourselves of the world's goals and values—or are not filled up by them—then the Dao dwells in us, never leaving us, and we retain our original virtue. This is why the title of the *Daodejing* itself is "The Scripture of the Way and Virtue." The term I have translated as scripture, *jing* 經, is often translated as "classic," but the ancient Chinese tradition regards these texts as sacred texts, which is why I think "scripture" comes closer to its sense in classical Chinese. Additionally, in modern English, we use the term "classic" not to designate sacred texts but to refer to works that have been heralded as culturally important. This is precisely the kind of designation the authors of the *Daodejing* are calling into question. The authors of this text urge us to question the hidden assumptions and judgments that we uncritically absorb through the process of socialization and education. Indeed, they eventually call on us to get rid of all written texts, because a scholarly way of life is not the best or most natural form of life for us (chap. 80). While it might strike us as self-contradictory for the authors of any text to call on us to get rid of all writings, the authors of the *Daodejing* wrote down their ideas in order to "spread the word" about what they believed was the solution to the crisis their society was facing. They aimed to convince people to embrace a way of life that they believed could bring peace during the aptly named Warring States Period of early China (403–221 BCE). Once people understand the kind of life we must lead, we will no longer need the *Daodejing*. At that point, we must leave the text behind and simply live in the way it describes, a bit like using a ladder to climb up to a rooftop, and then kicking away the ladder because it is no longer needed.[7]

What does their vision of a good society entail? The *Daodejing* maintains that we ought to live in small, scattered agrarian villages, and not in large, centralized cities and states (chap. 80). Our lives should revolve around working with our hands in the earth to plant, harvest, and gather food, and using natural resources to make the things we need—from raising barns and building furniture to making quilts, clothing, and baked goods—all in collaboration with other members of our community. This is the kind of education we will receive, as opposed to the academic education of the Confucians (or most modern societies). The *Daodejing* warns us not to use "labor-saving tools" or various forms of technology because of their corrupting influence on this way of life. Simplicity must be the cardinal virtue.

If you think this ancient vision of a good life is wholly untenable today, think again. It is a life that closely resembles that of Old Order Amish communities in North America, which have successfully sustained their way of life since the early 1700s, with a population that continues to grow rapidly. Another key resemblance between Amish communities and the simple agrarian communities described in the *Daodejing* is that they are both rooted in religious convictions: a belief in God, for the Amish, and for the Daoists, a belief in the Dao. Above all, the Amish seek to emulate the life of Jesus of Nazareth by practicing unconditional love and forgiveness, humility (including a giving up of self and yielding to God and the Church), obedience, nonviolence, gratitude, and simplicity. The authors of the *Daodejing* ask us to emulate the Dao by embodying some overlapping virtues such as humility, nonresistance, and simplicity, as well as some different ones: emptiness, nonaction or effortless action, and flexibility. But the Dao is not a personal God. Indeed, I believe this is one of the reasons why early Daoism is worth studying: this religious tradition offers an alternative to theism, or belief in God.

The text of the *Daodejing* tells us that the Dao "seems to be the ancestor of the Myriad Creatures. It blunts their sharpness; Untangles their tangles; Softens their glare; Merges with their dust. Deep and clear! It seems to be there" (chap. 4). The authors repeatedly express humility about their own perceptions of the Dao, saying that it "*seems* to be the ancestor of the myriad creatures" and "*seems* to be there" rather than boldly making objective statements about it. They have a keen sense of their own finitude in the face of the infinite Dao, and they are also focused on describing their own experiences of it. They view the Dao as the ancestor of the myriad creatures or "ten thousand things"—a metaphor for all the creatures in the world.

Here we see a number of important differences between the Daoist conception of the Dao and the Confucian conception of the Dao. First, the early Daoists conceive of the Dao as an entity or force that relates to humans therapeutically—blunting their sharpness and untangling their tangles, while the Confucians maintain that it is a path or way of life that is defined by cultivating virtues like filial piety, ritual propriety, and humaneness. Second, the Dao relates to all living things and not just humans, according to the *Daodejing*, while for the Confucians it is a human way of life; it does not apply to, nor is it followed by, other creatures. The Daoists understand it as the underlying force of nature that is observable in the growth of trees, the forming of bonds, and an animal's inclinations, whereas the Confucians saw it as a road map to goodness. Third, the text repeatedly describes the Dao as the ancestor or origin of all living things. The Confucians do not view the Dao as the origin of life; rather, it comes to us through sages who are called to teach us about Tian's plan for us to flourish. Tian, for the Confucians, is the origin of the Dao, and it is not the source or ancestor of creation.

This third characteristic of the Daoist conception of the Dao distinguishes it from a variety of other religious entities and especially God in the major monotheistic faith traditions. In the passage above, it is called the *ancestor* of the myriad creatures, and in multiple chapters, it is referred to as that which produces (in the sense of *gives birth to*) the world and all the creatures in it (chaps. 20, 40, 42, and 51). The Dao is often referred to as "Mother," and it is consistently referred to in feminine terms, and never as masculine (e.g., chaps. 6, 20, and 52). "The female" is repeatedly exalted over the male in the text, and we are urged to be like the Dao in this regard, as the text asks us, "Can you play the part of the feminine?" (chap. 10).

What are we to make of all this? For one, we are seeing what some traditions have called the Divine Feminine, although perhaps the term "divine" should be replaced with "infinite" here, as the divine typically references theism. At least two related characteristics of mothers and women in early China were appealing to the Daoists: their capacity to gently nurture and care for others (especially children), and their emptiness, both as a physiological characteristic that allows them to give birth and as a social characteristic (i.e., they were deprived of the kind of education men received). Early Daoists contend that mainstream society and culture values most of the wrong things, and that most of the things (and people) that are devalued are those we should value most. Whereas society prizes someone who is assertive, aggressive, and overtly strong, the authors of the *Daodejing* emphasize that gentleness is a virtue and a sign of true strength. This is one reason why the text repeatedly tells us "the highest good is like water," urging us to be more like water: it is "supple and weak," takes the shape of whatever it is poured into, and yet "nothing can surpass it for attacking what is stiff and strong" (chaps. 8, 43, and 78). Additionally, women in ancient China were empty in not having careers or official positions; mothers were expected to be self-sacrificing and inviting, emptying themselves for the needs of their children, and mothers with their wombs are empty, like valleys and canyons. Our goal, according to the *Daodejing*, ought to be making ourselves empty rather than filling ourselves up with the world's goals and values. If we remain empty, the Dao is able to dwell in us.

Indeed, emptiness and effortless action (*wuwei* 無為) are among the most important features of the Dao that we are to emulate. The text tells us, "the Way is like an empty vessel," or the empty space in between the spokes of a wheel, and that "the Way does nothing and yet nothing is left undone" (chaps. 4, 11, and 37). The Dao does not foist itself on us, does not manipulate or control us or other creatures in the world, but it is there for us to accord with through our natural rhythms and inclinations, and when we do so, nothing is left undone. Daoist landscape paintings highlight the way in which empty space and less activity are good: landscapes consist of waterfalls, clouds, lakes and mountains, with large patches of empty space in their midst. The humans in the frame—as well as their houses and boats—are miniscule, tucked into the landscape, blending so seamlessly into the hills and water that you must look closely in order to see them. Often, sages are depicted in reclining positions, at rest and at peace, "abiding in nonaction," as the *Daodejing* says (chap. 2).

In the Daoist tradition, this art is a way of illustrating our place in the world—both the truth about the way things are and the way we ought to live. From a Daoist perspective, we are one small part of a larger whole. We are neither the center of the world nor the most important part of it. In order to live well, we must recognize this fundamental truth and live in harmony with the rest of Nature (something else that we naturally do as young children, when we are drawn to the wonder of nature: young children do not usually rush past puddles and anthills, but stop to enjoy them). And Daoist landscape paintings are a notable contrast to traditional Confucian paintings, which prominently feature sages or scenes from sages' lives. Confucian sages are rarely depicted reclining or at rest: rather, they are in upright, ritually correct postures, visibly engaged in learning and self-cultivation.

Looking at all the descriptions of the Dao throughout the *Daodejing*, we see that this entity is at once transcendent and immanent; it is beyond us and greater than us, yet it is here in our midst, beating in our chests and pulsing through our veins, moving in our midst as it untangles our tangles and merges with our dust. It seems to be omnipresent: "Still and indistinct, it stands alone and unchanging. It goes everywhere and yet is never at a loss. One can regard it as the mother of Heaven and Earth. I do not know its proper name; I have given it the [name] 'the Way'" (chap. 25). It is also dynamic: it underlies the transformation and change of all things and regulates the universe's natural cycle. Change characterizes the world, and yet this change is orderly because it is regulated and driven by the Dao—the ultimate source of all living things.

The Dao is described using both impersonal and personal language, often in the same chapter: "How expansive is the great Way! Flowing to the left and to the right. The myriad creatures rely on it for life and it turns none of them away. When its work is done it claims no merit. It clothes and nourishes the myriad creatures, but does not lord it over them" (chap. 34). Qualities such as "expansive" and "flowing" are not personal (or person-like), but activities like "clothing," "nourishing," and "not claiming merit" are personal. Given this combination of characteristics, the Dao does not seem to be a theistic entity. Earlier in this work, I defined theism as involving the belief in a powerful spiritual entity of some sort that has personal characteristics or qualities. In the last chapter, we found that the Confucian concept of Tian is a quasi-personal entity or agent. The concept of the Dao in the *Daodejing* is even less personal than Tian in the *Analects*.

So how should we classify the Dao, from a religious perspective, if it is not a theistic entity? According to the *Daodejing*, the Dao is a force or entity that we can encounter, as well as something that works and moves within us. Throughout the text, the authors repeatedly describe their experiences of the Dao: "As for the Way, it is vague and elusive. Vague and elusive! Within is an image. Vague and elusive! Within is a thing. Withdrawn and dark! Within is an essence. This essence is genuine and authentic. Within there is trust. From ancient times until the present day, its name has never left it. It is how we know the origin of all things. How do I know what the origin of all things is like? Through this!" (chap. 21) It is difficult to find but it can be used: "Look for it and it cannot be seen; listen for it and it cannot be heard; but use it and it will never run dry!" (chap. 35) One of the things these passages tell us is that the Dao is greater than we can conceive or grasp, and beyond this world's categories, including language: "Looked for but not seen, its name is 'minute.' Listened for but not heard, its name is 'rarified.' Grabbed for but not gotten, its name is 'subtle'" (chap. 14). The text continues with a description of it, including its alignment with the ancient ways: "Trailing off without end, it cannot be named. . . . Greet it and you will not see its head; Follow it and you will not see its tail. Hold fast to the Way of old, in order to control what is here today. The ability to know the ancient beginnings, this is called the thread of the Way" (chap. 14). "Embracing your soul and holding on to the One, can you keep them from departing? Concentrating your *qi* 氣 'vital energies,' and attaining the utmost suppleness, can you be a child?" (chap. 10). Sages, the text tells us, "embrace the One and serve as models for the whole world" (chap. 22).

## Alternatives to Theism

As we saw earlier in this book, there are many varieties of theism, but they share a belief in a personal being or beings who intervene in history, in some way. One of the interesting features of the Dao is that it cannot be classified as theistic, since it is not a personal being; but it is not deistic, either, because it is at work in the world and interacts with the myriad creatures. The early Confucian and Daoist traditions each offer alternatives to theism and deism with their central religious concepts. Tian in the Confucian tradition and the Dao in the early Daoist tradition are both what we would call religious ultimates—central entities in a religion that are associated with the sacred, the divine, or the infinite. But since these entities are not personal beings, we lack clear terms for this type of religious view.

How do the authors of the *Daodejing* believe that we recover (or retain) our original goodness, if we are born into a world of Confucians, who socialize and educate us from so early in our lives? The Daoist answer to this is that if sages are able to preserve (or recover) their original harmony with the Dao, "the myriad creatures will transform themselves," and "without desire and still, the world will settle itself" (chap. 37). Because we are originally born in harmony with the Dao—that is, *having a particular kind of relationship with* the Dao, it is possible for us to return to it and recover our original goodness. The simple presence of sages plays a key role in helping us to do this.

What, fundamentally, does it mean to us to be originally good? For one, as we have already seen, it means that we exhibit good qualities—we are not competitive or aggressive, we find joy in simple yet wonderful things, like the beauty of nature and music, and we respond in kind to the love, compassion, and generosity that others show us. But another reason why the *Daodejing* insists we are naturally good is that we naturally know, resemble, and reflect the Dao. We are aware of its presence, and we exude its gentleness and humility. As a result of our relationship with the Dao, we exude a sense of oneness with others. A kind of giving up of oneself is a part of this, because in our original state, we do not have a sense of ourselves as fully separate from others. We give willingly and freely to others. We do not live in a world with the mists of "yours" and "mine," or in what my father called "an I-me world." (When I behaved in a self-centered way as a child, he would say, "You're living in an I-me world!" This phrase always reminded me to think of others.) This is why the text says, "If you are a canyon for all the world, constant virtue will never leave you. . . . If you are a valley for all the world, constant Virtue will always be sufficient, and you can return to being unhewn wood" (chap. 28). In such a state, the identities and needs of others naturally flow into us because we are empty, like canyons and valleys. And it is natural for us to follow the Way, just as water tends downward naturally: "Streams and torrents flow into rivers and oceans, just as the world flows into the Way" (chap. 32).

Those who have read about the Buddhist tradition may be aware that emptiness has an important place in that tradition as well. This Daoist sense of emptiness differs in important ways from Buddhist understandings of emptiness (although Buddhist conceptions of emptiness were deeply influenced by Daoism after Buddhist missionaries arrived in China in the first century). Buddhists focus on emptiness because they believe we do not possess a soul or self that endures, and in this sense, the emptiness in all of us is a fundamental truth that we must appreciate in order to progress toward enlightenment. For the authors of the *Daodejing*, however, being empty is good because it means we are not full of the world's goals and values and instead have room for the Dao to dwell in us. "Those who preserve this Way do not desire fullness. And, because they are not full, they have no need for renewal" (chap. 15). This is what leads them to be so interested in *wuwei* 無為—"effortless action": "Act, but through *wuwei*," the text tells us. "Be active, but have no activities" (chap. 194). We are to act in ways that are not aggressive, coercive, or assertive. The text repeatedly mentions the virtue of noncontention, which characterizes

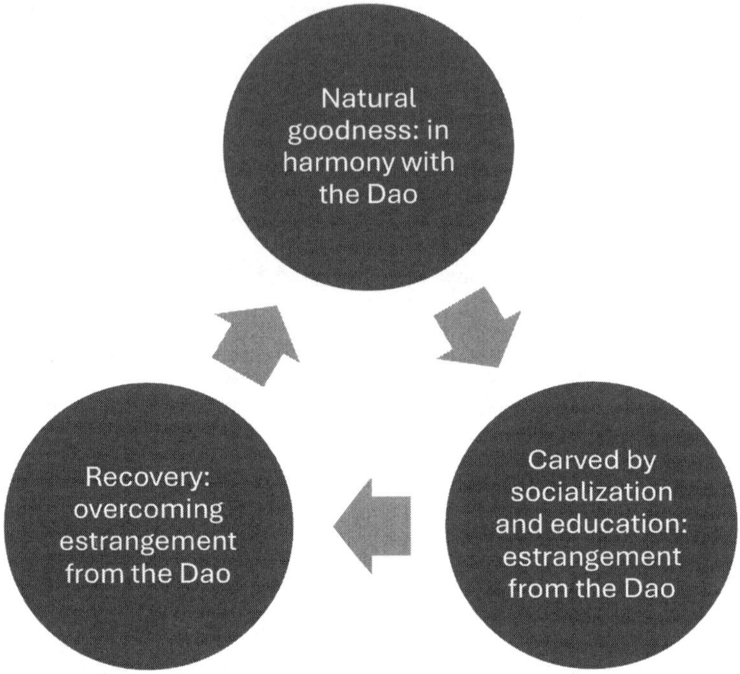


Figure 7.1 *Diagram of the Human Journey*

the Way and those who follow it (chaps. 68, 73, and 81). Additionally, as we engage with the world gently and humbly, we should not have *activities*. Thinking back to the story about Joshua Bell in the subway, activities are what led all the parents accompanying children that day to pull their children away from the music and move them along. Activities are things that we list on college applications and resumes. Activities are things that distinguish us from others. Activities belong to the world. They do not belong to the Dao.

The human journey, from the perspective of the *Daodejing*, can be sketched in a clockwise diagram, with three distinct stages. At the top of the cycle is where we begin: we are naturally good, knowing, and in harmony with the Dao. At the bottom of the circle is the second stage, which involves a downward fall and the diminishment of our naturally good state. This is caused by the society into which we are born, which carves and cultivates us through its particular forms of socialization and education. We are filled up with the world's goals and values, and we become estranged from the Dao in the process. The third stage, which moves us up the lefthand side of the circle, involves our journey back home from that fallen state. In the presence of sages—those who embrace and embody the Dao and who have a powerful therapeutic effect on those around them—we are able to begin to peel back the layers of socialization and education that have been heaped on us (figure 7.1).

The early Daoist tradition invites us to consider another dimension of the problem of God: the way in which culture and education can corrupt the original goodness that is a part of the fiber of our being, and for which we were originally created. Perhaps our task in this life is not simply to *become* good but to preserve the goodness with which we are endowed. In a world that teaches us to pursue wealth, power, and prestige, our socialization and education become destructive forces, and we must recover from (and resist) their influence. To use the Daoist metaphor of wood that has been damaged by carving, this process is a bit like the removal of injured bark from a damaged tree, which leaves healthy bark that is sound and tight to the wood and allows new growth to form and add to the sound wood. We remove the damage that has been done to us by emptying out the world's goals and values that have filled us, and as we do, we begin to remember and experience the presence of the Dao again. We overcome our estrangement from it. And as we undergo the process of undoing the damage that has been done to us, our natural goodness resurfaces and reclaims us. Our final destination, then, is precisely where we began. In the words of the *Daodejing*, we "return home to be a child" (chap. 28).

## Notes

Epigraphs:

Mary Oliver, "I Happened to Be Standing," in *Devotions* (New York: Penguin, 2017), 46–47.

The translation of the *Daodejing* here is my own. "Altar" is *ao* 奧—the southwest corner of traditional ancient Chinese homes, where the altar with household deities is located. All subsequent translations of the *Daodejing* are by Philip J. Ivanhoe, trans., *The Daodejing of Laozi* (Indianapolis: Hackett, 2003).

George Harrison, "The Inner Light," on *Lady Madonna / The Inner Light* (nonalbum single), The Beatles, Parlphone (UK) / Capitol (US), 1968.

1. Gene Weingarten, "Pearls Before Breakfast," *Washington Post*, April 8, 2007.
2. Weingarten.
3. Weingarten.
4. When I refer to early Daoism in this chapter, I am referring to an emerging group of thinkers and texts with certain commonalities (including their criticisms of Confucianism and their conception of the Dao), which later became part of the Daoist canon. I am not suggesting that they viewed themselves as part of a single religious tradition or school of thought, or that they all held exactly the same view.
5. Weingarten, "Pearls."
6. Matthew 18:3–5.
7. Wittgenstein uses this metaphor to describe the nature of his early work, in the penultimate proposition of the Tractatus Logico-Philosophicus (5.54), https://archive.org/details/tractatuslogicop1971witt/page/n5/mode/2up.

# 8

# AUGUSTINE'S GOD

## Overcoming Estrangement and Engaging Mystical Experience

One can distinguish two ways of approaching God: The way of overcoming estrangement and the way of meeting a stranger.
—Paul Tillich

Men go forth to marvel at the mountain heights, at huge waves in the sea, at the broad expanse of flowing rivers, at the wide reaches of the ocean.
—Augustine

On the windowsill in my office sits a small, framed photograph. It shows the silhouette of a person standing, facing the ocean, reading a book. He stands at the end of a long dock stretching out into the ocean before him, as the sun sets on the horizon. He is reading Augustine's *Confessions* to the sea. The photograph was taken by his wife, on their trip to the Outer Banks of North Carolina—the express purpose of which was to give him the opportunity to read the entire text, aloud, to the ocean.

I had the privilege of studying Augustine with the noted philosopher and theologian Carl Vaught throughout graduate school; and though he dedicated his life to studying and teaching the *Confessions*—even writing a trilogy of books about it—this photograph of him captures the magnitude of his personal engagement with the text unlike anything else.[1] Any text that could so captivate someone that they would read its three hundred–plus pages aloud, ought to intrigue us. Equally intriguing? The fact that they would read it *to the ocean*! In the *Confessions*—a text that Augustine addresses *to* God—the sea is a key metaphor for God: vast, powerful, beautiful, life-giving, and mysterious. And so, as we explore in this chapter the conception of God that anchors Augustine to the Christian tradition, the image of an individual facing the ocean is a perfect place to begin.

## Christian Understandings of God

The Christian tradition is full of remarkable sources that describe and elaborate on who God is, and we have already encountered some of them. We focus on Augustine's conception of God in this part of the book for a number of reasons. First, like the *Bhagavad Gita*, the *Analects*, and the *Daodejing* in their traditions, the works of Augustine have a unique place in the Christian tradition. Augustine, born in 354 in North Africa, is the most influential thinker in shaping the Christian tradition after the Apostle Paul (who wrote several books in the New Testament). As Vaught puts it, "Augustine stands like a colossus for more than a thousand years, casting his shadow over the development of the Middle Ages. . . . Augustine is one of the greatest psychologists since Plato, the greatest rhetorician since Cicero, and the greatest Christian thinker before the birth of Thomas Aquinas."[2] His influence on Christianity includes his synthesis of Greek and Roman philosophy with Christianity (including his use of Plotinus and the idea that all forms of existence flow from divinity and strive to return to it) and his conception of God's radical transcendence (seen in the idea that God creates but is not of the world because he transcends it). Augustine writes about God's omnipotence, omniscience, and omnibenevolence. He is also the author of the Doctrine of Original Sin, and his views on the nature of good and evil, the priority of grace in salvation, the doctrine of the Trinity, and Christian ethics and politics have had unparalleled influence in the Christian tradition.

Yet, as Vaught points out, "The most important fact about Augustine is that he combines philosophy and passion in equal proportions."[3] There is no better example of this than Augustine's *Confessions*: his spiritual autobiography, which is profoundly personal, grounded in his own descriptions of his encounters with God. It is also the first autobiography in the West, and the first example of real psychological introspection in Western religious literature. Though nothing like the discipline of psychology existed in Augustine's time, throughout the text he makes empirical observations and reflects on his own psychological experience in unprecedented ways. The influence of this work—both his theological and philosophical view and the way he writes about his experiences—is unmatched, and it is not an understatement to say, as one translator of the *Confessions* put it, that "every person living in the Western world would be a different person if Augustine had not been or had been different."[4]

The opening lines of the *Confessions* are some of the best-known in Western literature, and in religious literature more broadly: "You are great O Lord, and greatly to be praised: great is your power and to your wisdom there is no limit. And man, who is part of your creation, wishes to praise you. . . . You arouse him to take joy in praising you, for you have made us for yourself, and our heart is restless until it rests in you."[5] Here and throughout the *Confessions*, Augustine contends that we are created for the purpose of knowing God, and that our hearts are restless until we rest in God. This is the first place in the text where we encounter Augustine's view that as beings created by God, we have original goodness within us: we are created with a natural desire to seek and find joy in knowing and praising God.

The *Confessions* itself, in its very format—a prolonged prayer or meditation addressed to God—tells us a number of important things about God, from Augustine's perspective. The very act of addressing God tells us that Augustine believes God is listening to us: God takes an interest in us, desires to hear from us, and wants to be in a relationship with us. Over the course of the text, Augustine engages in "confession" in three distinct ways: he proclaims his love for God, he confesses his sins, and he affirms his faith in God. As he does so, he unveils a personal, loving God who hears and interacts with us, desires to know our innermost thoughts, and reaches out to us even in our most vulnerable moments of sinfulness.

Over the course of the *Confessions*, Augustine's view of God is developed alongside and in relation to his view of human nature. For him, the infinite and the finite are to be understood hand in hand, for the infinite (God) creates the finite (us) out of love and for the purpose of relationship. Made in God's image, we mirror God's love for us and God's desire to have a relationship with us in our natural longing for God: the fact is that "our hearts are restless until they rest in you." In a theological sense, for Augustine, we are hard-wired to seek God. This is true even for those who, like Augustine, find it difficult to enter into a relationship with God, and those who have never had a religious experience of any kind. Augustine insists that we originally *know* God, and even as we enter a world that distracts and tempts us and leads us to forget, there is a trace of the memory of our creator that is never eliminated. As a result, to use the words of the American theologian Paul Tillich, when we encounter God, we are not meeting a stranger, but overcoming estrangement from someone we already know.[6]

Augustine describes our estrangement from God as the process of forgetting what we originally know, represented as a fall or downward plunge, "wherein this world . . . tending down towards lower things, forgets you, its creator, and loves your creature more than yourself."[7] Thus, the goal of the human journey, for Augustine, is to remember and return home to the loving God we originally knew. Our hearts are no longer restless when we overcome estrangement, recovering our original goodness and unity with God. And here we see an interesting point of resemblance with the Daoist tradition, when it comes to the basic *shape* of our journey. Our goal is not to reach a new destination but to return home. Yet, undoubtedly, Augustine's personal God is a very different entity to return home to than the Dao.

One of my aims in this book is to explore different conceptions of the infinite. The *Confessions* serves as a remarkable window into Christian views of God, but to understand them, we must talk about one man: Jesus Christ. Christian views of God emerge against the backdrop of traditional Jewish views of God, and especially Jewish views of the Messiah or Christ (Hebrew: *masiah*; Greek: *Christos*)—the anointed one or chosen one of God, who is described in the Hebrew Bible as a liberator and redeemer of the Jewish people. The Jews expected the Messiah to be a future Jewish king from the Davidic line. Jesus of Nazareth was understood by his followers (and subsequent Christians throughout history) to be the Messiah, but Jesus was a very different kind of Messiah than the Davidic king that the Jews expected: instead of a military leader, Jesus was someone who healed, forgave, and loved. He also did not adhere to traditional Jewish laws in the strict way that Jewish leaders of his time saw fit; he was a reformer. He healed on the Sabbath, and he prioritized certain laws—loving God and loving your neighbor—over others.

In addition to believing that Jesus was the Messiah (and thereby accepting that traditional conceptions of the Messiah had been wrong or were misunderstood), Christians also believe that Jesus was God's son *and* that he was God incarnate. For Christians, Jesus is both fully human and fully divine. These beliefs are rooted in Jesus's expressions of continuity with God, such as his capacity to heal and forgive, and his contention that "the Father is in me and I am in the Father" (John 10:30–38), as well as his discontinuity with God, seen in his humanity. Jesus is raised by human parents, he experiences the full range of human emotions and experiences, and he eventually dies. He repeatedly refers to God as his Father and prays to the Father. These things all express various degrees of discontinuity with God the Father; in other words, they show that Jesus is not fully identifiable with the Father to whom he prays.

Yet Jesus is God incarnate, for Christians. In addition, he was very different from the military leader the Jewish tradition expected as the Messiah. To begin with, he was not born in a palace but to a couple from a small, backwater town—a poor infant, born in a stable surrounded by livestock because there was no room for them to stay anywhere else. The Gospels tell us that his mother, Mary (believed by most Christians to be a virgin), had a religious experience before becoming pregnant with Jesus, in which she was visited by an angel who told her:

> Do not be afraid, Mary, for you have found favor with God. And now, you will conceive in your womb and bear a son, and you will name him Jesus. He will be great and will be called the Son of the Most High, and the Lord God will give to him the throne of his ancestor David. . . . The Holy Spirit will come upon you, and the power of the Most high will overshadow you; therefore the child to be

> born will be holy; he will be called Son of God. . . . For nothing will be impossible with God. (Luke 1:26–35)

The idea that "nothing will be impossible with God" is a defining theme of Jesus's ministry (and one that was exceedingly important to Augustine), in which he repeatedly brought about change in the lives of people who seemed impossible to reach. Jesus asked people to leave their old lives behind, emphasizing that renewal, resurrection, healing, and redemption are possible for us as humans, no matter who we are and what we have done. Jesus embodies a God who loves humans deeply and wants to reconcile them to himself, no matter what they have done wrong or how they have sinned. In the Gospels, Jesus is described as healing people of spiritual, emotional, and mental anguish, as well as various kinds of physical afflictions (including diseases, disabilities, and demon-possession). Repeatedly, Jesus says to those he heals, "Your faith has made you well" (Matthew 9:22; Mark 5:34; Mark 10:52; Luke 11:19), emphasizing the centrality of *spiritual* healing. Their interactions with Jesus inspire a kind of faith, hope, and love that completely transforms their lives.

Two additional features of Jesus's ministry that decisively shape Christian views of God are, first, the fact that he welcomes all, turning none away. He calls all different kinds of people to follow him, while teaching that the lowly shall be lifted up. He pays attention to children, to the sick, to the poor, and to the forgotten and marginalized (including women). Indeed, his disciples include women, fishermen, and tax collectors, though he calls other rabbis to follow him, too. Second, Jesus emphasizes, and offers, *forgiveness*. He teaches that God loves us unconditionally and always stands with arms open, ready to redeem us, if only we will repent and seek forgiveness for our sins and commit ourselves to loving God and loving our neighbor (and *everyone* is our neighbor, in Jesus's view).

Jesus's capacity to heal and inspire change in people led large numbers of people in his time to believe he was the Messiah. Many Jewish leaders disagreed, viewing him as a dangerous blasphemer who was leading people astray. These leaders handed Jesus over to the Roman authorities, who crucified him. The Christian tradition has worked to make sense of his death—and especially the fact that he did not actively resist his own death or miraculously save himself. The Christian tradition also holds that Jesus was miraculously resurrected from being dead on the third day after his crucifixion, appearing to his disciples before ascending to Heaven. The most widely accepted theological view of Jesus's death in the Christian tradition is that Jesus died on the cross in order to pay the penalty for the sins of humanity, so that we could have eternal life after death. Indeed, Christian views center on a God who offers unconditional forgiveness and redemption to all people, regardless of who they are.

## Augustine's Journey Back to God

For Augustine—who did not find any of these theological claims easy to believe, and who actively rebelled against the Christian faith in which his mother tried to raise him—the promise of forgiveness, renewal, and redemption would turn out to be decisive. Over the course of the *Confessions*, Augustine tells his story by leading us from one garden to another, beginning in the Garden of Eden, where God created us with original goodness, but where we also stand beside Adam and Eve in their sin; to a pear orchard, where Augustine and his friends revel in rebellion and sin—an instance of evil that separates him from God.[8] He then leads us to a garden in Milan, where he begins to overcome his estrangement from God after hearing the voice of a child from beyond the garden wall. Finally, in a garden at Ostia, the port of Rome, Augustine allows us to witness the shared mystical experience that he and his mother have as their journey reaches its culmination. Vaught argues that these four gardens correspond to a four-stage metanarrative: Creation, Fall, Conversion, and Fulfillment (figure 8.1)—with the final stage bringing us back around, full circle, to the original goodness that is recovered when Augustine overcomes his estrangement from God.[9] For Augustine, this is the fundamental shape of the human journey, "in the light of which he believes that the lives of all his readers can be understood."[10]

Why are gardens so important for Augustine? For one thing, they are dynamic. Like our lives—which include continuous change and growth, rising and falling, living and dying—so too do these processes characterize gardens. Vaught points out that Augustine also uses gardens "to generate open spaces in his journey toward God. Gardens punctuate the metaphor of a journey with 'spatial' moments that often display a dimension of eternal significance."[11] As Augustine looks back on his life, he sees God at work in a variety of places, even though he was unaware of it (or willfully resisted the idea of it) at the time. But Augustine does not identify a wild field, a desert, or a forest as his setting: gardens are cultivated, requiring human intervention, just as we need to make space for God's loving care; the life and death of Jesus are just as essential for us as the planting, watering, weeding, and pruning by a patient gardener tending a flourishing garden.[12] Indeed, God is the planter of all that is good: early in the *Confessions*, Augustine articulates his view that all good things come from God, even if they come to us through other humans. This is because God, as Creator, not only creates all that is good but is Goodness itself. However, the reverse is not true: bad and evil things do not come from God, but solely from humans (and as we shall see, much of Augustine's work

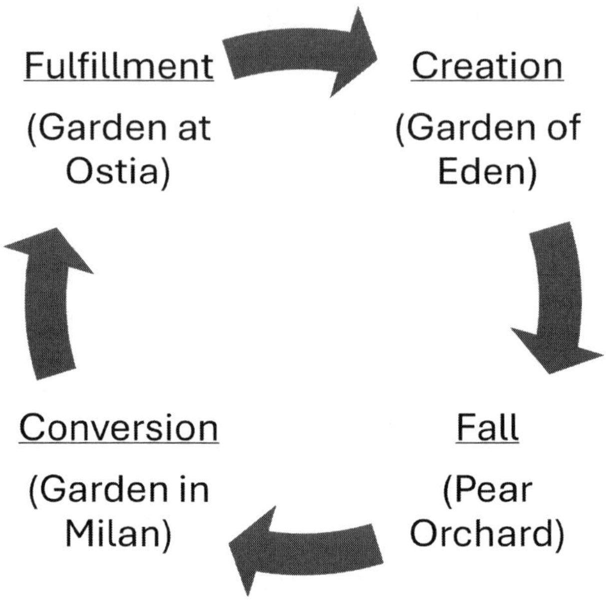


Figure 8.1 *Diagram of the Four-Stage Metanarrative*

is dedicated to understanding where and how evil originates). As an example, he discusses how he was nursed as a child, but

> neither my mother nor my nurses filled their own breasts. Rather, through them you gave me an infant's food in accordance with your law and out of the riches that you have distributed even down to the lowest level of things, . . . and you gave to those who nursed me the will to give what you gave to them; . . . yet it was not from them but through them. For from you, O God, come all good things.[13]

As he grows and becomes a teenager, Augustine discusses how his mother cared deeply for him, warning him about destructive behaviors—warnings he eventually realizes came from God:

> Whose words but yours were those that you sang in my ears by means of my mother, your faithful servant? Yet none of them sank deep into my heart, so that I would fulfill them. It was her wish, and privately she reminded me and warned me with great solicitude, that I should keep from fornication, and most of all from adultery with any man's wife. Such words seemed to be only a woman's warnings, which I should be ashamed to bother with. But they were your warnings, and I knew it not.[14]

Perhaps the most stunning dimension of the text is Augustine's stark honesty about his life up until his conversion. He by no means sounds like the bishop of Hippo (which he became) as he lays bare the realities of his early years. He does not paint the picture of himself that most of us would be inclined to paint: there are no claims of being divinely ordained for the role he would one day fill, or of remarkable intellectual or spiritual gifts, nor does he highlight his moments of glory. Rather, he paints an unflinchingly honest picture of himself as a child, and then a teenager, and then a young man, who struggled in every imaginable way. He describes hating school, being punished for his rebellious behavior, and, finally, his sexual sins beginning as a young teenager. But this is no sob story designed to elicit sympathy; Augustine fully owns his behavior and willfulness, maintaining that he had every opportunity to make different choices. Reflecting on himself, he notes that he did *not* feel guilt or remorse; rather, "I was pleasing to myself, and I desired to be pleasing to the eyes of men."[15] This is surely the most counterintuitive dimension of *The Confessions of Saint Augustine*: it certainly does not sound like the story of a saint.

Augustine writes, "I wish to bring back to mind my past foulness and the carnal corruptions of my soul. This is not because I love them, but that I may love you, my God."[16] For Augustine, the most important dimension of his journey is just how long, painful, and restless it was. His willingness to describe his sexual sins and how he "broke all your laws" is particularly stunning. And his language does not leave much to the imagination: "Clouds arose from the slimy desires of the flesh and from youth's seething spring. . . . I was tossed about and spilt out in my fornications; I flowed out and boiled over in them, . . . and farther and farther I went from you, into more and more fruitless seedings of sorrow, with a proud dejection and a weariness without rest."[17] Even in these vivid descriptions of his sins, Augustine refers to his original goodness, contending that he was journeying "farther and farther" from God, which of course assumes that he was originally close to God.

Much of the *Confessions* is dedicated to answering this question: How and why are humans so sinful if they were created by God, who is "not merely good, but goodness itself? Whence then comes it, then, that I will evil, and do not will the good? . . . Who has placed this in me and ingrafted in me this seedbed of bitterness, since I have been fashioned whole and entire by my most sweet God?"[18] This question is fundamental to the nature of God and the nature of humans. For Augustine and for the Christian tradition, we are made in the image of God (*Imago Dei*). In the book of Genesis in the Bible, in the ancient creation narratives that became a part of the Christian tradition, God creates *and* says that it is good. For Augustine, the only way to make sense of corruption is if a thing is originally good—but not supremely good, like God, which would make something incorruptible.[19] This is why evil, for Augustine, is the privation or loss of goodness; it does not exist as something on its own, because it is an *absence*. Indeed, "corruption" implies that there was something good to begin with that has been ruined and diminished somehow, like a piece of fruit that initially exists whole and then is slowly diminished, gradually rotting away.

Indeed, the fruit in the Garden of Eden is precisely where Augustine goes as he seeks an answer to how we can have a propensity for evil if we were created in the image of God, with original goodness and a longing for God implanted in us. The first garden Augustine entertains is the inspiration for his view of our original goodness: the Eden narrative. Augustine develops what comes to be the most widely accepted account of human nature in the Christian tradition—known as the Doctrine of Original Sin—under the influence of the Apostle Paul's views on the Eden narrative, and also as a result of his own experience of sin.[20] Augustine's view that evil is the privation of goodness is why any conversation we have about original sin must include a discussion of original innocence or goodness. In the *Confessions*, the first word to be said about the human person is original innocence, and the second word is original sin.[21] The second word comes quickly after the first, but original innocence is nevertheless prior to original sin: God expresses perfection not just by creating souls but also by creating embodied beings who are good.

In the Eden narrative, which follows the two creation myths in Genesis 1 and 2, the story continues. The serpent, which "was more crafty than any other wild animal that the Lord God had made," tells Eve that what God told them is not true—they will not die if they eat of the fruit of the tree that is in the middle of the garden of Eden. Rather, he tells them that their eyes will be opened and they will be like God, knowing good and evil. When the fruit ripens, Eve then eats it and also gives it to Adam, who eats it as well. "Then the eyes of both were opened, and they knew that they were naked, and they sewed fig leaves together and made loincloths for themselves." When they heard the Lord God walking in the garden, they hid themselves, and God called to them, asking, "Where are you?" Adam says he was afraid and hid himself because he was naked, to which God replies, "Who told you that you were naked? Have you eaten from the tree of which I commanded you not to eat?" Adam then says that Eve gave him the fruit and he ate, and God asks Eve, "What is this that you have done?" And she says, "The serpent tricked me, and I ate." Then God issues a punishment to the serpent, the woman, and the man. And he says, "See, the humans have become like one of us, knowing good and evil, and now they might reach out their hands and take also from the tree of life and eat and live forever," and God "sent them forth from the garden of Eden, to till the ground from which they were taken" (Genesis 3:1–23, NRSV).

In making sense of the Genesis story, it is always helpful to remember that the Bible contains many different kinds of literature. Genesis contains creation narratives that have their origins in Mesopotamian creation myths, which were knitted together and reinterpreted in different contexts over time. The views of God that we find in these stories are the product of multiple cultures and traditions, and they differ in significant ways from mainstream Christian views of God. For example, God is not presented as omniscient in this story, because he does not know where Adam and Eve are or that they have rebelled against him. Additionally, when God says "the humans have become like one of us," he is addressing other deities; we are not dealing with a monotheistic view but one that is explicitly polytheistic. So when Augustine reinterprets the story, as a way of understanding human nature in light of God's nature, he is working with a story that requires significant reframing in light of his tradition.

According to Augustine's interpretation, the condition God imposes as a punishment on Adam and Eve explains our propensity for evil: he writes that "sin dwells in me, sin that issues from punishment of a more voluntary sin, for I was Adam's son."[22] This punishment includes dispossession from a naturally perfect environment, loss of natural immortality, acquisition of susceptibility to bodily pain, fatigue, disease, aging, and rebellious bodily disorders (especially sexual lust). This condition is inherited, like a disease, infecting every descendent of Adam and Eve (and all humans). It is innate, not acquired, and notably, the *tendency* to sin is a part of the condition we inherit. As Vaught puts it, "Adam is the type of which we are tokens, and where the unity of original innocence [unity with God] is contaminated by the division of original sin [division or separation from God]."[23] As a result of Adam and Eve's sin, human nature is transformed; we are henceforth inclined toward sin. The cosmic battle between good and evil, then, is ultimately waged in the human heart. From an eternal point of view, we participate in original innocence and original sin simultaneously. The fall produces a split, or "a bifurcated consciousness in which two sides of the human person are in conflict with one another."[24] Yet the soul has an unbreakable connection to God. For Augustine, we are always capable of knowing and loving God; it is a capacity that can never be lost. So while sin is "original," in that it is a fundamental aspect of the human condition, God's goodness—and our goodness (since we are made in the image of God)—is even more original.

Close on the heels of the Garden of Eden, the second garden to which Augustine leads us in the *Confessions* is a pear orchard, where we witness Augustine's downward plunge toward evil. The story, while part of his autobiography, is also highly symbolic: it illustrates what he was capable of, what he was naturally inclined toward and did willingly, and how he felt about it:

> In a garden nearby to our vineyard there was a pear tree, loaded with fruit that was desirable neither in appearance nor in taste. Late one night—to which hour, according to our pestilential custom, we had kept up our street games—a group

> of very bad youngsters set out to shake down and rob this tree. We took great loads of stolen fruit from it, not for our own eating, but rather to throw it to the pigs; even if we did eat a little of it, we did this to do what pleased us for the reason that it was forbidden.[25]

I want to note three important features of what Augustine describes here. First, he says he willfully and intentionally did what was wrong. He says he knew it was wrong, and not just because the law punished theft but also because of "that law written on the hearts of men." He continues, "I willed to commit theft, and I did so, not because I was driven to it by any need. . . . For I stole a thing of which I had plenty of my own and of much better quality." Second, Augustine says repeatedly that he enjoyed doing it and that this motivated him, writing that he did not "wish to enjoy that thing which I desired to gain by theft, but rather to enjoy the actual theft and the sin of theft."[26] The cognitive and affective dimensions of this episode together lead Augustine to understand it not just as mischief but also as evil.[27] "Foul was the evil, and I loved it. . . . I loved my fault, not that for which I did the fault, but I loved my fault itself. Base in soul was I, and I leaped down from your firm clasp even towards complete destruction, and I sought nothing from the shameful deed but shame itself!"[28]

For Augustine, it would be different if he had not known the pears belonged to someone else, or had he not really understood that stealing is wrong. It would also be different if he had been wracked with guilt and fear the entire time he did it. But the combination of doing what he *knew* was wrong—willful rejection of the good—and the *enjoyment* of doing it, together lead Augustine to believe that it constitutes evil, enough to say that human nature *is* evil. Our minds and our hearts—the rational and emotional dimensions of the human person—are equally important, for Augustine. But so too is the fact that we are social creatures, and this is the third feature of the pear-stealing episode that I want to highlight: sin, for Augustine, is social, for we are social creatures. He writes that "alone, by myself, I would not have done it—such, I remember, was my state of mind at that time—alone I would never have done it. Therefore, I also loved it in my association with the others with whom I did the deed; . . . my pleasure lay not in the pears: it lay in the evil deed itself, which a group of us joined in sin to do"[29] So, for Augustine, we are by nature drawn to rebellion like a magnet, we enjoy rebelling, and we are especially inclined to do it (and to enjoy it) when we are together. He and his friends enjoyed "tricking those who did not know what we were doing and would most strenuously resent it," and they laughed together about it, in a way that no one laughs when they are alone.[30]

At this point in the *Confessions*, Augustine is at his most raw and vulnerable, asking, "Who can untie this most twisted and intricate mass of knots? It is a filthy thing: I do not wish to think about it; I do not wish to look upon it. . . . I fell away from you, my God, and I went astray, too far astray from you, the support of my youth, and I became to myself a land of want."[31]

## Overcoming Estrangement with Augustine

At this stage of Augustine's spiritual autobiography, several things are emphasized. Both personally and intellectually, Augustine casts about. We learn in book IV of the *Confessions* that he has a live-in girlfriend, with whom he has also had a child. He joins the Manichaeans, spending about ten years as a part of this religious movement founded by the Iranian prophet Mani. Part of what attracted Augustine to Manichaenism was its account of the nature of evil in the world. Manichaenism thrived in the third to seventh centuries and was one of the most widespread religions in the world, incorporating indigenous religions (including Hinduism and Buddhism) wherever it went. In Augustine's time, it was the main rival to Christianity and competed with it and traditional Greco-Roman paganism.

In the midst of all of this, no one's distress is greater than that of Augustine's mother, Monica, who was a devout Christian, and we can trace his fall through her grief; as she "wept more for me than mothers weep over their children's dead bodies. By that spirit of faith which she had from you, she saw my death, and you graciously heard her, O Lord. Graciously you heard her, and you did not despise her tears when they flowed down from her eyes and watered the earth beneath, in whatsoever place she prayed."[32] When Monica attempts to enlist a bishop to help set Augustine straight, the bishop refuses, knowing that Augustine is not yet open to counsel. But he tells Monica that her persistent faith and love for her son will be decisive: "As you live, it is impossible that the son of such tears should perish."[33]

Monica (b. 331) was possibly the descendant of indigenous Numidians who lived on the plateaus of North Africa in a lifestyle similar to that of the late Berbers. She raised Augustine in the town of Thagaste (modern Souk Ahras in Algeria), which was 300 years old at the time of Augustine's birth. Monica married Patricius, who sat on the town council of Thagaste but struggled financially.[34] Augustine frequently contrasts his father with Monica, noting that although he paid for an excellent education for his son, "this same father took no pains as to how I was growing up before you, or as to how chaste I was, as long as I was cultivated in speech, even though I was left a desert, uncultivated for you, O God, who are the one true and good Lord of that field which is my heart."[35] Patricius, who was a pagan, would not allow Monica to have their children baptized, was annoyed by her Catholic prayer and devotional habits, and was also known for his violent anger—something Augustine discusses in book IX, the only place in the entire text where he refers to his father by name.

Augustine describes Monica, conversely, as "moved by a holy fear and trembling," fearing "the crooked ways on which walk those who turn their back on you and not their face toward you,"[36] Notice the language he uses: when we rebel against God, we turn our backs on God, because we are originally facing God, our Creator, who is not a stranger to us originally. Our goal will be to turn back around, once again turning our faces toward God. Indeed, the most important symbol for God throughout the *Confessions* is Monica. "Did you in truth remain silent to me at that time? Whose words but yours were those that you sang in my ears by means of my mother your faithful servant?"[37] Repeatedly and persistently, God speaks to Augustine through his mother, never letting go of him, and never giving up on him. Perhaps surprisingly, his image of God, revealed through Monica, is not cold and patriarchal but matriarchal, nurturing, loving, and persistent. "I thought you kept silent and that only she was speaking, whereas through her you did not remain silent to me. In her person you were despised by me, her son, 'the son of your handmaid,' and your servant."[38] Augustine's view of God as one who loves us unconditionally and abides with us, never letting us go, is fully embodied in Monica.

The third garden to which Augustine leads us is a garden in Milan, which is the site of his conversion. By the time he reaches this garden, Augustine has been brought to the brink of conversion to Christianity; but even though he has been convinced intellectually, he has not yet experienced a conversion of the heart. He has resisted change in his life, even though he knows the way he lives is not making him happy or fulfilled:

> But when deep reflection had dredged out of the secret recesses of my soul all my misery and heaped it up in full view of my heart, there arose a mighty storm, bringing with it a mighty downpour of tears. . . . I flung myself down, how I do not know, under a certain fig tree, and gave free reign to my tears. The floods burst from my eyes, an acceptable sacrifice to you.[39]

Water in the form of tears of contrition here also alludes to God's vastness, like that of the ocean; like the water that sustains life in gardens; and like the waters of baptism that wash an individual clean. He cries out, "How long, how long? Tomorrow and tomorrow? Why not now? Why not in this very hour an end to my uncleanness?"[40] Then Augustine says that he heard the voice of a child—a gender-neutral voice, he notes: "I heard from a nearby house, a voice like that of a boy or a girl, I know not which, chanting and repeating over and over, 'Take up and read. Take up and read.' Instantly, with altered countenance, I began to think most intently whether children made use of any such chant in some kind of game, but I could not recall hearing it anywhere."[41] Here, Augustine's first thought is not "It's God speaking to me!" but rather "Those darn kids! What game are they playing now?!" Finally, Augustine says that he stopped crying and got up, as he realized that perhaps this was the voice of God, telling him to look at the Bible. When he picked it up, it opened to the following passage: "Not in rioting and drunkenness, not in chambering and impurities, not in strife and envying, but put you on the Lord Jesus Christ, and make not provision for the flesh in its concupiscences" (Romans 13:13–14). He says there was no need to read further. "Instantly, in truth, at the end of this sentence, as if before a peaceful light streaming into my heart, all the dark shadows of doubt fled away."[42]

There are several interesting features of this story. To begin with, the voice of God is that of a child—an allusion to our original goodness. The child's voice is also gender-neutral. Augustine's mother has been the primary symbol for God throughout the text, and now, it is a gender-neutral child's voice that takes over. Absent from the text is any reference to or image of God as a man. Additionally, the child's voice comes from the other side of the garden wall; as Vaught points out, "God's voice can reach beyond the garden wall to address Augustine directly."[43] As Augustine is well aware, the passage that he reads when he picks up the book seems like it was written for him, as rioting and drunkenness, chambering and impurities, and especially concupiscence have been at the root of Augustine's struggles. He refers to light streaming into his heart—the restless heart, finally about to reach a place of rest. After this moment of conversion, he immediately shares his experience with his friend Alypius and then with his mother—and we see a threefold conversion: Augustine and Alypius both become Christians, while Monica experiences a different kind of conversion:

> When she hears about the conversion of her son, turning her back on the worldly ambitions she entertains for her son, and accepting the fact that Augustine has now become God's son in a richer way than she could have ever imagined. Earlier Monica had wanted marriage, legitimate grandchildren, and professional success for Augustine, together with his conversion to Christianity. Now she is "converted" when she becomes willing to accept Augustine's Christian conversion to the exclusion of everything else.[44]

Just as sin is social, conversion, too, is social. Augustine immediately shares his experience in the garden with his friends and family, and their lives are changed as well. In turn, Augustine's life changes forever: he becomes a catechumen (receiving training in doctrine and discipline before baptism) and discerns a call to leave his former life behind in service of the Church.

The final garden to which Augustine leads us is the garden at Ostia, at the center of the house where Augustine and his mother are resting before sailing back to Africa, and where the journey begins to reach its culmination in a shared mystical experience. While religious experiences are a broad category of experiences of or encounters with the divine or a religious ultimate (and which are described in many different religions and cultures), mystical experiences are a narrower subset or type of religious experience. They are, as the term "mystical" suggests, more mysterious. William James argues that they are defined by being ineffable (they cannot be fully described), noetic (they involve insight, illumination, or revelation), transient (they last only a short time), and passive (they involve something that is received without participation, or that appears to the person without being elicited).[45]

When the mystical experience in the garden at Ostia occurs, Augustine and his mother are alone, leaning out of a window together, looking into the garden that is at the center of the house where they are staying. They are talking about "what the eternal life of the saints would be like." Then, they lift themselves up toward God, as Augustine describes it:

> raising ourselves up with a more ardent love to the Selfsame, we proceeded step by step through all bodily things up to that heaven whence shine the sun and the moon and the stars down upon the earth. We ascended higher yet by means of inward thought and discourse and admiration of your works, and we came up to our own minds. We transcended them, so that we attained to the region of abundance that never fails.[46]

All this happens while they are still talking, and they sigh in the presence of the eternal Word before the experience ends, and they "turned back again to the noise of our mouths, where a word both begins and ends."[47] Augustine describes the entire sequence of events in the first-person plural, indicating that they share this mystical experience, which is highly unique in mystical literature worldwide: moments of mystical ecstasy usually involve a single person's experience. It is most significant that Augustine shares this experience with Monica—ever-present, always having faith, always abiding with Augustine even at his worst. In the garden at Ostia, Augustine encounters God directly, and no other figure's presence could be more important in this moment than Monica's.

## Conclusion

Each time I look at the picture of my teacher reading the *Confessions* to the sea, I remember how excited he was when his publisher first sent a draft of the cover design for his trilogy of books on the *Confessions*. Each of the books is a different color, but they all feature the same illustration: Looking at the cover, it is as though you are looking up in a pyramid, with all its edges—all roads—leading directly to a single point or apex: God. The image illustrates the vastness of the world where we are lost and disoriented without God, "restless until we rest in you," finally overcoming estrangement from and returning home to our one true source. It also encapsulates human finitude, and God's infinitude—which is one of the reasons why my teacher so loved the image of the sea as a metaphor for God. To grasp God even in our finitude, we must be enlarged. As Augustine put it, "Too narrow is the house of my soul for you to enter into it: let it be enlarged by you."[48]

The second volume in my teacher's trilogy, which discusses Augustine's conversion in the garden at Milan and the encounter with God in the garden at Ostia, is a deep shade of blue. I suspect this is because it symbolizes the ocean—where we see and experience God's vastness in our finitude, as Augustine and Monica did in Milan and Ostia, and as my teacher did when he read the text aloud on that dock. There is a famous story about Augustine later in his life, walking along the seashore as he was working to explain the Doctrine of the Trinity (the Christian belief in one God who exists in the three persons of the Father; the Son, Jesus Christ; and the Holy Spirit). He came upon a young child running back and forth to the ocean, using a seashell to scoop seawater to try to fill up a hole in the sand. When Augustine asked him what he was doing, the boy said that he was trying to bring the entire ocean to the hole he had created. Augustine laughed and said that the ocean was far too vast to fit in the hole. The child replied, "It is no more impossible than what you are trying to do—comprehend the immensity of the mystery of the Holy Trinity with your limited understanding."[49] Astonished at what the child had said, Augustine looked up at the ocean, stretching out before him. When he looked back down, the child was gone.

## Notes

Epigraphs:

Paul Tillich, *Theology of Culture* (New York: Oxford University Press, 1959).

*The Confessions of Saint Augustine*, trans. John K. Ryan (New York: Image, 1960), book X, chap. 8, para. 15, 202–3.

1. See Carl G. Vaught, *The Journey toward God in Augustine's Confessions (Books I–VI)*, *Encounters with God in Augustine's Confessions (Books VII–IX)*, and *Access to God in Augustine's Confessions (Books X–XIII)* (Albany: State University of New York Press, 2003, 2004, 2005).

2. Vaught, *Journey toward God*, 3.

3. Vaught.

4. *The Confessions of Saint Augustine* (hereafter, *Confessions*), trans. F. J. Sheed (Indianapolis: Hackett, 1993), xxvii.

5. *Confessions*, book I, chap. 1, para. 1, 2.

6. I owe this insight to Vaught, *Journey toward God*, 155n4.

7. *Confessions*, book II, chap. 3, para, 6, 26.

8. Vaught, *Encounters with God*, 126.

9. Vaught, *Journey toward God*, 1.

10. Vaught, 1–2.

11. Vaught, 7.

12. I am indebted to P. J. Ivanhoe's analysis of agricultural metaphors in Confucianism for my views on this dimension of Augustine's thought. See Philip J. Ivanhoe, *Confucian Moral Self Cultivation* (Indianapolis: Hackett, 2000).

13. *Confessions*, book I, chap. 6, para. 7, 5.

14. *Confessions*, book II, chap. 3, para. 7, 26.

15. *Confessions*, book II, chap. 1, para. 1, 23.

16. *Confessions*, book II, chap, 1, para. 1, 23.

17. *Confessions*, book II, chap. 2, para. 2, 23–24.

18. *Confessions*, book VII, chap, 3, para. 5, 122.

19. *Confessions*, book VII, chap. 12, para. 18, 133.

20. While not all Christians accept the Doctrine of Original Sin—Eastern Orthodox churches never accepted it, and in the nineteenth century many liberal Protestants also began to reject it—it is nevertheless a central doctrine in Christian history.

21. Vaught, *Encounters with God*, 87.

22. *Confessions*, book VII, chap. 1, para. 22, 160.

23. Vaught, 87.

24. Vaught.

25. *Confessions*, book II, chap. 4, para. 9, 28.

26. *Confessions*, book II, chap. 4, para. 9, 28.

27. I owe this point to P. J. Ivanhoe. For his discussion of how Augustine's view contrasts with the Confucian Xunzi's view that human nature is bad (not evil), see Ivanhoe, *Confucian Moral Self Cultivation*, 32.

28. *Confessions*, book II, chap. 4, para. 9, 28.

29. *Confessions*, book II, chap. 8, para. 16, 33.

30. *Confessions*, book II, chap. 9, para. 17, 33.

31. *Confessions*, book II, chap. 1, para. 18, 34.

32. *Confessions*, book III, chap. 11, para. 19, 49.

33. *Confessions*, book III, chap. 12, para. 21, 51.

34. *Confessions*, book II, chap. 3, para. 5.

35. *Confessions*, book II, chap. 3, para. 5, 25–26.

36. *Confessions*, book II, chap. 3, para. 6, 26.

37. *Confessions*, book II, chap. 3, para. 7, 26.

38. *Confessions*, book II, chap. 3, para. 7, 26.

39. *Confessions*, book VIII, chap. 12, para. 28, 164.

40. *Confessions*, book VIII, chap. 12, para. 28, 165.

41. *Confessions*, book VIII, chap. 12, para. 28, 165.

42. *Confessions*, book VIII, chap. 12, para. 29, 165.

43. Vaught, *Encounters with God*, 91.

44. Vaught, 102.

45. William James, *The Varieties of Religious Experience* (New York: Penguin Classics, 1982).

46. *Confessions*, book IX, chap. 10, para. 24, 184.

47. *Confessions*, book IX, chap. 10, para. 24, 185.

48. *Confessions*, book I, chap. 5, para. 5, 4.

49. A written account of this story is found in *Legenda Aurea* (*Golden Legend*), a mid-thirteenth-century collection of saints' lives by the Italian Dominican Jacobus De Voragine.

# Part III

# WHY BELIEVE?

## Challenges to Faith and Responses

# 9

# THE PROBLEM OF EVIL AND THEODICY

He can only suppose that the things of goodness,
the most momentary, are in themselves
so whole, so bright as to redeem the darkness.
—Wendell Berry

Grief is the price we pay for love, and worth it, a million times over.
—*A Boy Called Christmas*

The highly acclaimed musical *Hamilton* does not often receive credit for its presentation of the oldest of all theological problems, but it should. In one of its most poignant songs, "It's Quiet Uptown," Alexander Hamilton and his wife Eliza grapple with the death of their nineteen-year-old son. In the aftermath of his son's death, Hamilton wrestled with his faith as he never had before. But he did not walk away from it. Indeed, as his biographer, Ron Chernow, writes, "It is striking how religion preoccupied Hamilton during his final years."[1] He prayed daily, wrote notes in the margins of the family Bible, and began examining logical proofs for God's existence, annotating his copy of William Paley's *A View of the Evidences of Christianity*. On his deathbed, less than three years after his son's death, his most urgent concern was to receive the last rites from the Episcopal Church.[2]

It is impossible for me to listen to "It's Quiet Uptown" and not think of my beloved friends who lost their daughter—a devoted mother, brilliant attorney, and activist—to suicide. She left behind two young children, her spouse and siblings, and her parents. Her father, the philosopher and theologian Robert M. Baird, writes:

> One of the most ecstatic, happiest experiences of my life was the moment I laid eyes on [her], our first-born. The moment of deepest sadness, nothing else comes close, was her death. . . . She grew from a baby to a little girl, and we loved her. She grew from a little girl to a teenager, and we loved her. . . . She moved through college and law school and we loved her. She became a mother herself and added

> more love to our lives with [her children]. . . . And then we lost her. For the first time in her life at the age of 46 she went into a depression. She came out of that depression once, but the remission did not last and at the age of 48 in a depression so deep she could not bear it, we lost her, a loss that is and always will be very much a part of who I am.[3]

Hundreds of years before the Christian era, Greek philosophers asked, "If God is all good and all powerful, why is there so much pain and suffering in life?" This is what we call the Problem of Evil. For those of us who are parents, the loss of a child is the most painful loss we can conceive of, which is why I have begun with it. But there are, as we all know, staggering, large-scale examples of pain and suffering. There are genocide and war. There are terrorist attacks. There are mass shootings, and school shootings that take the lives of young children. There are natural disasters such as earthquakes, hurricanes, and floods. There are diseases like cancer, and car accidents and plane crashes that take the lives of the best and brightest people we know.

Why do we call it "the Problem of Evil" when we are really talking about pain and suffering of many different kinds—not just the evil things that people do? The term "evil" does not just refer to moral wickedness but also, in this usage, refers to *a force that causes bad things to happen*. This force may be human choices in some instances, and the forces of nature in others. But in all instances, if one believes in an omnipotent, omnibenevolent God who creates the world to be a certain way, and who creates humans to be a certain way, then God becomes a part of the forces that are at work.

The traditional way of formulating the Problem of Evil is to state it as a dilemma: If God is perfectly loving (omnibenevolent), God must wish to abolish evil. If God is all-powerful (omnipotent), God must be able to abolish evil. If God is all-knowing (omniscient), God must know about all evil that exists. But evil exists. Therefore, God cannot be, at the same time, all-loving, all-powerful, and all-knowing. Put another way: God (so defined) does not exist. It is important to look very closely at the first two parts of the dilemma, because it is the joining of what God desires to do (as a result of being perfectly loving) and God's unlimited power (as a result of omnipotence) that creates the problem. For if God wanted to stop suffering but was incapable of it, there would not be a problem. And if God was capable of stopping suffering but did not desire to stop it, there would not be a problem. The dilemma is created by the fact that we cannot have it both ways: why, if God *wants* to stop pain and suffering and is *able* to put an end to pain and suffering, does God not intervene and stop them?

Many, if not most, people who leave the Christian and Jewish traditions of faith do so as a result of some form of the Problem of Evil.[4] Indeed, for some Jews, the Holocaust created an insuperable bar to belief in God, and this is one of the reasons why we have seen the rise of secular Judaism since World War II. When I ask my students what they think "the Problem(s) of God" could be, the Problem of Evil is consistently the first problem that they describe. In cultures where monotheistic traditions have been dominant, if you ask an atheist or an agnostic why they do not believe in God, you are most likely to get some version of the Problem of Evil as an answer. The magnitude of this problem exacerbates it: we do not simply face banal instances of evil in our lives. Rather, we live in a world where evil exists on a truly remarkable scale. As John Hick puts it, "It is the appalling depth and extent of human suffering, more than anything else, that makes the idea of a loving Creator seem so implausible."[5]

We traditionally distinguish between moral evil, which is pain and suffering caused by human choices, and natural (or nonmoral) evil, which is pain and suffering caused by things other than human choices. God is not off the hook for either one. In the case of moral evil, the question is why an all-good and all-powerful God creates humans who are capable of doing such things (especially since an all-knowing God knew that humans would use their freedom for such things as genocide, war, terrorism, rape, torture, and child abuse) and also why God does not intervene to prevent or lessen suffering. In the case of natural evil, the question is why God creates a world with so many sources of pain and suffering built into it (e.g., natural disasters and disease), and also why God does not intervene to lessen suffering. We cannot say that God did not know how things would turn out, or the outcome of the chain of events God set in motion, for God is understood to be omniscient. Additionally, even if God did not know how humans would use their freedom or how the natural world would evolve to produce so many sources of suffering, we are still left with the question of why God does not intervene. The Christian and Jewish traditions contend that God witnesses our suffering and is pained by it. And yet God apparently does not do anything about it. Why? God would seem to be a bystander to human suffering—like someone who witnesses another person being injured or killed and is fully capable of intervening to prevent it but chooses not to do so. We regard this as morally reprehensible when humans do it, and in some societies it is even punishable by law. Why do we still believe that God is all-loving and all-powerful when God does it?

## Theodicy

In response to the Problem of Evil, one can offer multiple solutions in order to preserve the rationality of belief in God. One is to simply eliminate one of God's attributes. One might conclude from the fact that God does not intervene to stop suffering that God is not omnipotent, or that God is not omniscient, because it appears that God did not anticipate the outcome of giving humans freedom. One could also conclude that God is not perfectly loving, on the basis that such a being would not have created a world with so much pain and suffering.

In contrast, a theodicy is a rational argument that offers a defense of God in the face of evil, while keeping all God's attributes intact. As Hick points out, theodicy "does not claim to explain, nor to explain away, every instance of evil in human experience, but only to point to certain considerations that prevent the fact of evil (largely incomprehensible though it remains) from constituting a final and insuperable bar to rational belief in God."[6] There are two main forms of theodicy in the Christian tradition, although you will encounter different versions of them. In this book, I refer to them as the Free Will Theodicy and the Soul-Making Theodicy. Let us consider each of them, in turn.

The Free Will Theodicy is rooted in the claim that humans are created as free and self-directing beings and can choose to act rightly or wrongly. Why did God create such beings? Why not create beings who would always freely choose to act rightly? The answer, according to the Free Will Theodicy, is that this would mean we are not genuinely independent persons. If our actions were preprogrammed by God only to do certain things, then we would not be freely choosing anything. Part of what it means to be a person is to have moral freedom. Why, then, does God create persons? Hick writes:

> God is able to create beings of any and every conceivable kind; but creatures who lack moral freedom, however superior they might be to human beings in other respects, would not be what we mean by persons. They would constitute a different form of life that God might have brought into existence instead of persons. When we ask why God did not create such beings in place of persons the traditional answer is that only persons could, in any meaningful sense, become "children of God," capable of entering into a personal relationship with their Creator by a free and uncompelled response to his love.[7]

Here we can see clearly that theodicies require us to offer an account of *why* God creates, and in this way, responding to the Problem of Evil requires probing the deepest possible theological questions about God's nature. *Why* does God create at all? And why *us*? Baird quotes James Weldon Johnson's poem "The Creation," asking us to imagine precisely this:

> And God stepped out on space,
> And he looked around and said
> I'm lonely—
> I'll make me a world.[8]

Note the significance of what Johnson asks us to notice here: God creates because God wishes to have company—to have a relationship. Continuing Johnson's line of thought and relating it to the Problem of Evil, Baird writes,

"We can imagine this God wanting to create a world that contained faith and hope and love, but just maybe there is no way to create the greatest of these: love, without permitting the most painful of these: the loss of what is loved."[9] And so, God said,

> I'm lonely. I'll make me a world.
> A world with love.
> But love without loss is not possible.
> So it will be a world with pain
> But I will so love this world that I too will experience the losses
> I too will share the pain.[10]

A part of what Baird's points help us to see is that in both Christianity and Judaism, the reality of evil and suffering are clearly acknowledged. They are discussed in both the Hebrew Bible (or Old Testament) and in the New Testament. Yet these traditions have different ways of dealing with it. The Hebrew Bible shows a higher tolerance for the idea that God tests us through hardship, as seen for example in the story of Job, where Job's hardship is intentionally inflicted upon him by God. Here, we can see that the Jewish and Christian understandings of God, even though they are frequently run together as "Judeo-Christian," are in fact quite distinct families of views, even though they are related. The Jewish tradition has also struggled to offer an explanation of how God's chosen people could be subjected to such enormous oppression. The Holocaust, for many modern Jews, made this problem unbearable, and this is why the distinction between cultural Jews (many of whom describe themselves as atheists or agnostics and who practice traditional rituals to remain connected to their heritage but not as a way of sustaining a relationship with God) and religious Jews (for whom maintaining a relationship with God remains central) has become so important. As the Holocaust survivor Simon Wiesenthal (who spent his life bringing Nazi war criminals to justice) was known to say: "God must have been on leave during the Holocaust."

The Christian tradition has taken a more robust interest in theodicy, and this is at least partly because of the resources of the New Testament.[11] Hick points out that "Jesus saw his execution by the Romans as an experience which God desired him to accept, an experience which was to be brought within the sphere of the divine purpose and made to serve the divine ends, so the Christian response to calamity is to accept the adversities, pains, and afflictions which life brings, in order that they can be turned to a positive spiritual use."[12] Indeed, Jesus's crucifixion

> provides the paradigm for the distinctly Christian reaction to evil. Viewed from the standpoint of the Christian faith, evils do not cease to be evils; and certainly, in view of Christ's healing work, they cannot be said to have been sent by God. Yet,

> it has been the persistent claim of those seriously and wholeheartedly committed to Christian discipleship that tragedy, though truly tragic, may nevertheless be turned, through [our] reaction to it, from a cause of despair and alienation from God to a stage in the fulfillment of God's loving purpose for that individual.[13]

I want to underscore the final words Hick uses here: *for that individual*. In many cases, it seems easier to accept theodicies in response to individual instances of pain and suffering than as explanations for large-scale suffering such as genocide.

Let us now turn to the Soul-Making Theodicy, which, unlike the Free Will Theodicy, seeks to address nonmoral or natural evil—those forms of evil that are embedded in the world, as opposed to human choices. Like the Free Will Theodicy, however, it requires us to specify the nature of God's purpose in creating the world as it is. The Soul-Making Theodicy hinges on showing that "the divine purpose as it is understood in Judaism and Christianity could not be forwarded in a world that was designed as a permanent hedonistic paradise."[14] Hick points out that the Problem of Evil stems in part from the assumption that God's purpose in creating the world was to provide a suitable dwelling place for us, as fully formed creatures, "similar to that of a man who builds a cage for some pet animal. Since our world, in fact, contains sources of hardship, inconvenience and danger of innumerable kinds, the conclusion follows that this world cannot have been created by a perfectly benevolent and all-powerful deity."[15]

Against these claims, the Soul-Making Theodicy maintains that God's purpose in creating the world was *not* to create a hedonistic paradise or to maximize human pleasure and happiness but rather to create a place of "soul-making" or "person-making." In this view, there are two stages to God's creative process. God is the ultimate author of life, but this is only the first stage of the process. The second is for us to become good people, and this can only occur in a world where "free beings, grappling with the tasks and challenges of their existence in a common environment, may become 'children of God,' and 'heirs of eternal life.' . . . Our world, with all its rough edges, is the sphere in which this second and harder stage of the creative process is taking place."[16] One might object that although some suffering undoubtedly plays a role in our positive development, it seems that there is more evil than is required for soul-making, and some that does not serve that purpose at all. For there are many examples of evil that result not in soul-making but selfishness, fear, hatred, or despair. In response, defenders of the Soul-Making Theodicy contend that "any divine purpose of soul making that is at work in earthly history must continue beyond this life if it is ever to achieve more than a very partial and fragmentary success."[17] Soul-making, then, is not just an earthly creative process but is completed in the afterlife, through the Love that enfolds us when we encounter God face to face.

The Soul-Making Theodicy contends that the only way we can become the kinds of beings that God wants us to be is to live in a world with pain and suffering. God wants us to become loving, compassionate, generous, and grateful people. The word "become" is key here: God does not make us morally perfect to begin with, any more than he designs the world to be a hedonistic paradise for us. God creates free beings who live in an imperfect world intentionally, because God wants us to play a role in the second stage of the creative process: just as the Free Will Theodicy contends that God wants us to freely choose to enter into a relationship or covenant with God (and so does not deterministically program us to be in that relationship), the Soul-Making Theodicy contends that God wants us to play a role in the process of our own moral self-cultivation. Logically, the only way for us to develop virtues like compassion—and the only way for virtues like compassion to have meaning or purpose—is for us to live in a world where there is suffering and, therefore, a need for compassion.

To test this claim, just imagine a world without any pain or suffering. Hick writes that the consequences would be very far-reaching:

> For example, no one could ever injure anyone else: the murderer's knife would turn to paper or his bullets to thin air; the bank safe, robbed of a million dollars, would miraculously become filled with another million dollars (without this device, on however large a scale, proving inflationary); fraud, deceit, conspiracy, and treason would somehow always leave the fabric of society undamaged. Again, no one would ever be injured by accident: the mountain climber, steeplejack, or playing child falling from a height would float unharmed to the ground; the reckless driver would never meet disaster. There would be no need to work, since no harm could result from avoiding work; there would be no call to be concerned for others in time of need or danger, for in such a world there could be no real needs or dangers.[18]

The 2023 film *Barbie*, directed by Greta Gerwig and written by Gerwig and Noah Baumbach, though it may at first glance appear to be light-hearted, in fact provides ample insight into this type of world and why one might not choose it. Barbie Land is a paradise of precisely the sort described above, free of difficulties, challenges, discomforts, and inconveniences of any kind. Every day is great; every Barbie is happy, kind, confident, and noncompetitive. (As Barbie puts it, "This is the best day ever, and so is yesterday and tomorrow and so is the day after tomorrow and even Wednesdays and every day from now until forever!"[19]) Gone are the problems of patriarchy and inequality. Injuries are rapidly and magically healed. Upon leaving Barbie Land and entering the human world, however, Barbie experiences the full range of emotions for the first time, including self-consciousness, fear, anxiety, and sadness. As a tear rolls down her cheek for the first time, she says, "That felt achy, but good."[20] What follows is one of the most poignant scenes from the movie, in which Barbie, sitting on a park bench, observes the people around her—some fighting, some laughing, some lonely and sad. She sees children playing, and she looks up at the trees and the sunlight, and then she looks at the elderly woman beside her and tells her she is beautiful. Indeed, Barbie finds beauty and meaning in the full range of human experiences.

In the end, Barbie discovers that the joys *and perils* of living among humans are preferable to the preprogrammed life of "perfection" that she had in Barbie Land. She says to the creator of Barbie, Ruth, "The real world isn't what I thought it was," and Ruth replies, "It never is. And isn't that marvelous?"[21] (Theodicies suggest: Perhaps this is what our Creator would say to us. Perhaps the uncertainty of life, and the accompanying opportunity to cultivate hope and faith, is a gift.) What Barbie discovers, ultimately, is that what she thought was "perfect" is not the life she wants. She expresses a desire to have freedom, because, "I want to be a part of the people that make meaning—not the thing that's made. I want to do the imagining." Ruth warns her that being a human is uncomfortable, that humans perpetrate moral evil and eventually die. Barbie asks permission to become human, saying, "You're the creator—don't you control me?" Ruth tells her that she does not control her, adding, "We mothers stand still so our daughters can look back to see how far they've come." (This is the voice of a creator who wants us to be free to make our own way, in part so we can take joy in what we achieve. Theodicies, too, describe a Creator who wants us to flourish not just because of what God has done for us but also because of our own free response.) Ruth then takes Barbie's hands and says, "Now, *feel*." All the scenes of a human life—joy, love, and sorrow—fly by, and Barbie says, "Yes."[22] This is precisely what theodicies are asking us to see: that perhaps the world that a perfectly loving, all-powerful God would create for us is *not* one where we lack freedom and live in a paradise but one where we experience and respond freely to the full range of human emotions and experiences. In this sense, the entire film offers a theodicy.

## Love and Evil

Still, if we think about God as a loving parent, as the Christian and Jewish traditions do, then we may wonder: Do the most loving parents truly desire their child to experience *the full range* of emotions and experiences? For the darker end of that range involves not just sadness but also loss of the greatest magnitude. Baird offers an interesting perspective on this matter, writing that "nothing in life is more intimately connected than is the relationship between love and loss. The depth of loss is directly related to the depth of love. And the depth of love is directly related to the fear of loss."[23] He points out that the Apostle Paul said, "There is faith and hope and love, but the greatest of these is love. That is right, but also from the greatest of these, our loves, comes the greatest of these, our losses, our pains."[24] He goes on to point out, "Maybe, just maybe, you cannot have the marvel of love without the darkness of loss. Maybe the connection between love and loss is so intimate that even God cannot pull them apart."[25] He goes on to quote an anonymous piece of writing about grief and loss: "I've never gotten used to people dying, never have, but here's my two cents about losing those we love. It tears a hole through me whenever somebody I love dies, no matter the circumstances. But I don't want it to 'not matter.' I don't want it to be something that just passes. My scars are a testament to the love that I had for that person. And if the scar is deep, so was the love."[26] The anonymous author of this piece on grief goes on to describe grief as resembling ocean waves:

> In the beginning, the waves are 100 feet tall and crash over you without mercy. They come 10 seconds apart and don't even give you time to catch your breath. After a while, maybe weeks, maybe months, you'll find the waves are still 100 feet tall, but they come farther apart. When they come, they still crash all over you and wipe you out. . . . You never know what is going to trigger grief, . . . and the waves come crashing. But in between the waves, there is life. Somewhere down the line, and its different for everybody, you find that the waves are only 80 feet tall. Or 50 feet tall. And while they still come, they come farther apart. You can see them coming: an anniversary, a birthday, or Christmas. . . . You can see the pain coming, and for the most part, prepare yourself. And when the wave washes over you, you know that somehow you will, again, come out on the other side. Soaking wet, sputtering, still hanging on to some tiny piece of the wreckage, but you'll come out.[27]

The inspiration for this metaphor was a famous woodblock print by the Japanese artist Katsushika Hokusai, "The Great Wave off Kanagawa" (c. 1830–32).[28] The name "Katsushika" refers to the North Star, which is associated with an important deity in Hokusai's religion of Nichiren Buddhism. The scene depicts stormy seas threatening to engulf three long boats (designed to transport live fish to traditional Japanese markets), with one enormous wave towering over them in a spiral. In the distance, below the wave that threatens to engulf the boats, stands Mount Fuji, whose name refers to abundance and sageliness (*fujisan* 富士山); but early sources suggest that it originally referred to immortality (*fuji* 不死).[29] For Nichiren Buddhists like Hokusai, Mount Fuji symbolizes eternal life. Indeed, Mount Fuji has long been associated with the divine in Japanese religion and culture. Furthermore, "The Great Wave" is the first in a series—*Thirty-Six Views of Mount Fuji*—which itself reminds us of *perspective*: there are many views of the divine.

Like the great wave, pain—evil—is larger than life to us. Yet from atop Mount Fuji, those waves look like nothing but ripples. This is an excellent illustration of what theodicies point toward. We are finite, trying to understand the infinite. But our perspective is not the only one. And it certainly is not the perspective of the infinite.

## Notes

Epigraphs:

Wendell Berry, *This Day: Collected and New Sabbath Poems* (New York: Counterpoint, 2014), 342.

*A Boy Called Christmas*, film, directed by Gil Kenan (Netflix, 2021); based on the book by Matt Haig (Edinburgh: Canongate, 2015).

1. Ron Chernow, *Alexander Hamilton* (New York: Penguin, 2004), 659.

2. Chernow, 706–8.

3. Robert M. Baird, "A Sermon for Old People Like Me and Actually for Younger People Too," Lake Shore Baptist Church, November 20, 2016, transcript, 2–3.

4. Many of the issues I discuss in this chapter more broadly apply to monotheistic faiths, including Islam. However, in order to avoid glossing over the nuances and differences, I confine my discussion in this chapter to Christianity and Judaism, and I focus particularly on the Christian tradition, which has produced most of the literature on the Problem of Evil in the field of the philosophy of religion. For an excellent study of the Problem of Evil in Islam, see Salih Sayilgan, *God, Evil, and Suffering in Islam* (New York: Cambridge University Press, 2023).

5. John Hick, "The Problem of Evil," in *Ten Essential Texts in the Philosophy of Religion*, ed. Steven M. Cahn (New York: Oxford University Press, 2005), 290.

6. Hick, 291.

7. Hick, 292.

8. James Weldon Johnson, "The Creation," in *God's Trombones: Seven Negro Sermons in Verse* (1927) (New York: Penguin, 2008).

9. Baird, "Sermon," 5.

10. Baird.

11. The early Hellenistic Fathers of the Christian Church, especially Irenaeus, followed some of the Apostle Paul's ideas concerning how we are made in the image of God, and yet in our sinfulness we do not resemble God (revealed in Jesus Christ). They lay the groundwork for the view that the pain and suffering we face in this world play a key role in making us more like Christ. See Hick, "Problem," 293.

12. Hick, 295.

13. Hick.

14. Hick, 293.

15. Hick.

16. Hick.

17. Hick, 295.
18. Hick, 291–92.
19. *Barbie*, film, directed by Greta Gerwig (Warner Brothers, 2023).
20. *Barbie.*
21. *Barbie.*
22. *Barbie.*
23. Baird, "Sermon," 2.
24. Baird, 3.
25. Baird, 5.
26. See GSnow, "Scars and Waves," www.reddit.com/r/Assistance/comments/hax0t/comment/c1u0rx2/.
27. GSnow.
28. See GSnow, www.reddit.com/r/Assistance/comments/hax0t/comment/l6psvpd/.
29. This is according to the ninth-century source, *Tale of the Bamboo Cutter*. The current *kanji* (characters) for Mount Fuji and those for immortality are homophones.

# 10

# THE PROBLEM OF EVIL AND ATHEISM

Doubt is not the opposite of faith; it is an element of faith.
—Paul Tillich

"Do you teach arguments for atheism, too?" This is a question I get quite often when people ask me what "The Problem of God" includes, and I tell them that, among other things, we discuss different arguments for the existence of God. People who ask this question usually seem to expect me to say no, which is why I especially enjoy answering yes.

To be an atheist is to have a religious outlook. Indeed, one might describe atheism as a religious view, not as the complete *lack* of a religious view. For atheism, by definition, involves the *denial* of God's existence, and surely this is every bit as ambitious as affirming God's existence. People often mistakenly assume that atheism requires no defense or justification. However, the denial of a spiritual or religious entity or reality also requires justification. Hence, the burden of proof falls equally to atheists and theists. Both must show why the view that God exists, or does not exist, is rationally justified. Some prominent atheists whom we encountered earlier in this book have owned this stance; Richard Dawkins and Daniel Dennett are examples. Each argues that there is evidence *against* God's existence, and that this evidence constitutes warranted belief in atheism. I do not share their view that evolutionary theory constitutes evidence against God's existence; for as we saw earlier in this book, even though one does not *need* God to explain the emergence of life on Earth, this alone does not demonstrate that God does *not* exist, nor does evolutionary theory explain *why* anything exists. However, I do believe there is a compelling rational argument against God's existence based on the Problem of Evil.

As we have already seen, the Problem of Evil looms large among problems relating to faith. Even if a theodicy strikes one as compelling, there nevertheless remain a series of thorny questions around the Problem of Evil. Among the most pointed of these questions is why there is *so much* evil—far more than seems to be necessary to bring about the greater goods that are a part of the Soul-Making Theodicy. Another is the question of how an omnipotent God could be limited in the ways that both the Free Will and Soul-Making Theodicies suggest: Why does God *have to* allow radical freedom (e.g., including the freedom to commit genocide) in order to give us the freedom to become children of God? And why does God *have to* allow the full range of natural and moral evil in order for the process of soul-making to occur? Any time we talk about an omnipotent God *having* to do anything, are we not in fact denying God's omnipotence by admitting that God's hand is forced? We will turn to the question of God's omnipotence and what it entails in the next chapter, but for now I would like to zero in on the first question—why there is *so much* evil, or what John Hick calls "the appalling depth and extent of human suffering," and its implications for belief in God.[1]

One response to the question of why God creates a world with so much evil, and does not intervene to lessen it, is simply to point to our own finitude and the limits of our understanding of the infinite. As we have already seen in this book, a part of what it means to be a person of faith is to acknowledge one's own finitude in the face of the infinite. In this view, our capacity to grasp the nature of the infinite is at best limited. There are significant resources in the Jewish tradition that respond to the Problem of Evil in this way, from the Book of Job in the Hebrew Bible, where God wonders how Job could question the author of creation, to the rabbinic literature, much of which avoids offering theological solutions in favor of emphasizing the limits of human understanding when it comes to the sufferings of the righteous.

At the same time, people sometimes read stories from sacred texts, such as the story of Job, as offering a *solution* to the Problem of Evil. But it is important to distinguish between stories that discuss pain and suffering in relation to God and a theodicy or rational explanation for the existence of evil in the face of an omnipotent, omnibenevolent God. A theodicy explains why God allows pain and suffering (and why God created a world with such vast amounts of it), even though God could stop it and desires to stop it. Additionally, ancient stories sometimes make the Problem of Evil even *more* difficult to grapple with. In the story of Job, for instance, God gives permission to Satan (an angel known as the "adversary") to take away everything from Job, in order to prove that Job is not being faithful to God just because God protects him. All this would seem to undermine God's perfectly loving nature: Why would God give permission for pain and suffering to be inflicted on someone just to prove that they are faithful for the right reasons? The story of Job is often read as suggesting that God tests us in order to determine if we are faithful. But why would an omniscient God need to test us? Does not an omniscient God *already know* how much faith we have? The Eden narrative is another clear example. Why does God punish all humanity in response to a transgression that occurred because Eve was deceived by another one of God's creatures, the serpent? And why did God create such a deceptive creature, knowing what would happen? These in no way seem like the actions of an all-loving, omniscient, wholly just God.

Of course, this is because the Eden narrative, like the book of Job, predates the concept of an omnipotent, omniscient, omnibenevolent God. Recognizing this is important, because it allows us to reconsider how we think about sacred texts. One of the most compelling views of the Bible I have ever encountered describes the Bible as a library, but also as art.[2] Such a view takes seriously that the Bible not only contains different kinds of literature written by different people, at different times, for different audiences, and with different agendas; it also views sacred texts as expressions of individual experiences, and the stories in them as efforts to make sense of the world and ourselves. One who holds this view might view the Bible as a sacred text not because it is infallible but because it expresses different experiences of God. Similarly, works of art give expression to different experiences. But just as it would not make sense to ask if Vincent Van Gogh's *Starry Night* is infallible, it similarly does not make sense to ask if the Bible is infallible.[3] The Eden story and the story of Job give expression to people's understandings and experiences of God in different times and places, but they do not offer us theodicies; nor do they give (or attempt to give) us warrant for belief in God.

One can also respond to the Problem of Evil by granting that there are no fully satisfying theodicies, while also maintaining that this is not enough to undermine one's belief in God. In these cases, the Problem of Evil allows us to appreciate that when we are talking about matters of faith, not just the head is involved but the heart as well. Faith, for many if not most people, is rooted in some type of religious experience, and more often than not, these experiences are not easily undermined by theological or philosophical problems. One can understand certain logical problems or challenges to one's beliefs but can also remain convinced by one's own firsthand experiences or encounters, and by other arguments.

However, for many people, and certainly for an increasing number of people in the English-speaking world, the opposite is true. The Problem of Evil is not a purely theoretical problem for most of us; it is a deeply personal problem. While our experiences of pain and suffering sometimes deepen our faith, they can also deal it a devastating blow. Indeed, the Problem of Evil is the most common problem relating to theistic belief that leads people to atheism. In this chapter, we examine an argument for atheism that is based on the Problem of Evil. We also examine different kinds of atheism, along with agnosticism, and some of the implications of committing oneself to such views.

## The Argument for Atheism Based on the Problem of Evil

In his essay "The Problem of Evil and Some Varieties of Atheism," the philosopher of religion William Rowe sets out to answer three questions. The first is whether there is an argument for atheism based on the existence of evil that would rationally justify someone being an atheist; as we shall see, this is a question he answers in the affirmative. The second question is how theists can best defend their position against the argument for atheism based on the existence of evil. Indeed, Rowe goes on to demonstrate what the theist's strongest possible response would be. Finally, Rowe asks, "What position should the informed atheist take concerning the rationality of theistic belief?"[4] This last question is, as we shall see below, the most interesting, because it leads Rowe to describe different kinds of atheism. Indeed, just as there are different kinds of Christians, Hindus, and Jews, there are also different kinds of atheists—including some who are more open-minded and inclusive toward those who do not share their religious outlook. But some atheists are very much of a fundamentalist variety.

Rowe specifies that he is only dealing with theism in the narrow sense: "someone who believes in the existence of an omnipotent, omniscient, eternal, supremely good being who created the world. By 'theist' in the broad sense I mean someone who believes in the existence of some sort of divine being or divine reality."[5] While to be a theist in this narrow sense is to also be a theist in the broad sense, the reverse is not true. All this reminds us that the Problem of Evil is a problem primarily for theists in the narrow sense, who believe in an all-powerful, all-loving God (who is *capable* of abolishing evil and who *desires* to do so as well). Rowe points out that similar distinctions are helpful when we talk about atheism: "To be an atheist in the broad sense is to deny the existence of any sort of divine being or divine reality," but to be an atheist in the narrow sense is only to deny the existence of an all-knowing, all-powerful, perfectly good divine being.[6] Again, to be an atheist in the broad sense is also to be one in the narrow sense, but the reverse is not true: one might deny the existence of the "omnipredicate" God but still believe in the existence of some type of divine reality. This means that one could be an atheist in the narrow sense (i.e., by denying the existence of the "omnipredicate" God) and yet also be a theist in the broad sense (i.e., by affirming the existence of some sort of divine being or beings or reality). All this is helpful to acknowledge, not only because it reminds us that the Problem of Evil is only a problem in relation to a particular conception of God but also because it reminds us of the wide range of religious outlooks.

Rowe begins his argument for atheism by focusing on intense human and animal suffering, which, as he points out, "occurs daily and in great plentitude in our world."[7] He says that "if the intense suffering leads to some greater good, a good we could not have obtained without undergoing the suffering in question, we might conclude that the suffering is justified, but it remains an evil nevertheless."[8] Rowe emphasizes that intense human or animal suffering remains an evil and is in itself bad, *even in cases where it leads to good things*; we must not confuse suffering with the good to which it might lead, because the good does not simply negate or eliminate the suffering. The key question is whether suffering is justified "by virtue of being part of, or leading to, some good which is unobtainable without it."[9] This last point is of the utmost importance, because if the good to which suffering leads *is* obtainable without it, then the suffering is not justified; that is, permitting it is not morally justified, because it is not necessary in order to achieve some greater good or prevent some worse evil. Against this background, Rowe lays out the premises and conclusion of his argument as follows:

1. There exist instances of intense suffering, which an omnipotent, omniscient being *could* have prevented without thereby losing some greater good or permitting some evil equally bad or worse.
2. An omniscient, wholly good being *would* prevent the occurrence of any intense suffering it could, unless it could not do so without thereby losing some greater good or permitting some evil equally bad or worse.
3. Therefore, there does not exist an omnipotent, omniscient, wholly good being.[10] (emphasis added)

Rowe's argument is valid, which means that if we have rational grounds to accept its premises, then we have rational grounds to accept its conclusion. Although Rowe offers a highly detailed discussion of this argument (much of which is geared toward specialists in the analytic philosophy of religion), I want to focus on certain dimensions of Rowe's argument as they pertain to our interests in this book. To begin with, it is important to distinguish the central theological claim that is a part of this argument—namely, that God allows evil because it is the only way to bring about a greater good or prevent a worse evil—from the common observation that good often comes from evil. The latter view is held by religious and nonreligious people alike, for it does not involve any theological claim whatsoever. While stronger versions of that claim (e.g., that good always comes from evil) seem to be demonstrably false, there is abundant empirical evidence to support the claim that good often comes from evil. But the theological claim that is at stake in Rowe's argument for atheism is different, not just because it is a theological claim (concerning God) but also because it focuses on the question of whether allowing evil is the *only* way to bring about *greater* goods (or prevent *worse* evils). I emphasize the words "only," "greater," and "worse" here because these are the linchpins in the argument. If there is some *other* way for God to bring about greater goods or prevent worse evils, then the evil God permits in order to achieve those ends is gratuitous. Likewise, if the goods that result from allowing evil are not truly *greater* goods (and if the evils prevented are not genuinely worse evils), then the evil is no longer justified.

To explain the depth and extent of human and animal suffering in light of an omnipotent, omnibenevolent God, we must show that God had no other choice but to allow the evil we see in the world. For no perfectly loving, all-powerful Being would create a world with so much suffering unless it was the *only* way to achieve some greater good or prevent some worse evil; otherwise, it would be inconsistent with God's perfectly loving nature. The second premise of the argument, which contends that God *would* prevent intense suffering if it were in any way possible to do so without creating greater suffering or preventing greater good, goes to this point. The first premise, by contrast, concerns God's *power*, and it contends that there are instances of evil that an omnipotent Being could have prevented without losing some greater good.

Indeed, this is the premise that Rowe says theists must attack, in order to best defend their position. The strongest response a theist can make, he argues, is to reject the first premise, arguing that "it is not the case that there exist instances of intense suffering which an omnipotent, omniscient being could have prevented without thereby losing some greater good or permitting some evil equally bad or worse."[11] In other words, the theist must contend that *no* instances of intense suffering could have been prevented by God without some greater good being lost. The central claim here is that God permits evil because it is the *only* way to bring about a greater good or prevent a worse evil.

At this point, it is reasonable to pose the question, *what* greater goods or worse evils, precisely, are we talking about? This is a particularly difficult question to answer if we are talking about large-scale instances of suffering such as the Holocaust. First, from a purely theoretical standpoint, we might ask: What worse evil could God possibly be preventing by allowing the Holocaust to occur? We can also make empirical observations that eliminate some potential answers. The Holocaust did not, for example, prevent genocide from ever occurring again; nor did it put an end to antisemitism. Additionally, it is difficult to specify why, precisely, an evil of the magnitude of the Holocaust would be *necessary*. But the truth is that it can also be difficult in cases of individual suffering to specify greater goods that are brought about or worse evils that are prevented. In a case where serious injuries from a car accident lead to the early detection of a deadly cancer, then yes, we can see how a worse evil was prevented. For some religious believers, if a person's death leads to the salvation of another person's soul, then that person's death has led to a greater good. But unfortunately, such goods are not always apparent. And while one might say that this is a matter of our own finite perspective, or of us "seeing through a glass darkly" (1 Corinthians 13:12), one might also say that in many cases we cannot observe a greater good because there *is* no greater good.

To take the latter position is to deal a devastating blow to belief in God. And here is why: as Rowe points out, all it takes is one instance of gratuitous evil—one instance of pain and suffering that does not lead to some greater good or prevent some worse evil—for the first premise of the argument to be true. Note the language of that first premise; it begins, "There exist instances." All one needs to show is that *there are* instances of evil that do not lead to a greater good, and the first premise is true. Even if *some* instances *do* lead to a greater good, this does not matter for Rowe's argument. A God who would allow even one instance of gratuitous evil is not perfectly loving, and a God who is incapable of preventing such an instance is not omnipotent.

To illustrate his view, Rowe offers a carefully crafted example of intense pain and suffering—one in which it is exceedingly difficult if not impossible to come up with any possible greater good that could be brought about or worse evil that is prevented:

> Suppose in some distant forest lightning strikes a dead tree, resulting in a forest fire. In the fire a fawn is trapped, horribly burned, and lies in terrible agony for several days before death relieves its suffering. So far as we can see, the fawn's intense suffering is pointless. For there does not appear to be any greater good such that the prevention of the fawn's suffering would require either the loss of that good or the occurrence of an evil equally bad or worse. Nor does there seem to be any equally bad or worse evil so connected to the fawn's suffering that it would have had to occur had the fawn's suffering been prevented. Could an omnipotent, omniscient being have prevented the fawn's apparently pointless suffering? The answer is obvious, as even the theist will insist. An omnipotent, omniscient being could have easily prevented the fawn from being horribly burned, or, given the burning, could have spared the fawn the intense suffering by quickly ending its life, rather than allowing the fawn to lie in terrible agony for several days. Since the fawn's intense suffering was preventable and, so far as we can see, pointless, doesn't it appear that premise (1) of the argument is true.?[12]

## Different Kinds of Atheism

The last part of Rowe's essay is dedicated to outlining different versions of atheism. His discussion allows us to explore what being an atheist can look like and what it can mean for different people, giving texture to atheism as a religious outlook. Rowe is especially interested in what kind of posture different kinds of atheists might take toward religious believers. While an atheist "will view the theist as having a false belief, just as the theist will view the atheist as having a false belief; . . . what position should the atheist take concerning the *rationality* of the theist's belief?"[13] Here, Rowe invites us to distinguish between what one believes is *true* and what one believes is *rational*. The distinction hinges on what you actually believe is the case, versus what you think other people might, in some cases, have good reasons to believe.

Rowe contends that there are three basic positions, which he introduces as three different kinds of atheism, starting with what he calls "unfriendly atheism," which characterizes the atheist who believes that no one is rationally justified in believing that the theistic God exists. Note that this type of atheist believes anyone who does not share their view holds irrational beliefs: unfriendly atheists find no rational justification for anyone believing in God. The second type of atheism is "indifferent atheism," seen in the atheist who holds "no belief concerning whether any theist is or isn't rationally justified in believing that the theistic God exists," even though the indifferent atheist is committed to atheism. Indeed, the indifferent atheist takes a "live and let live" approach, resolving the issue for themselves but declining to make any further judgment concerning the rationality of others' beliefs. The final type of atheism is what Rowe calls "friendly atheism." Friendly atheists believe that some theists *are* rationally justified in believing that the theistic God exists—despite the fact that friendly atheists do not themselves find any rational justification for belief in God compelling.

Before looking more closely at friendly atheism, I want to take a moment to discuss agnosticism. Indeed, many people would not go as far as atheism in describing their religious view, preferring a more noncommittal position of suspended belief. But traditional agnosticism differs in some significant ways from religious uncertainty. Agnosticism is much more recent than either theism or atheism, as it developed in the nineteenth century with figures such as the English biologist and anthropologist Thomas Huxley (1825–95). Although many people today use the term "agnosticism" to describe an "undecided" position on God's existence, traditionally it involves a commitment to two claims: (1) We cannot know whether God exists or does not exist, and (2) It is not permissible to believe in the absence of knowledge. From a practical standpoint, agnosticism is the same as atheism, even though it is theoretically different. Although traditional agnostics do not *deny* God's existence, their behavior usually closely resembles that of atheists in that they do not normally participate in religious rituals, services, or other forms of religious practice. But note the importance of the theoretical difference: traditional agnostics are not indifferent to the rationality of theistic belief, as is the indifferent atheist, described above. While the indifferent atheist refuses to judge whether any theists are rationally justified in their theistic belief, the agnostic believes that no one is rationally justified in believing that God exists *or* in denying that God exists.

So what is "friendly atheism," and why would one be committed to it, if one is, indeed, an atheist? To begin with, Rowe points out that "the truth of a belief is not a necessary condition of someone's being rationally justified in having that belief," which means that "the friendly atheist is not committed to thinking that the theist has a true belief. What he is committed to is that the theist has rational grounds for his belief, a belief that the atheist rejects and is convinced he is rationally justified in rejecting."[14] He offers an illustration:

> Suppose your friends see you off on a flight to Hawaii. Hours after take-off they learn that your plane has gone down at sea. After a twenty-four hour search, no survivors have been found. Under these circumstances they are rationally justified in believing that you have perished. But it is hardly rational for you to believe this, as you bob up and down in your life vest, wondering why the search planes have failed to spot you.[15]

Just as you believe that your friends are rationally justified in thinking you have perished, even though you are not justified in believing that, so too, Rowe insists, can atheists be rationally justified in their atheistic beliefs and yet hold that some theists are rationally justified in believing in God. Rowe points to three different kinds of rational grounds for religious belief—all of which we have encountered in this book. First, one might justify theistic belief by appealing to one or more of the traditional arguments for God's existence—such as the Teleological, Cosmological, or Ontological arguments. Second, one "might appeal to certain aspects of religious experience, perhaps even his own religious experience."[16] Third, one might justify theism "as a plausible theory in terms of which we can account for a variety of phenomena."[17] Rowe argues that an atheist can believe that God does not exist, and yet also believe that some of these justifications for theism *do* rationally justify some theists in their belief in God. A part of what Rowe is trying to get us to see is that human reason can have different outcomes. We can find different reasons, often for competing views, convincing. As a result, we can be rationally justified in holding opposing views, while also knowing they cannot both be true.

Rowe allows us to better understand the different textures that are a part of informed atheism. But we must go further in order to understand these textures more fully, because atheism in its different varieties sometimes enables very different forms of life—something that is also true of different varieties of theism. Religious belief often has a deep and dramatic impact on the way we live our lives, and this is one of the reasons why it is worth studying. As we saw clearly in the book's introduction, religious faith can lead people to do extraordinary things—such as establishing a truce in war—but it can also motivate people to do horrific things, as we see in the actions of jihadists who believe God commands them to fight against those they perceive as enemies of their faith. The example of jihad is particularly apropos, because it represents a type of fundamentalism, and one of the things Rowe highlights in his discussion of unfriendly atheism is a type of fundamentalist atheism. Fundamentalists are defined in part by an unwavering attachment to a particular set of beliefs (the "fundamentals"), often involving a strict, literal interpretation of particular texts, teachings, or ideologies. Fundamentalism is opposed to fallibilism, which is the attitude that Rowe invites us to take seriously in his discussion of friendly atheism. If you are a fallibilist, you may be strongly committed to the beliefs you believe to be true (and rationally justified) but you also acknowledge that you *could* be wrong. Fallibilism takes human finitude very seriously, and it often shows itself in one's willingness to entertain the possibility that those who believe differently are rationally justified in their beliefs. Rowe's friendly atheism involves a fallibilist attitude, whereas unfriendly atheism does not. This is precisely what makes it "unfriendly": one who embraces such a view believes they are rationally justified in their beliefs concerning God's existence, but anyone who disagrees is not. Religious fundamentalists—both theistic and atheistic—do not believe that they could be wrong about their religious beliefs, and in this sense, their own finitude does not figure into matters concerning the rationality of their beliefs.

What is troubling about fundamentalism of different kinds is that it can lead one to do things that harm others, or that harm oneself, because one does not believe in one's own fallibility when it comes to certain matters. The intolerance and certitude of both fundamentalist theism and fundamentalist atheism can lead us away from a number of goods that are central to human flourishing. But especially in this post–9/11 era, we are much more familiar with the dangers of fundamentalist theism. What about fundamentalist atheism? One of the most powerful descriptions of the dangers of fundamentalist atheism that I have ever read is offered by the writer Anne Lamott. It details the heartbreaking loss of an alcoholic friend who relapsed because she could not stand the "God stuff" of Alcoholics Anonymous, even though she had gotten sober—and stayed sober for ten years—in AA. When she stopped going to meetings, Lamott asked her, "don't they let you come up with a higher power of your choice? Like the mountain, say, or the ocean? What about your dog? Dog love is god love." Despite all her best attempts—including suggesting the meetings designed for atheists—her friend insisted, "Dogs are dogs. Friends are friends. I don't believe in a higher power. It's infantilizing."[18] As Lamott puts it, "She refused to doubt her atheism. She was a fundamentalist."[19] Her friend started drinking again and, after an extended and painful downward alcoholic spiral, died by suicide. Lamott asks, "What if she had been willing to give up 3 percent of the identity she was committed to being, the fundamentalist atheist, and entertain the concept that there was something, anything, greater than herself?"[20]

One of many things this story helps us to see is that faith has a variety of *practical* implications, but so too does mere *openness* to belief in something greater than ourselves, even if we do not wish to call it God or understand it as God. There are a variety of observable ways in which faith can enhance people's lives. One of them is seen in programs like AA, which have a remarkable track record of helping people to bring about positive change in their lives and the lives of those around them, and which are often life-saving. Indeed, perhaps one is rationally justified in holding certain beliefs if they make an observable difference in one's life, for the better. In other words: alcoholics may be rationally justified in believing in a higher power if this belief, among other things, results in their sobriety.

Rowe's "friendly atheist" would be precisely the sort of atheist who could be comfortable with the "God stuff" in AA, in large part because friendly atheists are fallibilists. I opened this chapter with the claim by the American theologian Paul Tillich that doubt is not the opposite of faith but an element of it. Along those same lines, the poet and novelist Rainer Maria Rilke (1875–1926) urges us to "live the questions"—leaning into them, not avoiding them, and seeing them as avenues for growth, wherever they may lead you: "Be patient toward all that is unsolved in your heart and try to love the questions themselves, like locked rooms and like books that are now written in a very foreign tongue. Do not now seek the answers. . . . Live the questions now. Perhaps you will then gradually, without noticing it, live along some distant day into the answer."[21]

## Notes

Epigraph:

Paul Tillich, *Systematic Theology, Volume 2* (Chicago: University of Chicago Press, 1975), 116–17.

1. John Hick, "The Problem of Evil," in *Ten Essential Texts in the Philosophy of Religion*, ed. Steven M. Cahn (New York: Oxford University Press, 2005), 290.

2. Mike McHargue, *Finding God in the Waves* (New York: Convergent Books, 2017).

3. McHargue.

4. Wiliam Rowe, "The Problem of Evil and Some Varieties of Atheism," in *Ten Essential Texts in the Philosophy of Religion* (New York: Oxford University Press, 2005; orig. pub. in *American Philosophical Quarterly* 16, 1979), 301.

5. Rowe.

6. Rowe.

7. Rowe, 302.

8. Rowe.

9. Rowe, 303.

10. Rowe.

11. Rowe, 307.

12. Rowe, 303–4.

13. Rowe, 308.

14. Rowe.

15. Rowe.

16. Rowe, 309.

17. Rowe.

18. Anne Lamott, *Almost Everything: Notes on Hope* (New York: Riverhead, 2018), 127–28.

19. Lamott, 132.

20. Lamott, 143.

21. Rainer Maria Rilke, *Letters to a Young Poet*, trans. M. D. Herter Norton (New York: W. W. Norton, 1993), 27.

# 11

# THE PROBLEM OF EVIL AND GOD'S OMNIPOTENCE

He is God, there is no god other than Him; who knows all things both secret and open. He is the Most Beneficent, the Most Merciful. He is God, there is no god other than Him, the Controller, the Holy One, the Source of Peace, the Guardian of Faith, the Preserver of Safety, the Exalted in Might, the Irresistible, the Supreme.

—Qur'an

His omnipotence means power to do all that is intrinsically possible, not to do the intrinsically impossible. . . . It remains true that all things are possible with God: the intrinsic impossibilities are not things but nonentities. It is no more possible for God than for the weakest of His creatures to carry out both of two mutually exclusive alternatives; not because His power meets an obstacle, but because nonsense remains nonsense even when we talk it about God.

—C. S. Lewis

The 2022 film *Spirited*, a comedic retelling of Charles Dickens's 1843 work *A Christmas Carol*, presents the story of the deeply narcissistic, pessimistic, and morally "unredeemable" Clint Briggs, and the attempts of the Ghosts of Christmas Past, Present, and Future to redeem him.[1] The film revolves around the question of whether it is really possible for people to change and become better, as well as the reality that true character change is a process that takes considerable time. At the end of the film, Clint finally demonstrates that he has been redeemed by jumping in front of a bus to save a friend's life. The bus hits him, and he dies. Clint's spirit stands in disbelief that this is the end, insisting that he had only just begun to live a good life. In response, he is told, "But your sacrifice would have no meaning if it had no consequence." This point is at the heart of the Soul-Making Theodicy: it is logically impossible for someone to become good in a world without real consequences, including pain and loss. If Clint had known that he could not really be hurt or killed, then his willingness to sacrifice his life for another would have had no significance whatsoever. It was the fact that he was willing to put his life on the line that showed he had really come to love and care about others, and had truly been redeemed.

Indeed, the Soul-Making Theodicy insists that it was necessary for God to create a world with challenges and suffering in order for us to develop virtues such as love and compassion. As the plot of *Spirited* shows, real change does not come easily or instantly. This is undoubtedly true of the cultivation of most virtues: in the absence of an object of compassion or someone for whom we might demonstrate it, we cannot become compassionate. This is why so many parenting books stress the importance of not shielding children from your (or others') experiences of emotions like sadness, along with the importance of allowing them to fail: for without these experiences, they cannot become caring, resilient people. Virtues are like muscles: they are only built by exercising them. We must demonstrate compassion and resilience in order to further develop these traits. From the perspective of the Soul-Making Theodicy, we must live in a world with evil if we are to undergo the kinds of challenges that are required in order for us to become good people.

Now, one might be tempted to challenge the entire enterprise of theodicy by asking why God did not just create humans to *be* good in the first place. This is a fair question, and one that theodicies are attempting to answer by offering an explanation for why God permits evil in the world. As we have seen, however, theodicies do not assert that God should have created a different kind of world; nor do they offer arguments for such a claim. Rather, theodicies offer a rational explanation for how and why an all-powerful, all-knowing, perfectly loving God created *this* world, with its combination of moral and natural evil. In this way, theodicy is not a speculative task but a very practical one, fully grounded in reality. According to the Soul-Making Theodicy, God creates a world with pain and suffering so that we can experience and participate in the process of becoming good, and the Free Will Theodicy contends that God gives us free will so that we can experience freedom and agency. As the *Barbie* movie so aptly puts it, we are "part of the people that make meaning," and who do the imagining. In this way, we are "co-creators" with God. Both these theodicies contend that God's ultimate aim is for us to know and be in a loving relationship with God. (Remember the words of James Weldon Johnson's God: "I'm lonely—I'll make me a world.") But God elects not to control us. The Soul-Making Theodicy contends that God gives us the gift of a richer, more meaningful life as a result of giving us all of these things—instead of simply creating us to be perfect beings who live in a perfect world. To be sure, if God had created perfect beings, then the purpose of creation would have been altogether different. Part of what the film *Spirited* is trying to get us to see is that the purpose of our lives—of the process of "redemption"—is to come to truly love others, to the point where we would even lay down our lives for someone else. Would this be possible if we didn't live in a world with pain and loss? As we saw in chapter 9, the philosopher Robert Baird suggests, "Maybe, just maybe, you cannot have the marvel of love without the darkness of loss. Maybe the connection between love and loss is so intimate that even God cannot pull them apart."[2]

Take note of Baird's language here: perhaps even God *cannot* pull them apart. As we have seen, one of the central, lingering problems relating to the Problem of Evil concerns why God creates a world with so much evil, and why God does not intervene to alleviate at least some of the suffering in the world. If God did not realize the appalling depth and extent of the moral evil that humans would perpetrate when he created us with free will, then God appears not to be omniscient. The fact that God does not intervene to fix this problem makes it appear that God is either unable or unwilling to do so. William Rowe contends that the theist's only real defense is to contend that allowing evil is the *only* way for God to bring about a greater good or prevent some worse evil. Following Baird's analysis, we might propose that the greater good is love, and the worse evil is a world without love. Anyone who has experienced love will surely find this proposition tempting. (Think of the people you love most. Would you prefer a world without the possibility of loss but also without the experience of love?) But note what we must accept in order for this solution to work: it must be the case that the *only* way for God to bring about the greater good of love is for loss to also be a part of our world.

## Aquinas, Mavrodes, and Self-Contradictory Tasks

The basic problem here, theologically, concerns God's omnipotence. If God's hand is forced, and the only way for God to bring about some greater good like love is to permit evil, does this not mean that God is restricted? And does this, in turn, not mean that God is not omnipotent?

The question of what we mean when we say that God is omnipotent is a very old question in Christian theology and philosophy. (And it is worth noting that the very idea of an all-powerful God is a religious peculiarity: the belief in God's omnipotence is a feature of the Abrahamic faiths but not other religions, which conceptualize deities as having various limitations.) If God is omnipotent, does this mean that God can do *anything*—even logically impossible tasks? For instance, could God give us free will and all its benefits, yet also ensure that we will always choose rightly (or place certain safeguards on our freedom, in order to prevent us from making choices that result in harmful consequences)? Could God create a world where we can become loving, kind, and compassionate people, and that also does not have pain, suffering, or the possibility of loss? For that is what would be required if God's omnipotence means that God can do *anything*—even the logically impossible.

In this chapter, we examine two different understandings of omnipotence: the first is a more limited view of omnipotence, and the second is what I call radical omnipotence.

One of the first theologians to wrestle with this problem was Thomas Aquinas, who maintained that when it comes to the claim that God can do anything, "anything" should be understood to refer only to objects, actions, or states of affairs whose descriptions are not self-contradictory.[3] This is a more limited view of omnipotence. As the philosopher George Mavrodes explains in his essay "Some Puzzles Concerning Omnipotence," omnipotence here is only understood to include "such things whose nonexistence might plausibly be attributed to a lack of power in some agent. My failure to draw a circle on the exam may indicate my lack of geometrical skill, but my failure to draw a square circle does not indicate any such lack. Therefore, the fact that it is false (or perhaps meaningless) to say that God could draw one does no damage to the doctrine of His omnipotence."[4] In other words, the claim that God cannot perform self-contradictory tasks does not undermine God's omnipotence, just as my failure to draw a square circle does not undermine my geometrical skill. The difference between my inability to draw *a circle* and my inability to draw *a square circle* is that the latter is an impossible task; there is no such thing as a square circle. My failure to draw a figure that has four right corners *and* no corners is no failure of mine, because it is not logically possible to do it. To claim that anyone—human or divine—can draw a figure that has four right corners and no corners is a meaningless statement.

However, Mavrodes writes, a more involved problem is posed by the question, "Can God create a stone too heavy for God to lift?"[5] This is because it poses a dilemma: "If there might be a stone too heavy for Him to lift, then He is evidently not omnipotent. But if we deny that God can create such a stone, we seem to have given up His omnipotence already. Both answers lead us to the same conclusion."[6] Whereas "x is able to draw a square circle" involves a contradiction, no contradiction is involved in the claim that "x is able to make a stone too heavy for x to lift." Artists, for instance, sometimes create sculptures that are too heavy for them to lift. But Mavrodes points out that "God" is not "x," where x is understood as *any* subject. God, in our definition, is a particular *kind* of subject—one with omnipotence. If we understand God to be omnipotent, then the assertion that "God is able to make a stone too heavy for God to lift" *becomes* contradictory: "For it becomes 'a stone which cannot be lifted by Him whose power is sufficient for lifting anything," and "its failure to exist cannot be the result of some lack in the power of God," because the existence of such a stone is impossible.[7] Mavrodes thus follows Aquinas in arguing that God's inability to perform self-contradictory tasks in no way undermines God's omnipotence. As Mavrodes puts it, "Such pseudo-tasks, not falling within the realm of possibility, are not objects of power at all.

Hence the fact that they cannot be performed implies no limit on the power of God, and hence no defect in the doctrine of omnipotence."[8] What Mavrodes means by "pseudo-tasks" is that we cannot logically make any sense of their descriptions using our language. Indeed, part of what we mean when we call something "logically impossible" or self-contradictory is that it does not make sense using language; our statements about it are rendered meaningless. What does it mean, for instance, to say that God can draw a square circle, or that God can create a stone that is both too heavy for God to lift and not too heavy for God to lift? We might be inclined to say that we must be mistaken about the meaning of terms like "circle," "square," and "heavy," because these statements are incomprehensible. The claims are what we call mutually exclusive: a figure cannot both have corners *and* no corners, and God cannot be capable of lifting any object *and* be unable to lift *some* objects.

All this has a direct bearing on the Problem of Evil because, according to this view of omnipotence, God could not give us free will *and* make us always choose rightly; nor could God have created a world without pain and suffering and still have it be a place of soul-making. Similarly, God could not have created a world with love without the possibility of loss. The view of omnipotence articulated by both Aquinas and Mavrodes here is the view of omnipotence that is required to support the Free Will Theodicy and the Soul-Making Theodicy, because it explains why God has limited options, despite being omnipotent. It is also the view of omnipotence that is required of theists who wish to reject the first premise of Rowe's argument for atheism based on the Problem of Evil. For to defend the claim that God *could not* have prevented instances of intense suffering in this world without thereby losing some greater good or permitting some evil equally bad or worse, one must be able to offer an account of why an omnipotent God is restricted in this way. As we have seen, for Aquinas and Mavrodes, self-contradictory tasks do not undermine divine omnipotence. If the greater goods that God is bringing about by permitting suffering are freedom, goodness, and love, then it is self-contradictory to say that God could bring about these ends without permitting suffering. The self-contradiction is clearest in the case of freedom: God cannot create beings who have free will *and* who always or even usually choose rightly. For that is to negate the very idea of freedom.

From this perspective, creating persons who have free will is an all-or-nothing decision on God's part: we either have free will or we do not. There is no middle ground, because if God limits our choices by creating us to choose rightly all or most of the time, then we do not really have free will. It is also helpful to note that God giving us free will is very much unlike the freedoms that human parents allow their children to have as they grow, or the freedoms that citizens have in a society, both of which have degrees and limits. Certainly, we are finite beings and live in a world that limits our freedom in a variety of ways, for our choices are shaped by when and where we are born, our families of origin, and many other circumstances, including the experiences we have over the course of our lives. But when we talk about God giving us free will, we are talking about the capacity to make choices for ourselves at all. The very existence of moral evil is evidence of our freedom, for it shows that humans sometimes choose to do wonderful things and, other times, horrific things. In other words, a brief survey of human behavior does not suggest that God has preprogrammed all of us to always or usually choose rightly.

But the reality is complex: people do not always seem to be fully determined by their circumstances, yet some people are more strongly shaped by them, and those circumstances vary widely. People also seem capable of real change, and sometimes even dramatic transformation (something we saw in Augustine and will discuss further in chapter 14). While some are tempted by the allure of strong forms of hard determinism (the view that our "choices" are not really choices at all but are fully determined by the events and circumstances of our lives), the course of human lives and our responses to our circumstances are messier and more difficult to predict than one would expect if determinism were true. Additionally, the existence of regulations and systems that punish moral evil, in every human culture and society around the globe, highlights the widely shared human belief that we have free will, and thus can justly be held responsible for our actions.

Much like the claim that we could have free will *and* be made to always or usually choose rightly, claims that we can develop virtues like compassion without the existence of suffering, or experience love without loss, are problematic. As Mavrodes points out, following Aquinas, "It is only such things whose nonexistence might plausibly be attributed to a lack of power in some agent" that can undermine God's omnipotence. Put another way: these things are not logically possible. To say that we can develop the virtue of compassion without ever encountering suffering involves a contradiction, because compassion *is*, by definition, a response to suffering. Similarly, to say that we can experience love without the possibility of pain or loss involves a contradiction, because a part of what it means to love someone is to care so deeply for them that it pains you to see them suffer. (Remember the anonymous author who describes grief for us at the end of chapter 9, who says it "tears a hole in me whenever somebody I love dies, no matter the circumstances. But I don't want it to 'not matter.' I don't want it to be something that just passes. My scars are a testament to the love I had for that person.") Our scars are a testament to our love and affection for others because a defining feature of love and affection—one of the ways you *know* that you love or care deeply for someone—is that it pains you to lose them. To illustrate this, when I tear up at the university's commencement, it is because I have come to care deeply for my students. My sadness to see them go (alongside my happiness for them) is a reflection of my love and affection for them. (As Parker Palmer puts it, "teaching tugs at the heart, opens the heart, even breaks the heart."[9]) Another defining feature of love is that you share in others' pain and suffering; indeed, witnessing the suffering of someone you love is sometimes even more painful than your own suffering, as any parent who has witnessed their child's suffering can attest. In all these ways, having love without pain and loss is an impossibility. To use Aquinas's words, "It is more appropriate to say that such things cannot be done, than that God cannot do them."[10] They are, as Mavrodes says, "pseudo-tasks," since it is logically impossible to perform them. As we have seen, since their descriptions render language meaningless, we cannot even make sense of what they are.

### Frankfurt and God's Radical Omnipotence

A year after Mavrodes published his work on omnipotence, the philosopher Harry Frankfurt published a response.[11] Frankfurt grants that for God to create a stone too heavy for God to lift is indeed self-contradictory. But he also argues that we have some good reasons to question Mavrodes's principle concerning self-contradictory tasks—namely, that God need not be supposed capable of performing them. For one thing, this principle was explicitly rejected by one of the most influential philosophers in the history of Western philosophy: René Descartes (1596–1650), who wrote,

> In general we can be quite certain that God can do whatever we are able to understand, but not that He cannot do what we are unable to understand. For it would be presumptuous to think that our imagination extends as far as His power. . . . I would not even dare to say that God cannot arrange that a mountain should exist without a valley, or that one and two should not make three; but I only say that He has given me a mind of such a nature that I cannot conceive a mountain without a valley or the sum of one and two which would not be three, and so on, and that such things imply contradictions in my conception.[12]

Frankfurt (like Mavrodes) does *not* believe the dilemma concerning whether God can create a stone too heavy for God to lift is ultimately a threat to God's omnipotence. But instead of qualifying God's power, Frankfurt does just the opposite. Following Descartes, he argues that there is no reason to believe that God cannot do things that appear logically impossible or self-contradictory to us. Against Mavrodes, he argues that God *can* perform self-contradictory tasks: "What the critic [of divine omnipotence] wishes to claim, of course, is that when God has created a stone which He cannot lift He is then faced with a task beyond His ability and is therefore seen to be limited in power. But this claim is not justified."[13]

What is Frankfurt's solution? He argues that God can create a stone that is too heavy for God to lift *and God can lift that stone*. God's omnipotence, in Frankfurt's view, is not constrained by the laws or limits of logic, such as the principle of noncontradiction (which states that contradictory propositions cannot both be true in the same sense at the same time). As he puts it, "If God is supposed capable of performing one task whose description is self-contradictory—that of creating the problematic stone in the first place—why should He not be supposed capable of performing another—that of lifting the stone?"[14] In this view, God's omnipotence exceeds our powers of conception or imagination. Indeed, we might call this *radical* omnipotence, because God has no limitations whatsoever: "If an omnipotent being can do what is logically impossible, then he can not only create situations which he cannot handle but also, since he is not bound by the limits of consistency, he can handle situations which he cannot handle."[15]

What bearing does this have on the Problem of Evil? Throughout this chapter, we have focused on God's omnipotence as something that is not a merely theoretical concern but one that has practical implications for belief in God. If we take Frankfurt's view seriously, then its implications for theodicy are devastating; for in this view, God could have created free beings who would always (or usually) choose rightly, and so, too, could God have created a world that is a hedonistic paradise and yet also a place of soul-making. For if God can create a stone too heavy for God to lift and lift that stone, then God can give us free will without the possibility of moral evil, along with opportunities to develop compassion without any objects of compassion, and the opportunity to love and be loved by others, without the possibility of pain and loss.

The question is left to us: Which view of divine omnipotence do we find more compelling? Is God's omnipotence defined by the capacity to perform any *possible* task, or does God possess radical omnipotence, including the ability to do self-contradictory things? These are two competing views of God. The first insists that God is infinite and we are finite, but that God has given us the capacity to understand some dimensions of God's nature. One merit of this view is that it allows us to more easily make sense of what it means to be made in God's image—a fundamental tenet of both the Jewish and Christian traditions. The second contends that God's infinite nature, compared with our finite nature, translates into a reality that far surpasses our powers of understanding, and of which we cannot even conceive or make sense. While the former, more limited view of omnipotence allows us to defend the Free Will and Soul-Making theodicies, the latter view does not. One who defends God's radical omnipotence, insisting that God could have done anything (even the logically impossible) when creating the world, is likely to reject the idea that we have any hope of understanding difficult theological problems. Indeed, there are real limits to theology, in such a view. For one could maintain, as

Descartes does, that "it would be presumptuous to think that our imagination extends as far as His power." One who takes this view is likely to respond to the Problem of Evil with the claim that simply because *we* cannot resolve this problem logically is no reason at all to think that there is not an answer known only to God, which lies beyond our understanding.

## Notes

Qur'an 59:22–23, trans. Salih Sayilgan, quoted by Salih Sayilgan, *God, Evil, and Suffering in Islam* (New York: Cambridge University Press, 2024), 38.

C. S. Lewis, *The Problem of Pain* (New York: HarperOne, 2015; reprint), 1.

1. *Spirited*, film, directed by Sean Anders (Apple Original Films, 2022).
2. Robert M Baird, "A Sermon for Old People Like Me and Actually for Younger People Too," Lake Shore Baptist Church, November 20, 2016, transcript, 5.
3. Saint Thomas Aquinas, *Summa Theologiae*, 1a, q. 25, a. 3.
4. George Mavrodes, "Some Puzzles Concerning Omnipotence," in *Ten Essential Texts in the Philosophy of Religion*, ed. Steven M. Cahn (New York: Oxford University Press, 2005; orig. pub. in *Philosophical Review* 72, 1963: 117).
5. Mavrodes.
6. Mavrodes.
7. Mavrodes, 118.
8. Mavrodes, 119.
9. Parker Palmer, *The Courage to Teach: Exploring the Inner Landscape of a Teacher's Heart* (New York: Jossey-Bass, 2007), chap. 1.
10. Saint Thomas Aquinas, *Summa Theologiae*, 1a, q. 25, a. 3.
11. Harry G. Frankfurt, "The Logic of Omnipotence," in *Ten Essential Texts*, 119–21 (orig. pub. in *Philosophical Review* 73, 1964).
12. Frankfurt, 121n3. Frankfurt quotes Descartes's letters to Marsenne (April 15, 1630) and Arnauld (July 29, 1648).
13. Frankfurt, 120.
14. Frankfurt.
15. Frankfurt.

# 12

# PASCAL'S WAGER

It is not like a child that I believe in Christ and confess him.
My hosanna has come forth from the crucible of doubt.
—Fyodor Dostoyevsky

The finite dissolves in the presence of the infinite
and becomes pure nothingness.
So it is with our mind before God.
—Blaise Pascal

A print of *Jesus in the Workshop of Saint Joseph* (Van Honthorst, 1620) hangs on my living room wall. The painting shows Joseph working with a hammer and chisel at his workbench while Jesus, still a young boy, holds a candle for him to see by. The light illuminates both their faces. Jesus is staring directly into Joseph's face with a penetrating gaze. Joseph's eyes are trained on the chisel.

I remember staring at this painting every day after we learned we would need to sell our first home due to a highway-widening project that would likely take our backyard. With great trepidation, we put our house on the market, praying that someone would be willing to buy it. A colleague brought me a small statue of Saint Joseph, with instructions for burying it in the yard to help the house sell—an old Catholic tradition. A professional stager went room by room, removing everything personal, including most of our artwork. But when she reached the painting of Joseph, she exclaimed, "Oh that works. That can stay." And so, day after day, I looked up into Joseph's face. I admired how steadily his eyes were trained on that chisel. I thought of the statue buried in the yard. And a little faith grew in me, not because of the statue's power but because Joseph inspired me.

One day, I ran into a colleague on campus, and spontaneously shared all this. He smiled. "You know Joseph is my middle name? Born on Saint Joseph's Day. And as an adoptive father, I always felt a connection with him." He told me that the Protestant theologian Karl Barth had once told the pope that Joseph should have been more important in the Church, "because Joseph had faith when he didn't know anything!" Mary had the Annunciation—when an angel appeared to her and foretold much of what would happen, including Jesus's conception and birth, and when Mary offered her consent (Luke 1:26–38). Joseph, however, had faith with no window into the future.

## Pascal's Mathematical Theology

The French mathematician, physicist, and philosopher Blaise Pascal (1623–62) believed that a complete lack of knowledge or understanding was characteristic of faith in God—not just sometimes, but all the time. Accordingly, those who find themselves frustrated with attempts to rationally make sense of belief in God and the various problems associated with it find a kindred spirit in Pascal. While we focus on his philosophical and theological views in this book, Pascal is perhaps best known for his work as a mathematician. A child prodigy who wrote a treatise on projective geometry at age sixteen, he went on to make important contributions to probability theory (and was also one of the first two inventors of the mechanical calculator). His way of thinking and general approach to different problems reflect his orientation as a mathematician, as the opening line of his work "The Wager" shows: "*Infinity nothingness*. Our soul is thrust into the body, where it finds number, time, dimension. . . . A unit added to infinity does not increase it at all, any more than a foot added to an infinite length. The finite dissolves in the presence of the infinite and becomes pure nothingness. So it is with our mind before God."[1]

Pascal's theology is a mathematical one. He begins by considering our finitude in relation to the concept of an infinite God. From a purely mathematical perspective, any number "dissolves" in the presence of the infinite, becoming "pure nothingness." Based on this mathematical truth, he contends that this must also be true of our own finitude by comparison with God: "We therefore know the existence and nature of the finite, because we too are finite and have no extension."[2] Pascal concludes, "If there is a God, he is infinitely beyond our comprehension, since, having neither parts nor limits, he bears no relation to ourselves. We are therefore incapable of knowing either what he is, or if he is."[3]

Pascal's entire approach to religious faith differs from most of the approaches we have encountered in this book, because he gives up the ground to religious skeptics who say that we cannot prove God's existence rationally. Unlike the arguments for God's existence offered by Anselm, Aquinas, and Paley, and unlike theodicies that explain how God's nature is compatible with evil, Pascal grants from the start that God is *infinitely* beyond our comprehension. For him, this means that we cannot demonstrate whether God exists, or understand God's nature; as Pascal says, we are incapable of knowing either *what* God is or *if* God is. But this does not mean, for Pascal, that we should not believe. He puts the question this way: "God is, or is not. But towards which side will we lean? Reason cannot decide anything. There is an infinite chaos separating us. At the far end of this infinite distance a game is being played and the coin will come down heads or tails. How will you wager?"[4]

If Pascal's approach strikes you as a bit irreverent, you are not the first to feel that way. It is not uncommon to view Pascal as cheapening religious faith with the suggestion that it is a wager. But it is important to understand that this is not what Pascal intends. Rather, in using the terminology of a wager, he means to emphasize that we cannot decide the question of whether God exists by reasoning or arguments. Yet we *have* to choose. Indeed, we *will* choose, through our very actions, in the way we lead our lives, and this is why he calls it a "wager." Pascal insists that we must step out with faith—with *blind* faith—and simply *decide*. He urges us not to try to avoid the unavoidable by saying we are "suspending belief." For Pascal is aware that one who suspends belief, like an agnostic, typically behaves just like an atheist. To suspend belief, from his perspective, translates into wagering "no," and living as if God did not exist. In reality, there is no third alternative: we must wager "yes" or "no" regarding God's existence.

## Why Wager Yes?

Pascal contends that we ought to wager that God exists, because "if you win, you win everything; if you lose, you lose nothing. Wager that he exists then, without hesitating!"[5] This is because we stand to gain "an eternity of life and happiness"; but if we lose, we lose nothing, because "what you are staking is finite." Here, Pascal operates purely as a mathematician, insisting, "That removes all choice. Wherever there is infinity and where there is no infinity of chances of losing against one of winning, there is no scope for wavering, you have to chance everything."[6]

The key to understanding Pascal's insistence that we ought to wager "yes" is his mathematical point concerning the relation between infinity and any finite number: any number dissolves (or becomes zero) by comparison with infinity. This is why he says that if you lose, you lose nothing. If you wager "yes," and it turns out that God does not exist, any amount—or any quantification of your time and energies spent attending religious services, and the like—that we would consider in comparison with the possibility of gaining infinity simply dissolves into nothingness, or zero. (Note that for Pascal, religious devotion is a part of what is necessary for salvation. He also believes that real faith in God is evident in what one does.) If you wager "yes" and it turns out that God does exist, you gain an eternity of life and happiness. But if you wager "no," and it turns out that God exists, you have lost an eternity of life and happiness and have gained nothing, for if God does not exist, the game is over. Note that Pascal views the gains here as nothing because, even though we might think of the satisfaction of living your life with true beliefs, there is no satisfaction to be had in this case, for life simply ends; you would not even be aware that you were right. Thus, Pascal concludes, "You have to have discarded reason if you cling on to your life, rather than risk it for the infinite prize which is just as likely to happen as the loss of nothingness."[7]

Some of the most poignant passages in Pascal's work describe the limits of reason when it comes to faith. He writes, "It is the heart that feels God, not reason: that is what faith is. God felt by the heart, not by reason."[8] When Pascal says that the heart *feels* God, he seems to be describing his own experience of God as something that he perceives through his affective capacities, as opposed to something he comes to believe in through reasoning. In fact, Pascal was motivated to begin writing about philosophy and theology by a mystical experience he had in 1654, which resulted in a complete change in his lifestyle, intellectual interests, and personal ambitions.[9] So when Pascal writes, "The heart has its reasons which reason itself does not know: we know that through countless things," he is, among other things, drawing upon his own religious experience.[10] Pascal suggests that there are different ways of knowing, one of which is reason. But another way of knowing is through the heart, and for Pascal this is the *only* possible way we can know God. Yet he insists that the heart "has its reasons." That is, for Pascal, faith is warranted. But it is the experience of the heart that gives us warranted belief.

## Two Critiques of Pascal

In his critique of Pascal's wager, the contemporary philosopher Simon Blackburn provides us with a helpful visual illustration of Pascal's view, which, as table 12.1 shows, consists of a two-by-two box of the options.[11]

The zeros in table 12.1 represent the mathematical point on which Pascal grounds the wager: the fact that the finite is nothing compared with infinity. As Blackburn puts it, "This life is of vanishingly little account compared to what is promised to believers. The plus-infinity figure corresponds to infinite bliss. The minus-infinity figure corresponds to the traditional jealous God, who sends to Hell those who do not believe in him."[12] Blackburn is correct to point out the conservative religious outlook that informs Pascal's work. Pascal identified with a religious movement within Roman Catholicism known as Jansenism, which was in conflict with the Jesuits during the 1600s over how to interpret Augustine's views on divine grace and free will in salvation. Their criticisms coincided with a growing hostility on the part of Roman Catholic clergy toward the Jesuits, and Pascal led the Jansenist charge by attacking the Jesuits for being overly tolerant of sin and of practices associated with other religions.[13] Indeed, Pascal concludes "The Wager" with a series of remarks about Christianity that make clear that he is a staunch religious exclusivist

**Table 12.1** Simon Blackburn's Illustration of Pascal's View

| | God exists | God does not exist |
|---|---|---|
| I believe in God | +infinity! | 0 |
| I do not believe in God | – infinity! | 0 |

who maintains that Christianity is the only path to salvation (and the only path to moral goodness).

Blackburn admits, however, that the wager still looks good, even in the absence of the harsher elements of Pascal's theology. Indeed, he says it looks good "even if God does not punish disbelief, because there is still that terrific payoff of '+infinity' cranking up the choice."[14] So even if we replace "–infinity" with "0," Blackburn argues that "in decision-theory terms, the option of belief 'dominates,' because it can win, and cannot lose."[15]

Blackburn goes on to offer two critiques of Pascal's wager. The first is what we will call the Objection from Metaphysical Ignorance, and it is rooted in the fact that Pascal begins from a position of metaphysical ignorance, since he insists that we cannot know anything about God's nature. "But the set-up of the wager presumes that we *do* know something. We are supposed to know the rewards and penalties attached to belief in a Christian God. This is a God who will be pleasured and reward us for our attendance at mass, and will either be indifferent or, in the minus-infinity option, seriously discombobulated by our nonattendance."[16] Yet Blackburn argues that we have no good reason to think that God would reward belief. If we know *nothing* about God's nature, then it is possible that God would reward unbelief in the absence of evidence. In such a view, "The good human beings are those who follow the natural light of reason, which is given to them to control their beliefs. These good humans follow the arguments, and hence avoid religious convictions. These ones with the strength of mind not to believe in such things go to Heaven. The rest go to Hell."[17] Blackburn's basic point is that if Pascal is correct and we cannot know anything about God's nature, then we have no basis for deciding what would be gained or lost by wagering yes or no, if God in fact exists.

Blackburn's second critique is the Objection from Religious Pluralism. He argues that "whilst for Pascal it was a simple two-way question of mass versus disbelief, in the wider world it is also a question of the Koran versus mass, or L. Ron Hubbard versus the Swami Maharishi."[18] In other words, it is not as simple as Pascal suggests, because in addition to deciding whether we believe, we must also decide *what* we believe and which religion to practice. This question does not seem to have occurred to Pascal, most likely because in his time and place, one did not typically have the opportunity to make informed choices about a wide range of religions. (It is helpful to remember that Pascal was embroiled in a series of debates and disagreements *within Catholicism*, which is but one branch—albeit the dominant branch, at the time—of just one religious tradition: Christianity.) Even today, for a majority of the world's people, it is not a "live option" to simply choose from a buffet of different religions, as most people are not exposed to a wide range of religions, at least not in any depth. We might say that the choice is ultimately between those religions we *do* encounter—those that we have the opportunity to learn about, and which have places of worship and communities of faith that are easily accessible to us. Yet we do live in a world that presents historically unprecedented choices of this sort to some of us, and Blackburn is surely correct that it complicates Pascal's wager. (The variety of problems posed by religious pluralism are the subject of the next chapter of this book.)

In conclusion, I want to note a couple of limitations to Blackburn's critiques. First, Blackburn is correct to point out the inconsistency between Pascal's claim that God rewards belief with infinity and his contention that we cannot have any knowledge of God. It seems clear that Pascal—like so many of us—was not fully aware of the extent to which his own religious beliefs and experiences informed his thinking. Blackburn goes on to say that if God rewards those who follow the light of reason, then God will reward those who "follow the arguments, and hence avoid religious convictions."[19] Yet as we have seen, it is not at all clear that reason is on the side of *un*belief, rather than belief. Throughout this book, we have examined arguments both for *and* against God's existence. And it is not clear that the bulk of the evidence falls on one side or the other. William Rowe argues quite convincingly that there are theists *and* atheists whose religious beliefs are warranted. If Rowe is correct, then perhaps Blackburn's critique of Pascal is not quite as devastating as it seems. After all, there is no evidentiary basis for Blackburn's claim that a God who punishes belief is "a lot more reasonable."

Nevertheless, Blackburn's basic critique—that Pascal's wager rests on the theological claim that God might reward belief *with infinity*, when Pascal says we cannot know anything about God—still stands. We might, however, defend Pascal by stressing that infinity, *as a possibility of what one might gain*, is the linchpin in the wager. Remember, Pascal insists that we cannot know what the outcome will be, only that gaining infinity would be a possible outcome. Why should we believe this is the most likely possible gain? Some knowledge of different religious traditions might be a helpful resource here, for one of the commonalities between a majority of religions is, indeed, what we might call infinity: the promise of a final end state of liberation, enlightenment, union with God, or a perpetual spiritual existence that surpasses this one. Different religions even use some of the same metaphors for this, with Buddhists describing being "ferried over" by Buddhist teachings and practices to "the farther shore" of enlightenment or nirvana—an indescribable, infinite state in which there is no suffering. Christians describe "crossing over Jordan" as a metaphor for crossing over from death to eternal life, to Heaven, where "every tear will be wiped away" and there will be no death, mourning, or pain, and one dwells in the presence of the infinite God (Revelation 21:4). (This metaphor is based on the Hebrew Bible's account of the Israelites crossing the Jordan River after forty years of wandering in the desert, before they could enter the Promised Land.)

This final state is described as eternal and infinite in almost every major religion (and quite a few of the minor ones, too), despite important differences in how they understand it. Additionally, not a single major religious tradition contends that a *lack* of faith will be rewarded in the end. This is true even in traditions that do not clearly articulate a final spiritual state of liberation after death. The teachings of Judaism, for instance, consistently affirm the importance of faithfulness, even in the midst of persecution, insisting that faith in God will lead not only to our well-being in this life but also that of our descendants, who will follow in our footsteps. (The story of Job expresses such a view.) As a result, if we understand "+infinity" in broader terms than Pascal did—to represent the infinite state that an overwhelming majority of the world's major religions understand to be the final outcome or result of religious faith—it might be possible to defend the wager against Blackburn's critique. I will have much more to say about the similarities and differences between religions in the next chapter, but I would argue that a clear majority of the world's peoples—grounded in their own diverse religious experiences, throughout history—have viewed religious faith in this way. Of course, they might be wrong. But their shared orientation toward religious faith and the infinite, I think, gives us a good reason to consider that "+infinity" may indeed be what is involved in the wager.

## Conclusion

I once taught a student in "The Problem of God" who had been raised attending Mass regularly. When she and her brothers grew older, her family stopped attending church, and one day she asked her dad why they had stopped—and also why they had attended in the first place. He responded that the reason she and her brothers were baptized and had attended Mass for so long was that when he was a student at Georgetown, he had read "Pascal's Wager" in his "Problem of God" course. Thirty years later, in her reflection paper on Pascal for my course, she wrote, "This reading will always stick with me because it is the reason I was brought up the way I was, and I had not had the chance to actually read it until this course. And knowing my dad and his love for math, it makes perfect sense to me that 'The Wager' had this impact on him."[20] I am struck by her awareness that a faith community helped to define the way she was brought up, even though her family eventually stopped attending church. One of the most interesting yet neglected dimensions of Pascal's work is his insistence upon the goods that come from being part of a faith community—including the way faith communities help to nurture a variety of virtues in us. Pascal emphasizes that a life of faith involves certain ethical commitments, and a corresponding rejection of materialism. In "The Wager," he outlines some of the defining virtues of faith communities in his response to someone who is worried about the finite "losses" that are associated with wagering "yes":

> But what harm will come to you from taking this course? You will be faithful, honest, humble, grateful, doing good, a sincere and true friend. It is, of course, true; you will not take part in corrupt pleasure, in glory, in the pleasures of high living. But will you not have others? I tell you that you will win thereby in this life, and that at every step you take along this path, you will see so much certainty of winning and so negligible a risk, that you will realize in the end that you have wagered on something certain and infinite, for which you have paid nothing.[21]

Of course, not all faith communities succeed in fostering goodness in the ways they aim to. Like governments, religious communities are human institutions, and therefore deeply flawed and capable of harm. But just as we should not reject all governments (or particular forms of government) because of how some governments have harmed people, neither should we reject all religions because of how some religious communities have harmed people. Both are human institutions, capable of helping people and harming them, as history shows. (Democratic governments have harmed people, and so have Christian churches. Think, for example, of the history of slavery and racism in America, the treatment of LGBTQIA persons in many Christian churches, and the clergy abuse scandal. But this does not mean that democratic governance or Christian communities are not worth having. Just think of the role of democracy in the Women's Suffrage Movement, and Christianity's role in the Civil Rights Movement.) As the Reverend Amy Butler puts it, "The invitation to become who we are meant to be happens at the intersection of human pain and divine hope, and almost always in the context of relationship."[22] Pascal draws our attention to this important dimension of religious life: the dimension of religion that has helped to promote basic human rights and social justice in many societies around the globe. This contributes to his view that we have nothing to lose—even by finite standards—by wagering "yes."

This brings me back to the painting of Saint Joseph that I described at the beginning of this chapter, because for Joseph, faith was not just a commitment to believe in the midst of uncertainty. It was a commitment to live a certain kind of life, and to be a certain kind of person. While Joseph is the patron saint of families, fathers, adoptive parents, expectant mothers, travelers, immigrants, house sellers, craftsmen, engineers, and working people (among others), the uncertainty he faced in many of these roles is the same uncertainty we all face in different contexts and in different ways.

The day we moved out of our house, the painting of Joseph was the last thing to come down off the wall. I drove it to our new house myself and carried it inside, pausing to look once more at the person who stood by his pregnant fiancé and married her even though he knew the child was not his, who could find nowhere for them to stay but a stable the night she went into labor, and who raised and loved that child as his own. As Karl Barth said, Joseph had faith even though he knew nothing. This is precisely the lack of knowledge that, for Pascal, we all have, when it comes to God. For it is impossible for us to have knowledge of the infinite. In Pascal's view, this is why we must *wager* "yes." This is why we must have faith, which differs from trust that is supported by knowledge or reason. Indeed, faith involves waiting for that which is yet to come—most importantly, for Pascal, the outcome of our wager. As the writer and poet Wendell Berry puts it, we must "love where we cannot trust, trust where we cannot know, and must await the wayward-coming grace that joins living and dead, taking us where we would not go—into the boundless dark."[23]

## Notes

*Epigraphs:*

Fyodor Dostoyevsky, *The Grand Inquisitor* (New York: Continuum, 1981), introduction, xx.

Blaise Pascal, "The Wager," in *Ten Essential Texts in the Philosophy of Religion*, ed. Steven M. Cahn (New York: Oxford University Press, 2005), 361.

1. Pascal, "Wager." "The Wager" is part of Pascal's larger work, *Pensées*.
2. Pascal.
3. Pascal, 361–62.
4. Pascal.
5. Pascal, 362.
6. Pascal, 363.
7. Pascal.
8. Pascal, 365.
9. He describes a lighted vision and being in the presence of Jesus Christ. His notes from the experience are recorded in the *Memorial*, and he carried this brief description of the experience with him at all times, sewn into the lining of his coat. For a translation, see www.ccel.org/ccel/pascal/memorial.i.html.
10. Pascal, "Wager," 365.
11. Simon Blackburn, "Pascal's Wager: A Critique," in *Ten Essential Texts*, 365. Originally published in *Think*, by Simon Blackburn (New York: Oxford University Press, 1999).
12. Blackburn, 366.
13. Pascal's influential pseudonymous work, *Lettres Provinciales*, is a series of eighteen fictional letters that attack (and mock) Jesuit casuistry and moral laxity and defend the

Jansenist cause. They criticize the Jesuit view that sin is in part defined by a person's knowledge of the immorality of their actions (which Pascal viewed as excusing them). The letters also include a passing reference to the Chinese Rites Controversy, in which the Jesuits insisted that Chinese ancestral sacrifices were not religious but secular rituals and therefore compatible with Catholicism. (This controversy concluded in 1704, when Pope Clement XI banned the rituals, a position that was overturned in 1939 by Pope Pius XII.)

14. Blackburn, "Pascal's Wager," 366.

15. Blackburn.

16. Blackburn.

17. Blackburn.

18. Blackburn, 366.

19. Blackburn.

20. P. K., "Most Thought-Provoking Texts," paper for "The Problem of God," May 2021, 2.

21. Pascal, "Wager," 365.

22. Amy Butler, *Beautiful and Terrible Things: Faith, Doubt, and Discovering a Way Back to Each Other* (New York: Dial Press, 2023).

23. W Berry, *This Day: Collected and New Sabbath Poems* (Berkeley, CA: Counterpoint, 2013), 64.

# 13

# THE PROBLEM OF RELIGIOUS PLURALISM

It's not so much us seeking God, tracking Her down with a butterfly net; it's agreeing to be found. The Old Girl reaches out to everyone and wants to include us in this beautiful, weird, sometimes anguished life.
All people: go figure.
—Anne Lamott

Religion is like going out to dinner with friends. Everyone may order something different, but everyone can still sit at the same table.
—the Fourteenth Dalai Lama

I had not seen her in years. But there she was, crossing the parking lot, her flowing burgundy robes brushing the wet pavement as her prayer beads swayed and the rain fell on her shaved head—all marks of the Buddhist vows she had taken halfway around the world a year earlier. Smiling, she called my name. I was struggling to unbuckle my daughter's car seat while my three-year-old son splashed exuberantly in a giant puddle beside my car, so I was admittedly distracted as she opened her arms for an embrace. My son stopped jumping and gaped at her. We had what seemed like an ordinary conversation between old friends and then said good-bye.

The next day, I received a phone call from her.

"This will sound strange," she said, "But I know who your son is." Her next words were at once unsurprising to me (because I am a professor of Chinese philosophy and I teach Buddhism) and utterly surprising. She believed my son was a *tulku*—an enlightened Tibetan Buddhist master who returns to Earth, reincarnated, to pass on traditional teachings and guide others toward enlightenment. *Tulkus* are identified as children.

"Your family would be a natural choice for his rebirth because of your work. I knew when I saw your son. He is crying out to be noticed."

I was speechless. *What should I say? Do I tell her we're not Buddhists? That I don't believe in reincarnation?* But when she finally asked a question, I was relieved that it was an easy one for me to answer.

"He is *very* special. But you know that, don't you?"

"Well, yes—yes I do!" I said, breathing a sigh of relief.

As the conversation ended and in the months that followed, I kept thinking about what she had said, but our theological differences loomed large for me. When I told a Jesuit friend the story, he suggested focusing on the last thing she said: "*He is very special*—maybe that's what is important here." I did not realize just how important it would become, until my son's doctors began talking with us about his developmental disabilities, eventually making an autism diagnosis. And the promise that my son is special—despite disabilities that are a daily challenge—became very important, and spoke to the very essence of my faith.

## Exclusivism, Inclusivism, and Pluralism

The problem of religious pluralism that loomed large for me in this story is that for all that they share in common, the world's religious traditions also make several incompatible claims. All religions are not the same at the top, and all mystics do not seem to be describing the same experience. What are we to make of this? We encountered this problem in the last chapter, in Simon Blackburn's response to Pascal's wager: How are we to choose which religion on which to wager "yes"? For in many cases, they require different responses from us. Do we observe the Sabbath as Judaism teaches, practice Zen Buddhist meditation, or attend Mass at a Catholic Church? And how do we decide what to believe? It cannot be the case that the divine reality is at once both personal *and* impersonal; nor can it be the case that we only live once on this Earth and are repeatedly reborn through reincarnation. Think of the contrast between Augustine's view of God and the early Daoist conception of the Dao, between Christian views of Heaven and Hindu and Buddhist conceptions of reincarnation. How are we to adjudicate who is right? How can we know which path is the correct one to follow?

As the theologian and philosopher John Hick puts it, the fact that different religious or spiritual traditions have their own "distinctive beliefs, spiritual practices, ethical outlook, art forms, and cultural ethos, creates an obvious problem for those who see them, not simply as human phenomena, but as responses to the Divine. For each presents itself, implicitly or explicitly, as in some important sense absolute and unsurpassable and as rightly claiming a total allegiance."[1] This does not mean that all members of different religions condemn members of other religions, but it does mean that a key reason why they follow their own tradition is that they believe it gets things right. Conversely, it is also the case that different religions share much in common. How are we to make sense of their overlapping views, and of the deep and important commonalities between them?

Hick argues that one way of approaching these questions is to view different traditions as offering different paths of salvation. Although "salvation" is primarily a Christian term, Hick uses it here in a broader sense, "to include its functional analogies in the other major world traditions." While acknowledging the important differences between (for example) Christian conceptions of salvation through Jesus Christ, Buddhist conceptions of enlightenment or nirvana, and Hindu conceptions of liberation or *moksha*, Hick contends that "if we stand back from these different conceptions to compare them, we can, I think, very naturally and properly see them as different forms of the more fundamental conception of a radical change from a profoundly unsatisfactory state to one that is limitlessly better because [it is] rightly related to the Real."[2] Here, Hick offers a broad definition of salvation that allows us to discuss how different religions offer different contexts for personal transformation. He also proposes a broader term for God or the infinite: "the Real." When we look at different religions around the world today, Hick argues, we see that they each describe and conceptualize in their own way "the wrongness of ordinary human existence"—a fallen state, a condition of moral weakness, the fragmentation of the One into the many, or a self-centeredness that undermines human flourishing.[3] Each tradition also proposes a remedy to that state, or a "limitlessly better possibility" that, again, is understood in different ways. But all these remedies are "specifications of what, in a generic formula, is the transformation of human existence from self-centeredness to a new orientation, centered in the divine Reality."[4] They all concern a relationship with or to the Real, which is the right kind of relationship with or to divine Reality.

This last point is important: Hick is talking about religion, not just moral change: the process of transformation that he calls salvation *is centered in some sort of divine Reality*. Each religion, he argues, "sets forth the way to attain this great good: faithfulness to the Torah, discipleship to Jesus, obedient living out of the Qur'anic way of life, the Eightfold Path of the Buddhist *dharma*, or the three great Hindu *margas* of mystical insight, activity in the world, and self-giving devotion to God."[5] To these, of course, we can add many others, including the ritual practices and virtues of the Confucian Way (which is Tian's plan for human beings), the life of simplicity that allows us to accord with the infinite Dao of the Daoist tradition, and the reverence for all Nature in its oneness with the Great Spirit that is central to many Indigenous and First Nations cultures in North America.

Hick emphasizes the diversity that exists not only across different religions but also *within* religions. Saints in the Christian tradition, for instance, are examples of individuals so transformed. Although Hick points out that we find them or their equivalents in different traditions, within the Catholic tradition alone, we find different patterns of transformation: some withdraw from the world to prayer or meditation, and others go out and seek to change the world (seen, respectively, in the examples of Julian of Norwich, who lived in permanent seclusion, and Joan of Arc, who died fighting for her faith).[6] But his key point is that different traditions use the same criterion to assess transformation: "the unselfish regard for others that we call love or compassion."[7] In other words, there is ethical evidence of salvation: the internal spiritual change that different traditions describe leads to an observable change in a person's life. Hick notes that we even find similar or shared ethical teachings across different religions, including the Golden Rule, which originates independently in Indian and Chinese religions, as well as in the Zoroastrian, Christian, Jewish, and Islamic traditions. They extol many of the same virtues, even though their understandings of those virtues differ.

This ethical evidence of salvation is important because, as Hick points out, "We cannot directly observe the inner spiritual quality of a human relationship to the Real; but we can observe how that relationship, as one's deepest and most pervasive orientation, affects the moral and spiritual quality of a human personality."[8] He is not denying or minimizing the fact that salvation is defined by a spiritual experience; recall that in his definition it is a radical change from a profoundly unsatisfactory state to one that is limitlessly better *because it is rightly related to the Real*. But we cannot observe the inner state of the human person, except as it is expressed in their conduct. This allows us to see that different traditions are not only paths of salvation; they are *effective* paths of salvation. This, for Hick, is a matter of empirical observation: religions, all around the world, frequently and consistently help people to become more compassionate, grateful, and generous. Yet based on our current state of knowledge, we are in no position to reasonably claim that any one religion has proven itself to be a more effective context of salvation than the others, or that the net goods of one tradition outweigh those of the others.

For Hick, this tells us that we do not have good reasons to judge one religion as superior to the others, from an objective standpoint. As we look at social-scientific data from around the world, as well as literary sources and stories of firsthand encounters, it is not clearly the case that, for instance, Buddhists are more loving and less self-centered than Hindus.[9] Instead, we find that different religio-cultural settings prove to be effective contexts for nurturing self-giving love. But we also see "apparently spread more or less equally in every society, cruelty, greed, hatred, selfishness, and malice."[10] As we all know, throughout history right up to the present, religions around the globe have often incited violence and warfare. None have managed to avoid this. For Hick, this suggests that none of the major world religions is "salvifically superior" to the others.

So, he asks, what are we to make of the "often contradictory doctrines of the different traditions?"[11] Who is right? In Pascalian terms, who will win the wager? Hick presents three possible answers. The first is one with which we are all familiar: religious exclusivism. Exclusivists maintain that their own religion has the truth and offers the one correct path to salvation. In this view, there will only be one "winner" of the wager among the world's religions. Christian exclusivists, for example, are united by their belief that God is revealed exclusively in Jesus Christ (*solus Christus*) and that only those who hear the Gospel (*fides ex auditu*) and confess it in their hearts can be saved. While those in the English-speaking world are perhaps most familiar with religious exclusivism through Christian and Muslim fundamentalists, there are religious exclusivists in every major religious tradition around the world. The early histories of most religions are defined by various forms of exclusivism, seen in missionary religions like Buddhism (which was spread to East Asia by Buddhist missionaries who believed that the only way to free all beings from suffering was to convert them to Buddhism).

A position known as religious inclusivism offers a different answer to the question of how to understand the competing claims of different religions. In contrast to exclusivists, inclusivists maintain that while their religion offers the true and correct account of the Real, at least some members of other religions are, nevertheless, having real experiences with and experiencing salvation through the Real—even though they understand it in different terms and call it by another name. Christian inclusivists, for instance, believe that salvation is possible outside Christianity (including through other religions), although this salvation is always from Christ. A Christian inclusivist might, for instance, believe that non-Christians sometimes encounter God and experience Jesus Christ's love without knowing that it is Christ. Inclusivists maintain that there can be salvation outside Christianity, even though this is always the work of Christ, even if the person is unaware of it. One of the best-known phrases associated with religious inclusivism is "anonymous Christians," used by the Jesuit theologian Karl Rahner (1904–84) to describe individuals who are not Christians but whose lives clearly demonstrate the truth of Christianity. Christian inclusivists typically argue that "anonymous Christians" who are members of other traditions misunderstand (and thus misdescribe) their religious experiences, interpreting them through the lens of their own religions and cultures. But they lead good lives, both by the standards of their own religious tradition and by Christian standards, even though they have not converted to Christianity. The religious inclusivist insists, then, that when it comes to who is truly saved, "you will know them by their fruits" (Matthew 7:15–20), with fruits understood primarily in ethical terms: the kind of lives they are leading, the sort of people they are. For the Christian inclusivist, the difference between a Buddhist who is an "anonymous Christian" and a Christian is that the Christian knows that their salvation is due to Christ. For the Buddhist inclusivist, Christians who are truly loving and compassionate people have become that way by unknowingly following Buddhist teachings (i.e., they are "anonymous Buddhists"). They simply lack the understanding that Buddhists have: that they are moving closer to enlightenment (nirvana) because they are following Buddhist teachings. In both cases, people are saved without knowing they are being saved and without explicitly accepting the source of their salvation.

Religious inclusivism allows one to recognize the spiritual values of other religions while also preserving one's conviction of the ultimate superiority of one's own religion over others. For it maintains that all salvation is really salvation in one's own tradition. Hick points out that different kinds of religious inclusivism are widespread: Christian inclusivism, for example, characterizes the view of most Christians who have reflected on other faith traditions today (including the official position of the Catholic Church starting with Vatican II). Yet Hick argues that it presents particularly acute challenges for Christians, since Christianity developed later than most of the world's major religions. Specifically,

> The Christian inclusivist is . . . by implication, declaring that . . . various spiritual paths are efficacious, and constitute authentic contexts of salvation, because Jesus died on the cross; and, by further implication, that if he had not died on the cross they would not be efficacious.
>
> This is a novel and somewhat astonishing doctrine. How are we to make sense of the idea that the salvific power of the *dharma* taught five hundred years earlier by the Buddha is a consequence of the death of Jesus in approximately 30 CE? Such an apparently bizarre conception should only be affirmed for some very good reason. It certainly was not taught by Jesus or his apostles. It has emerged only in the thought of twentieth-century Christians who have come to recognize that Jews are being salvifically transformed through the spirituality of Judaism, Muslims through that of Islam, Hindus and Buddhists through the paths mapped out by their respective traditions, and so on, but who nevertheless wish to retain their inherited sense of the unique superiority of Christianity.[12]

In a moment we will turn to the alternative view that Hick proposes to avoid these difficulties. But first, let us not lose sight of the deep and important contrast between religious exclusivism and religious inclusivism: exclusivists maintain that conversion to their religion is necessary for salvation, while inclusivists do not. There can be no anonymous Christians or Buddhists for the exclusivist, because having true beliefs is an essential part of salvation, in their view; salvation is not, as the inclusivist believes, simply a matter of ethical transformation.

There are many different versions of religious exclusivism and religious inclusivism, and it is helpful to envision them on a spectrum representing different religious outlooks, from more conservative to more liberal. Strong forms of religious exclusivism, which characterize the views of more conservative members of different religions, lie at one end of the spectrum. Different forms of religious inclusivism lie in the middle of the spectrum, since it allows that members of other religions are sometimes saved but insists that their salvation occurs through the salvific power of one religion. But what if one is willing to let go of the latter claim? What if you believe that members of different religions are indeed experiencing salvation but through their own tradition, and not yours? If one moves further down the theological spectrum, we find Hick's third alternative, a view that he calls religious pluralism. (It is important here to distinguish between the *fact* of religious pluralism, or the mere fact that there are different religions, and the theological position that Hick calls religious pluralism. ) Religious pluralism holds that all religions are or can be paths to either the one divine reality or plural divine realities. According to Hick, this position is defined by the view that "an infinite transcendent divine reality is being differently conceived, and therefore differently experienced, and therefore differently responded to from within our different religio-cultural ways of being human. This hypothesis makes sense of the fact that the salvific transformation seems to have been occurring in all the great traditions."[13]

The line between religious inclusivists and religious pluralists is important: the former contend that they have privileged access to the Real, while the latter see themselves on equal footing with members of other religions. The difference can be diagramed in the following way: We have two sets of concentric circles, one of which represents religious inclusivism and the other of which represents religious pluralism (figures 13.1, 13.2, and 13.3). The concentric circles represent a series of personal, religious, cultural, and societal factors that serve as lenses through which we view the world and our experiences of God, the infinite, or the Real. (We are all aware of how we sometimes perceive and describe the same events or objects differently from others, even within the same culture and religion.) In the center of the innermost circle is the object of our religious experiences and beliefs: God, the infinite, or the Real. Around the outermost circle in both diagrams are members of different religions: Christians, Jews, Muslims, Hindus, Daoists, and so on.

There are three differences between the diagrams of the religious inclusivists and the religious pluralist: (1) At the center of the circle is something different: for the religious pluralist, it is the Real, while for the religious inclusivist it is the being, entity, or experience that is central in their own tradition: the Holy Trinity for Christians, the Dao for Daoists, YHWH (Yahweh) for Jews, Allah for Muslims, Brahman for Hindus, and so on (figures 13.1 and 13.2).[14] (2) In the religious pluralist diagram, one of the lenses that stands in between members of different traditions and the Real (at the center) contains each religion's specific conception of the Real. So, for instance, from the perspective of the religious pluralist, the Holy Trinity is a lens through which the

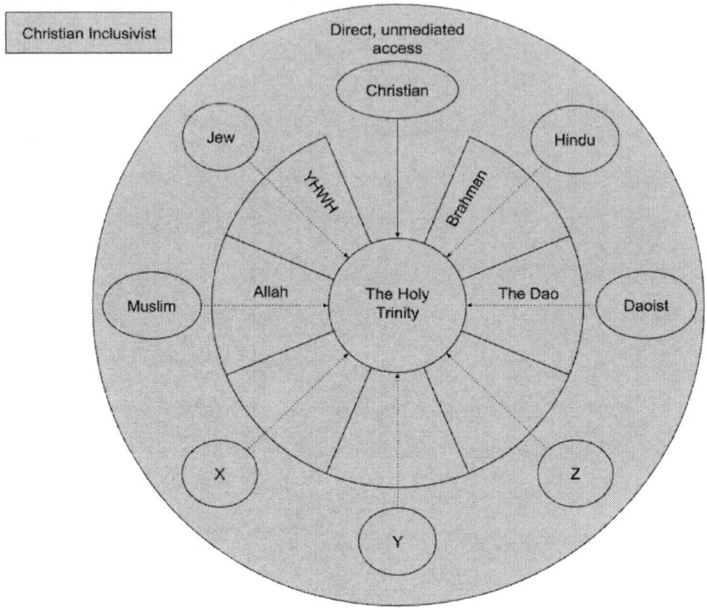


Figure 13.1 *Diagram of Christian Religious Inclusivism*

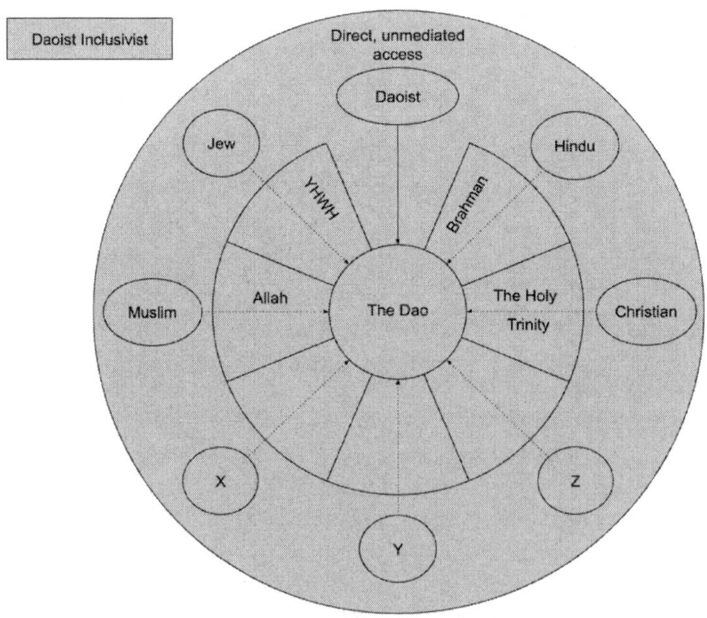


Figure 13.2 *Diagram of the Daoist Religious Inclusivism*

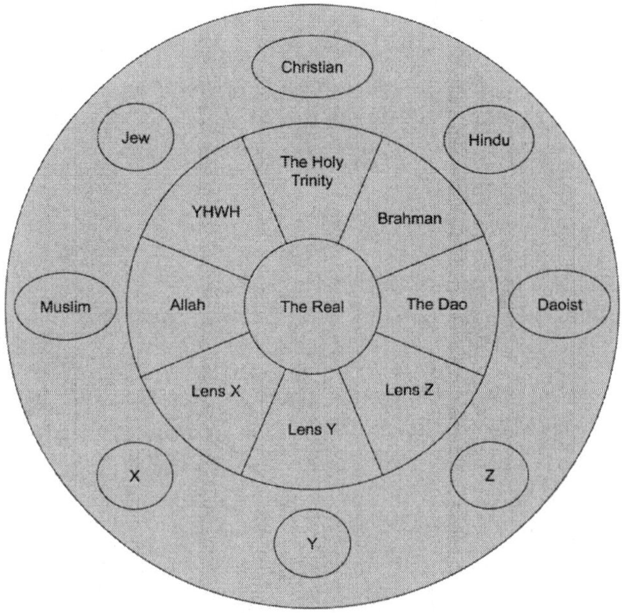


Figure 13.3 *Diagram of Religious Pluralism*

Christian perceives and understands the Real, as is the Dao for Daoists, Allah for Muslims, YHWH (Yahweh) for Jews, Brahman for Hindus, and other religious ultimates for other religions. This presents a notable contrast with the religious inclusivist diagram, which places these entities at the center, positing them as the true and correct conception of the Real. (3) In the religious pluralist diagram, the concentric circles are continuous and unbroken all the way around, standing between *all* human beings and the Real, equally. But in the religious inclusivist diagrams, the circles are broken in one place: in between members of the inclusivist's own tradition and their conception of the Real. So, as the diagrams show, the Christian inclusivist has direct and unmediated access to the Holy Trinity, but members of other religions view the Holy Trinity through the lenses of their own religious ultimates. The Daoist inclusivist has direct and unmediated access to the Dao, but members of other religions are experiencing their own religious ultimate as a lens through which they view the Dao. Only members of the religious inclusivist's tradition have direct, unmediated access to the entity at the center of the circle.

Let us consider the Christian inclusivist diagram (figure 13.1). If we look around the outside of the circle and locate the Christian, then if we follow the track from the Christian to the center of the circle, we will find that the concentric circles—the lenses or filters through which our experience of the divine reality flows—are broken, which illustrates the Christian inclusivist's privileged access to God. Even though members of other religions are also experiencing the Holy Trinity (God the Father, Son, and Holy Spirit), they view God through their own religious lenses, which leads them to misperceive God in, for example, Jewish, Muslim, Hindu, or Daoist terms. They perceive and conceptualize their religious experience differently because of their own religious lenses or filters. The same is true, as we can see, in the diagram of the Daoist inclusivist (figure 13.2). In contrast, in the diagram of the religious pluralist, no one has privileged access to the Real; rather, one of the filters through which we experience and conceptualize the Real is that thing we call the Real in our own individual traditions. Hick puts it this way:

> The religious tradition of which we are a part, with its history and ethos and its great exemplars, its scriptures feeding our thoughts and emotions, and perhaps above all its devotional or meditative practices, constitutes an uniquely shaped and coloured "lens" through which we are concretely aware of the Real specifically as the personal Adonai, or as the Heavenly Father, or as Allah, or Vishnu, or Shiva, . . . or again as the non-personal Brahman, or Dharmakaya, or the Void or the Ground. . . . Thus, one who uses the forms of Christian prayer and sacrament is thereby led to experience the Real as the divine Thou, whereas one who practices advaitic yoga or Buddhist zazen is thereby brought to experience the Real as the infinite being-consciousness-bliss of Brahman, or the limitless emptiness of *sunyata* which is at the same time the infinite fullness of immediate reality as "wondrous being."[15]

Now, to be clear, Hick does not believe we are *fully* determined by the religious traditions in which we are raised; indeed, many people leave their home traditions and convert to other religions. On one hand, we are shaped by our religious backgrounds and will inevitably avail ourselves of the concepts and terms we have in order to describe our experiences. On the other hand, our experiences also lead us away from certain traditions and toward others, based on the degree to which they align with, or have concepts that accurately capture, our religious experiences. People sometimes convert because another tradition's account of reality more closely aligns with their spiritual experiences or because another tradition helps them to be a better person. But the reason why, for example, a Jew might convert to Buddhism is that she has become intimately familiar with Buddhist concepts, texts, and practices, and they more closely align with her experience (and perhaps give rise to more powerful religious experiences) than the concepts, texts, and practices of Judaism. This affirms, rather than undermines, the idea that we all use particular lenses to understand our experiences. These play an important role in what religions we remain in or convert to. (I am reminded of John Stuart Mill's claim in *On Liberty* that the same causes that make someone a Christian in London would have made them a Buddhist or a Confucian in Beijing.[16]) Of course, it would behoove us all to familiarize ourselves more fully and deeply with different religious traditions, if we are interested in encountering the Real and if we wish to be able to more accurately and fully describe our religious experiences. This is really an extension of the broader point that many of us know is true: that studying and experiencing different cultures is enriching for us in a variety of ways, one of which is that we sometimes encounter richer forms of life that allow us to lead better lives.

In seeking to explain why members of different faith traditions seem to have such diverse spiritual experiences, Hick argues that we need not say that only one of them is correct—as religious exclusivists and religious inclusivists argue. The religious pluralist contends that there is a way to make sense of religious differences without arguing for the unique superiority of one tradition and that this position has the added merits of acknowledging our own distinctive backgrounds and the role they play in shaping our perception of the world and our experiences. We each have at our fingertips a different set of concepts and terms that we reach for when we seek to understand and describe our experience. So, according to Hick, when the Christian experiences a loving spiritual presence, she is likely to understand it as the presence of God. A Buddhist or Daoist would understand it differently. Some lenses might be thicker than others due to societal or cultural influences on (or control of) religious institutions. None of them has unmediated access to the Real, however, so they all fall short of fully understanding it. And the Real can never be fully grasped or described by anyone, because we are finite and the Real is infinite—or at least much greater than us. This view, Hick points out, is widely shared across different religions.[17]

So for Christians who are religious pluralists, Jesus Christ is one revelation among many different and potentially equally important revelations. Why would one be a Christian, then? One possible answer is autobiographical. One might say, for instance, that while they do not believe that Christ is everyone's way to God, Christ has been and is their way. In other words, one might commit oneself to a particular religion based on one's own experiences—which, one can freely acknowledge, are in part a product of one's own background—and yet also acknowledge that others have different, yet equally valid experiences of the Real.

### Potential Objections to Religious Inclusivism and Religious Pluralism

Atheists tend to object to these views because they all contend that religious people are having real encounters with or experiences of a divine reality. Indeed, one important feature of religious exclusivism, inclusivism, and pluralism is that they all represent forms of religious realism, which holds that the objects of religious experiences are real, and not a figment of our imagination. This is one reason why Hick calls this object "the Real." Religious antirealists, in contrast, reject the view that religious or spiritual experiences have real objects. If we again consider our diagram with the concentric circles, the religious antirealist contends that there is nothing at the center of the circles. There are only the lenses or filters, and these lead members of different religions to believe they are experiencing something real. Yet their experience is wholly constructed. Prominent defenders of this view of religion include two very influential figures from the nineteenth century, Freud and Marx.

Unlike religious antirealists, religious inclusivists and religious pluralists take seriously the claims of people from different cultures and traditions that they are experiencing something real, despite the fact that they conceptualize it in different ways. They argue that we should not dismiss the experiences of so many people, across such diverse times, places, and contexts. They also reject the view that these experiences can be dismissed as simply an imaginary product of the brain (vs. an experience of reality). There are, after all, many theological explanations of why humans might be inclined toward religious and spiritual experience. We encountered two such explanations earlier in this book, in the Daoist tradition's contention that we originally know the Dao and long to return to it, and in Augustine's contention that the same is true of God. Both traditions contend that we are created by the Real with a longing for the Real as a part of our nature.

One feature of religious antirealism is that it tends to assume an objective view of reality. But why should we believe that religious antirealists are able to perceive and understand objective reality, if religious people cannot? In other words, why should we not believe that *their* view of religion is simply constructed by, or a product of, their background? It is unclear why we should believe that *they* have privileged access to reality, instead of religious believers. We could, for instance, place atheists on our diagrams for religious inclusivism and religious pluralism and argue that the lenses of atheists are thicker than those of religious people—so thick as to fully block or obscure their perception of the Real, however it is understood.

Another common objection from nonreligious people is that they are left out of the picture entirely by theologians like Hick. Their question is: Where am *I* on the diagram? Do we not find "ethical evidence of salvation" in nonreligious people, too? Religion, after all, is not the only way of cultivating virtue. None of the positions we have been examining dispute this fact. Religious exclusivists, inclusivists, and pluralists are not arguing that only religious people are good. Rather, they are working to explain the conflicting claims of different religions and what we are to make of them. Must we condemn others and insist that only we are right? Or is it possible that more than one tradition gets things right? Theologians like Rahner and Hick do not deny that people can become good without religion. But they also make an important observation: religious communities are especially good at helping us to become better people. This is at least partly due to the way in which religious communities help people make sense of religious experiences and what they mean for how we live our lives. And as a historical fact, we owe much of our understanding of morality to religious traditions. This is true of cultures all over the world.

At the other end of the spectrum, some scholars have objected that a position like religious pluralism places too much emphasis on morality, as opposed to spirituality. The theologian William Reiser, SJ, critiques the use of ethical evidence of salvation, writing that "religion is not coterminous with morality; the 'cash value' or spiritual measure of ascetical practice and contemplation is not simply higher ethical standards and noble, humanitarian actions."[18] Reiser goes on to write that "spirituality is ultimately about the human being's living more deeply in God and experiencing divine life in our communities and our common humanity. While spiritual people are expected to be moral, spirituality touches first, not on morality, but on what happens as the mystery of God penetrates one's life. It is about relationship."[19] Here, Reiser defines spirituality in exclusively monotheistic terms, but we have seen throughout this book that spirituality exists even in religions without God. This is precisely what theologians like Hick are trying to take account of, and why he uses the broader term "the Real." Again, a reminder of Hick's primary task is helpful: he aims to help us to judge different religions' claims to be effective contexts for becoming centered in a Divine or spiritual reality. He explicitly acknowledges that there is much more to spiritual life than morality, but he uses ethical evidence of salvation for this particular task because "we cannot directly observe the inner spiritual quality of a human relationship to the Real, but we can observe how that relationship, as one's deepest and most pervasive orientation, affects the moral and spiritual quality" of a person's life and their relationships with others.[20]

## Conclusion

For as much as I struggled, as a Christian, with the idea that a Buddhist nun might be able to identify my son as a reincarnated Buddhist deity, the truth is that I am always aware that my finitude limits my ability to grasp religious truth. We make reasoned commitments in the face of uncertainty; but at times, we are reminded more of the latter than the former. This is precisely what I think of when I recall my Buddhist friend's insights about my son.

Both my parents were schoolteachers—my dad having given up a career as an anthropologist in order to raise us in a small Alaskan town and fulfill his vocation as an elementary school teacher. Two things my dad loved about teaching elementary school were nurturing his students' love of aquatic life and science, and finding ways to help kids who struggled in school. When I was in the sixth grade, he was awarded a grant to raise salmon with his fifth-grade class and release them at year's end. Each morning before school, I would help him tend the hundred-plus tiny salmon fry (as young salmon are called) in the large aquarium at the back of his classroom, rescuing the adventurous ones who, at less than an inch long, had jumped into the back regions of the tank overnight.

My father did not live to see my son reach the sixth grade; but that year, I realized my son was just like the kids my dad had loved working with the most: he loved learning about aquatic life, and he struggled with school, attending a special program for children with disabilities. After hearing my son's stories about catching frogs, crayfish, minnows, and sunfish in the creeks near our house, one of his special education teachers introduced him to the biology teacher at his school who, it turns out, had won a grant to have his classes raise trout for release at the end of the school year. He invited my son to help, and for the next three years, he helped to maintain the tanks in that classroom in the mornings before school.

I think of my dad's love of nature, and his gift for reaching kids who struggled. Then I think of my mornings as a sixth-grader in his classroom rescuing wayward salmon fry, and teachers who cared enough to nurture my autistic sixth-grader's love of all creatures, great and small. One of the defining features of the Buddhist tradition is a belief in the deep interconnectedness of all things, and the view that our present life is only one in a beginningless series, each of which is determined by the good we have done. The karma of our past lives is carried into the next, and everything we do comes back around.

I have to admit, it certainly seems like the fruits of my dad's labors came back around to us that year, even in his absence. Was it simply a coincidence that my son had landed in the classrooms of such caring teachers, who also happened to be raising trout? The commonality between the Buddhist and Christian answers here is striking: whether we understand it as part of God's plan or as an instance of karma at work in the oneness of all things, it is best understood as a gift. Perhaps we found ourselves in one of the "thin places" referred to in ancient Celtic theology, where the veil between this world and the eternal world grows thin, and it becomes easier to encounter the sacred. As the old Irish saying goes, "Heaven and Earth are only three feet apart, but in thin places the distance is even shorter."

## Notes

Epigraph:

Anne Lamott, *Almost Everything: Notes on Hope* (New York: Riverhead, 2018), 138.

1. John Hick, "Religious Pluralism and Salvation," in *Ten Essential Texts in the Philosophy of Religion*, ed. Steven M. Cahn (New York: Oxford University Press, 2005), 450. The original source for much of this work is Hick's book, *An Interpretation of Religion* (New Haven, CT: Yale University Press, 1989).

2. Hick, "Religious Pluralism," 451.
3. Hick.
4. Hick.
5. Hick.
6. Hick, 452.
7. Hick.
8. Hick, 451.
9. Hick, 453–54.
10. Hick, 453.
11. Hick, 454.
12. Hick, 461.
13. Hick, 454.
14. Of course, different members of these traditions might articulate their Religious Ultimate differently. For instance, some Hindus are devotees of particular deities in the Hindu tradition and would have those deities at the center (even though they are all a part of Brahman). I have not included Buddhism in the diagram because Buddhists are exceptionally diverse when it comes to this matter. Some Buddhists would place the experience of ultimate emptiness at the center, while others would have particular Buddhist deities or bodhisattvas at the center.
15. Hick, "Religious Pluralism," 455.
16. John Stuart Mill, *On Liberty and the Subjection of Women* (New York: Penguin, 2007), 25.
17. Hick, "Religious Pluralism," 456.
18. William Reiser, SJ, "The Spiritual Exercises in a Religiously Pluralistic World," *Spiritus* 10 (2010): 143.
19. Reiser.
20. Hick, "Religious Pluralism," 451.

# 14

# RELIGIOUS EXPERIENCE AND CONVERSION

The God with whom you are having problems, or whom you hate or ridicule, is not the God we are talking about. When we talk about goodness, an animating intelligence in the universe and in our hearts or a pervasive positive unity or presence, we are not talking about an old bearded guy in the sky, Parvati, or a Jewish Palestinian baby. We are talking about a higher power, a power that might be called Not Me, a kindness, a patience, a hope, which is everywhere, even in our annoying, self-centered, fraudulent selves. . . . It opens us and heals us and brings us together and turns our hearts of stone into human hearts. Any time you are experiencing love, you are experiencing the God we are talking about.
—Anne Lamott

Listen to your life. If indeed there is a God . . . one of the ways he speaks to us, and maybe one of the most powerful ways, is through what happens to us.
—Frederick Buechner

"Prayer can change your life!" The minister's wife looked at me with a huge grin on her face. "You should join my Sunday school class!" she continued. "That's what it's called: Prayer Can Change Your Life!" My schedule as a busy college student did not permit me to join her class, but Pam took me under her wing anyway, weaving me into a warm community at church that felt like a family. She also never stopped telling me about her Sunday school class. But as a young philosophy major, I remained skeptical: the idea that God intervenes in the world, answering some prayers and not others? That serves the Problem of Evil up on a platter. It was not until many years later that I found myself thinking about her prayer class in a new light.

Each year a small group of faculty and staff at Georgetown University participate in a year-long retreat, during which they experience the Spiritual Exercises of Saint Ignatius in the midst of daily life. Called Spiritual Exercises because they reflect Ignatius's belief that like the body, the human spirit requires exercise in order to stay healthy, these different ways of praying, meditating, and reading Scripture give shape to the spiritual lives of Jesuits. They offer a way of learning to recognize God's ongoing presence in one's life and work, and of deepening one's relationship with God. They also involve an expansion of how most of us think about prayer.

When I was invited to participate in the retreat, I hesitated. It involved devoting at least 30 minutes to personal prayer every day, meeting with a spiritual director each week, and meeting as a group with the other participants once a month. I wanted to say yes, but I had two kids under the age of five and worked full time. How would I find the time? But I said yes, and over the course of the next year, I learned just how much prayer can change your life, but not in the ways I had considered when Pam talked about it. Ignatian ways of praying are different from petitionary prayer, where we make requests of God; there is less talking and more listening, and it is more meditative. Yet it is also a very active way of praying, often involving the use of our imagination and memory. (Instead of simply reading Scripture or thinking about it, Ignatian prayer often involves using your imagination to place yourself in Biblical scenes and accompany Jesus and his disciples.) While 30 minutes of prayer was initially daunting, I began to long for my daily time with God, and soon, 30 minutes was not enough. (A colleague who made the retreat that year noted that he started out setting a 30-minute timer, but by the end of the year, he was not setting that timer anymore.) I also began to notice subtle changes in my daily life. I was more patient with my children. I was more attentive to small graces. I was able to see opportunities instead of stumbling blocks. I started to feel that wherever I went, God was walking beside me—something I had always believed but had never before experienced so consistently on a daily basis. And this all stemmed from an eclectic collection of spiritual practices that a Spanish saint developed in the 1500s.

## The Life of Ignatius of Loyola and the Jesuit Tradition

One of the most stunning facts about Georgetown is that it exists because of one man's religious experiences. This is because Georgetown is a Jesuit university. The Jesuits are members of the Roman Catholic religious order called the Society of Jesus, which was founded by Iñigo Lopez de Loyola—known to us today as Ignatius of Loyola (1491–1556)—and a group of his friends. Religious orders are communities, lineages, or institutes of people (often comprising monks or nuns who live in monasteries, friars or religious sisters, and clerics or priests) who live in some way set apart from society in order to devote themselves to a particular religious mission or teachings. They are found throughout the world in many different religions and usually consist exclusively of men or women. The largest and best-known religious orders today are Roman Catholic and Buddhist orders that require vows of celibacy, obedience to one's superiors, and poverty. The Society of Jesus is the most influential Roman Catholic religious order of the last five hundred years, and its influence is due in part to the fact that Jesuits took an interest in education, founding schools all over the world, including colleges and universities like Georgetown. With over 16,000 members spread across 112 countries worldwide, it is also the largest male religious order in the Catholic Church, and its members serve in wide-ranging contexts, including ministry in hospitals, churches, retreat centers, schools, colleges and universities, social and humanitarian ministries, research, and ecumenical and interreligious dialogue.[1]

Long before he ever conceived of the Society of Jesus, however, Ignatius was a young, ambitious and (by his own admission) self-absorbed Spanish courtier and soldier. But in 1521 he was seriously injured by a cannonball during a battle defending the honor of the Spanish crown, and he spent six months convalescing at his family castle. As the bones in both of his legs were broken and reset repeatedly, the pain was nearly unbearable, and he spent months in traction. In a state of dejection and with little to do, he began to pay closer attention to what he called the "interior movements" of his soul: his feelings, attractions, passions, ambitions, and dreams. While reading Ludolph of Saxony's *Life of Christ* and a version of *The Lives of the Saints*, which were among the few books available to him as he recovered, he began to imagine a life that differed from his life as a knight, which was filled with the pursuit of riches, fame, and worldly honors. He pictured a life similar to the saints he read about; and when he imagined devoting his life to the service of God and others, he found himself uplifted by a deep sense of joy. In contrast, when he revisited his familiar daydreams of serving as a valiant knight, he was left with feelings of discontentment and unhappiness. He came to believe that God was speaking to him through these interior attractions and reactions, and once he had recovered, he decided to test his desires on a pilgrimage. The result was a journey in which his soul was exercised through a profound set of experiences and encounters with God. Throughout this time, he kept a record of his insights and his ways of praying and meditating, hoping that his experiences might one day be able to help others. He was right: his journal was the beginning of the manual of prayer that is now known as the Spiritual Exercises.

Religious orders each have distinctive identities and defining features. Ignatius and his friends decided to call their community the Society of Jesus because loving, serving, and emulating Jesus Christ was their sole aim. The Jesuits have always understood themselves as "contemplatives in action," due to the fact that their origins lie in the religious experiences of Ignatius and the contemplative practices he designed to help others to have such experiences. (Contemplative practices refer to all different kinds of prayer and meditation, sometimes including physical postures or movements. A "contemplative" is one who is dedicated to such practices.) While many traditional contemplatives are cloistered or spend most of their time disengaged from the world, the Jesuits always believed in the importance of living in and serving the world, because that is how Jesus lived. This is what makes them contemplatives "in action." Contemplative practice, for Ignatius, leads us to want to engage more deeply and fully with others, helping them to encounter and follow Jesus as well. This led the Jesuits to define themselves as a global order from the beginning, dedicated to missions around the world. Indeed, two additional Jesuit values are being "people for others"—living a life in service of others—and "finding God in all things." The Ignatian Spiritual Exercises are designed to help us recognize God's voice everywhere—in creation, in others, and in our own feelings and desires.

While these practices became a central feature of the Jesuit order, Ignatius always intended them for men and women from all walks of life. So he developed different "retreats" that would allow people to experience the Exercises, in part or in whole, based on their particular needs and backgrounds. Ignatius's instructions guide us in using our imagination and memory to pray and meditate on a variety of things—from the consideration and experience of God's unconditional love to our own limited response and patterns of sinfulness, to the account of the life, death, and resurrection of Jesus Christ that is presented in the Bible. Ignatius insisted on the importance of adapting the Exercises to meet each person's individual needs and background, which means that one should not mechanically run through all of them at the same pace or even in the same order as others. Rather, under the guidance of a spiritual director (often a Jesuit priest, but many lay Christians are trained to offer the Exercises as well), each person should move through the Exercises following the lead of the Holy Spirit.

Something called "the discernment of spirits" underlies the Exercises. Inspired by his own experience of God calling him to lead a different sort of life, Ignatius designed the Exercises to be a tool for discernment—practices to help people make decisions grounded in their faith. For some, this means making what Ignatius calls an "election"—a momentous decision or life choice—while for others it simply means checking to be sure one is heading in the right direction or deepening a call one has already embraced. Throughout the Exercises, one learns what Ignatius learned during his convalescence: that God speaks to us through the "interior movements" of our thoughts, feelings, desires, attractions, and resistances. Indeed, Ignatius insists that God does not just speak with us in the way we often expect—as a voice from the Heavens—but more often, as a voice from inside us, through our deepest desires and longings. But as we all know, there are many different voices inside our heads. The Exercises are designed to help us discern God's voice from all the others through a careful, systematic, prayerful examination of our interior movements.

### A Contemporary Moral Conversion

Ignatius's life is an example of what John Hick called "a radical change from a profoundly unsatisfactory state to one that is limitlessly better because it is rightly related to the Real." Ignatius had been seduced by wealth, fame, and prestige in his early life as a courtier and soldier. But his injury and convalescence began a chain of events that led to both a religious and moral conversion: he decided to turn his life over to Christ and change his way of living entirely.

I want to consider a contemporary story alongside that of Ignatius of Loyola's that involves seduction not by wealth and fame but by an ideology that taps into hate and fear. It is a conversion story that, like those of Augustine and Ignatius, involves both the head and the heart, but it is not the story of a *religious* conversion. It is, rather, the story of a moral conversion, but one that critically involves one's attitudes toward and beliefs about others, including particular cultural and religious groups. It is also a story that highlights how critically bound up together religious and moral education are, as well as how critical it is that we encounter people of diverse backgrounds (and especially diverse religious backgrounds) over the course of our education, both inside and outside the classroom. Finally, it is a story that invites us to grapple with the depth and extent of religious discrimination and, in particular, antisemitism in American society.

The story of R. Derek Black is remarkable for many reasons. One is that Black was, by every standard, the leading light and heir apparent of the white nationalist movement in America. In November 2008, just a few days after Barack Obama was elected president, Black offered one of the keynote speeches at a meeting of white nationalists in Memphis. Black had just turned nineteen but was already hosting a radio show; had won a local election for a Republican committee seat in Palm Beach County, Florida; and had launched a white nationalist website for children. Black stepped up to the podium and told the audience, "The way ahead is through politics. We can infiltrate. We can take the country back."[2] As Eli Saslow writes,

> Years before Donald Trump launched a presidential campaign based in part on the politics of race and division, a group of avowed white nationalists was working to make his rise possible by pushing its ideology from the radical fringes ever closer to the far conservative right. Many attendees in Memphis had transformed over their careers from Klansmen to white supremacists to self-described "racial realists," and Derek Black represented another step in that evolution.[3]

Contrary to what one might expect, Black never used racial slurs or advocated violence. Instead, Black focused on "the ravages of political correctness, affirmative action, and unchecked Hispanic immigration."[4] This outlook reflects the changing face of antisemitism and white supremacism in America, which has increasingly made immigration, multiculturalism, and globalism its central targets. This is a strategic choice: it has allowed white nationalists to appeal to Americans who might not otherwise support their ideology but who are worried about things like immigration and who feel left behind. Unfortunately, they are particularly vulnerable to ideologies driven by fear and hate. White nationalism seeks to *affirm* the fear that they have lost their place, or will lose it, to immigrants, minorities, and others, through what is called *replacement theory*: a white nationalist, far-right conspiracy theory that particular white populations are being demographically and culturally replaced by other racial, ethnic, and cultural groups. (This type of view is also a part of the long history of antisemitism.)

Black was born into a prominent white nationalist family. Black's father is a former Ku Klux Klan leader who went on to found the first major white nationalist website, describing himself as a "white civil rights activist" and a "racial realist." Black's mother had been previously married to the former KKK leader, neo-Nazi, and politician David Duke (who also happens to be Derek's godfather), who is well-known for promoting antisemitic conspiracy theories, including Holocaust denial. It is unsurprising, then, that Black grew up believing that America was intended for white Europeans and that we should be suspicious of other cultures and races. It was also an atheist household, something that eventually led Black to "a particular interest in learning about where and how religious ideology had tracked through time and what it meant to different communities across the world"—but something they would not have an opportunity to explore in depth until college.[5] After third grade, Black's parents withdrew them from public school in West Palm Beach and began home-schooling, often attending white nationalism conferences together throughout the Deep South. Black was smart and "sought out logic and science to confirm [their] worldview, reading studies from conservative think tanks about biological differences between races, IQ disparities and rates of violent crimes committed by blacks against whites."[6] Black used radio programs, websites, and speeches to promote the idea of white genocide: "that whites were losing their culture and traditions to massive, nonwhite immigration."[7]

Black finished high school and eventually applied to New College of Florida after deciding to study medieval history. Its strong History Department notwithstanding, New College was an odd choice for Black. It was one of the most liberal schools in the state, but when someone asked Black's dad if he was concerned about sending his child to a "hotbed of multiculturalism," he laughed and replied, "If anyone is going to be influenced here, it will be them. Soon enough, the whole faculty and student body are going to know who they have in their midst."[8]

His words could not have been more prophetic on the latter count. Upon arrival at New College, Black initially was successful in concealing their ideological views, realizing that ostracization would follow if other students found out. But Black continued to call into their radio show every weekday morning, talking about white genocide and "massive, nonwhite immigration." Black then went to study abroad in Germany. But while Black was gone, a fellow student who had been researching extremist groups online discovered Black's status in the white nationalist community and shared the information on an online student message board. "How do we as a community respond?" the student asked. There were more than a thousand replies by the time Black returned to campus. After securing off-campus housing, Black was for the most part ostracized at New College. At the same time, Black's views on white genocide were being popularized on their father's website and on conservative talk radio, while David Duke was building an alliance with the Tea Party movement and Donald Trump began promoting the false claim that President Obama was not born in the United States and was secretly a Muslim. As the movement thrived, New College students continued to track Black's activities and post them to the online forum. Finally, one student wrote, "Ostracizing Derek won't accomplish anything. We have a chance to be real activists and actually affect one of the leaders of white supremacy in America."[9]

A student named Matthew Stevenson, an acquaintance of Derek's from their first semester, was the first one to act on that suggestion. He was also the only Orthodox Jew at New College. Stevenson almost always wore a yarmulke, and at the weekly Shabbat dinners he hosted for his fellow students, he "always drank from a kiddush cup and said the traditional prayers, but most of his guests were Christian, atheist, Black or Hispanic—anyone open-minded enough to listen to a few blessings in Hebrew."[10] Stevenson had read Black's offensive online posts about Jews but "decided his best chance to affect Derek's thinking was not to ignore [them] or confront [them], but simply to include [them]. 'Maybe [Derek had] never spent time with a Jewish person before,' Matthew remembered thinking."[11] So one week, Stevenson invited Black to his Shabbat dinner. It was the first time Black had been invited to anything since returning to campus, and they accepted the invitation. Only two other students who usually attended the Shabbat dinners were willing to come that week, and Matthew instructed them to try to treat Black like anyone else, in the hope that Black would come again. It worked. Black kept coming back, week after week, and over time, more students returned to the Shabbat dinners. Stevenson and Black became friends and started playing pool together.

Finally, some members of the Shabbat dinner group began to ask Black about white supremacy. In response, Black distinguished white supremacy from white nationalism, insisting that massive immigration and forced integration would result in white genocide and that each race was better off in its homeland, living separately.[12] Black's friends continued the conversation both in person and in email exchanges, asking Black to clarify the white nationalist view and explaining why they disagreed. In response to the purported evidence Black produced, they shared studies showing that racial disparities in IQ were accounted for by factors like prenatal nutrition and educational opportunities and how discrimination affects job performance and mental and physical health. They worked to help Black learn to interpret and distinguish between different kinds of studies and shared articles about white privilege and the history of genocide against Jews, Rwandans, Armenians, and others.

Over the course of several months, Black's views gradually began to soften. It was incremental at first: Black "no longer thought the endpoint of white nationalism was forced deportation for nonwhites, but gradual self-deportation, in which nonwhites would leave on their own."[13] But Black stopped posting on their father's website and began to avoid calling in to their radio show. Then, during Black's senior year, while taking classes on Jewish Scripture and German multiculturalism, Black "learned that Western Europe had begun not as a great society of genetically superior people but as a technologically backward place that lagged behind Islamic culture." Black studied the eighth century to the twelfth century, trying to trace back the modern concepts of race and whiteness, but could not find them anywhere, eventually concluding, "We basically just invented it."[14]

With the encouragement of friends, and partly out of a sense of respect for Black's own parents, who had taught Black that you should speak your mind even when doing so is unpopular, Black emailed a statement to the Southern Poverty Law Center explaining their reasons for slowly but steadily disaffiliating from white nationalism. It included an apology for the harm that Black's words and actions had caused people of color, people of Jewish descent, and others. In the years that followed, Black began to share this story widely and became a passionate antiracist activist.

Black's story shows, first and foremost, the extent to which people can undergo a thoroughgoing moral conversion. If anyone in the white nationalist movement would have been deemed an impossible case, it would have been Black. But Black's story shows that we are never fully—or permanently—determined by the views we are raised with, no matter how strongly we believe in them. In order for our views to change, however, we must critically examine them, and this usually does not happen in isolation from others. Who would Black be today if the other students had been unwilling to engage in dialogue and debate? Who would Black be if Stevenson had not reached out?

Black's story is a case study in how real and profound change happens in a person: slowly, and through the engagement of both the head and the heart. On one hand, Black's friends asked questions about white nationalism, listened to the answers, and offered reasoned counterarguments, presenting evidence, and engaging Black regularly and repeatedly in discussion. Courses on history, culture, and religion played key roles, as well. But the shift in Black's beliefs was not only a product of reasoned argument and evidence; it was also a product of firsthand experience, and a matter of the heart. It was not just *anyone* who discussed these issues with Black; it was friends. Even more importantly, Black experienced knowing and having friends who came from different backgrounds, races, religions, and cultures. And Black developed real affection for them. Black listened to their experiences and empathized with them. It is not just that Black's mind was changed. Black underwent a change of heart, as well.

To me, one of the most interesting elements of this conversion story is that it unfolded within the context of a weekly ritual meal in Judaism. Stevenson showed Black real hospitality, and in Judaism the practice of hospitality is particularly important. The commandment to welcome and embrace the stranger appears thirty-six times in the Torah (the first five books of the Hebrew Bible). Jewish tradition also teaches that we should view others as made in God's image. The tradition of welcoming the stranger is seen in a wide range of traditional Jewish stories, including the story of Abraham, who rushes out into the desert to meet three strangers and invites them into his tent, helps them to wash, and serves them a meal (Genesis 18:1–8). Jewish Biblical exegesis known as Midrashic tradition holds that his tent opened on all four sides so that he could see and welcome anyone who approached, from any direction. In another story, Abraham ushered an elderly man into his tent, welcoming him just as he had welcomed the three strangers. But after dinner, the man took out an idol and began to worship it. Abraham was enraged and threw the man and his idol out of the tent. Abraham then heard the voice of God, telling him, "Abraham, Abraham! I have put up with that man and his idol worship for 75 years! Could you not have tolerated him for even a single night?" Ashamed, Abraham ran out into the night, apologized to the man, and welcomed him back into the tent.[15]

Stevenson's invitation to Black is an example of welcoming someone who approaches from *any* direction, and of showing them hospitality even if they offend you. Further, Stevenson did not invite Black to just *any* dinner. The relationship between these students developed in the context of Shabbat dinners—a weekly ritual observance in Judaism that commemorates the beginning of the Sabbath (the day of completion and rest that commemorates the seventh day of Creation) every Friday at sundown. As a ritual occasion, Shabbat dinner is the first of three sacred meals that are a part of the Sabbath. Rabbi Abraham Joshua Heschel writes, "There is a realm of time where the goal is not to have but to be, not to own but to give, not to control but to share, not to subdue but to be in accord."[16] Shabbat is that time.

The Torah refers to two commandments concerning Shabbat: to keep it (i.e., to observe it by refraining from forbidden activity) and to remember it (in one's words, thoughts, and actions). Shabbat dinners typically begin shortly before sundown with the lighting of two candles that symbolize these two commandments and the reciting of the traditional blessing: "Blessed are You, our God, Sovereign of the universe, who has sanctified us through Your mitzvot and commands us to light the Shabbat candles."[17] After the recitation of Genesis 2:1–3 (which describes the origins of the Sabbath in the Creation story), a blessing called Kiddush ("sanctification") is recited in Hebrew over a cup of wine:

> Blessed are You, our God, Creator of time and space, who enriches our lives with holiness, and who delights in us. With love and desire You have given us the holy Shabbat, a taste of the days of Creation. For it was the first among Your sacred days, a reminder of our liberation from Egypt. For you chose us from among all the nations, and You made us holy. With love and pleasure You gave us the holy Shabbat. Blessed are You, who hallows Shabbat.[18]

As these words show, the observance of Shabbat in Judaism serves as a reminder that the world has purpose and that humans have a role in this purpose. It involves giving thanks to God and affirming that the Jewish people are loved and chosen by God. Indeed, Shabbat cultivates and keeps alive the fundamental values of Judaism; as Ahad Ha'am put it, "Even more than the Jews have kept Shabbat, Shabbat has kept the Jews."[19]

The words of the Kiddush also recall God's deliverance of the Jews from slavery in Egypt. In this sense, Shabbat is *all about* redemption. Several ritual elements of Shabbat express this. Two loaves of *hallah* symbolize the miracle of God providing food for the Israelites as they wandered in the desert after the Exodus. Rabbi Nina Beth Cardin points out, "Some people don't cut the hallah with a knife; instead, they tear it with their hands as a reminder that Shabbat is a time of peace, when we dream that the nations will put aside their weapons of war."[20] These rituals, together with Jewish views of hospitality, form the basis of the view that all humans have dignity and worth—even if they hold vicious views that personally wound and offend us. The Torah commands us not only to observe Shabbat with a day of rest but also to *remember* it, making it special or sacred with our words, thoughts, and deeds. What Stevenson did in opening his apartment to his friends was precisely this. He made Shabbat even more sacred by opening himself and his home to Black and the possibility of redemption. As Stevenson recited blessings in Hebrew and tore the *hallah* at every Shabbat meal, even those who did not share his beliefs entered into and became a part of the sacred space at his table.

By creating sacred spaces like this, religions have real power. It is in part through these kinds of rituals that salvation occurs, both in the traditional sense and in Hick's ethical sense. While the conversations and friendship between Black, Stevenson, and their friends were the direct source of Black's moral conversion, the context for it was Shabbat. Rituals—as we have already seen in our study of Confucianism—are one of the primary ways in which religions do the work of conversion. This is often theological work, but it is also ethical work. Just imagine the power of this particular ritual, for an ostracized white nationalist who professed antisemitism and yet was still welcomed to the table by a Jewish friend. To be welcomed in this manner, week after week, may very well have had just as much effect on Black's conversion as the arguments and evidence their friends produced.

## Conclusion

Like the Jewish tradition's emphasis on hospitality, the Jesuit ideal of being "contemplatives in action" fundamentally concerns our willingness to engage with others. The Ignatian Spiritual Exercises are designed to lift us up from our knees and lead us to reach out to others, no matter who or where they are, especially in the most broken experiences and places. I experienced this firsthand when I made the *Exercises*, and they affected virtually every aspect of my daily life. It is important to notice the deep resonance between the Jewish and Christian traditions here concerning our obligations to the stranger. The Christian tradition, too, recognizes the Torah's commandment to welcome the stranger, and it is indebted to Judaism for the teaching that we ought to love our neighbor as ourselves. The Hebrew Bible tells us, "Do not neglect to show hospitality to strangers, for by doing that some have entertained angels without knowing it" (Hebrews 13:2). In the Gospels, Jesus tells his disciples, "In a little while the world will no longer see me, but you will see me" (John 14:19). Maybe—just maybe—Jesus meant that if we truly follow him, we will see him in the faces of all. In the words of the Christian contemplative (and contemporary of Ignatius) Saint Teresa of Avila (1515–82): "Christ has no body but yours, no hands, no feet on earth but yours. Yours are the eyes with which He looks compassion on the world. Yours are the feet with which He walks."[21]

And is this not what religious life is ultimately all about? Every major religion has at its core a set of ethical teachings, which are at once an outgrowth of and an expression of human encounters with God, the infinite, or the Real. These encounters do not leave us unchanged; nor do encounters with each other leave us unchanged, when we welcome each other to our tables and tents, opening them on all sides.

## Notes

Epigraphs:

Anne Lamott, *Almost Everything: Notes on Hope* (New York: Riverhead, 2018), 125–26.

Frederick Buechner, *Now and Then: A Memoir of Vocation* (New York: HarperOne, 1991). Quoted by Michael Gerson, "Frederick Buechner Was a Writer Tuned into the Frequency of Grace," *Washington Post*, August 22, 2022.

1. Historically, the Jesuits are known for spearheading the Catholic Reformation (or "Counter-Reformation") in the sixteenth century, which was a response to the Protestant Reformation. Beginning with Martin Luther's critiques of the Catholic Church in his *Ninety-Five Theses* (written in 1517), the Protestant Reformers' split from the Catholic Church launched a new branch of Christianity known as Protestantism, which would flourish globally and change Christian history forever. (Today, roughly half of the world's Christians are Catholic, while nearly 40 percent are Protestant and about 10 percent are Eastern Orthodox.) The Jesuits were instrumental in defending and reshaping Roman Catholicism in response to and as an alternative to the Protestant Reformations at the time.

2. Eli Saslow, "The White Flight of Derek Black," *Washington Post*, October 15, 2016. See also Eli Saslow, *Rising Out of Hatred: The Awakening of a Former White Nationalist* (New York: Doubleday, 2018); and R. Derek Black, *The Klansman's Son: My Journey from White Nationalism to Antiracism—A Memoir* (New York: Harry N. Abrams, 2024). In the latter work, Black comes out as transgender, using the pronouns they/them and she/her. I therefore use they/them pronouns for Black in this chapter.

3. Saslow, *Rising Out of Hatred*.

4. Saslow.

5. Black, *Klansman's Son*, 167.

6. Saslow, "White Flight."

7. Saslow.

8. Saslow.

9. Saslow.

10. Saslow.

11. Saslow.

12. Saslow.

13. Saslow.

14. Saslow.

15. Rabbi Stephen Lewis Fuchs, "What We Need to Know about Welcoming the Stranger," November 17, 2016, https://reformjudaism.org/blog/what-we-need-know-about-welcoming-stranger.

16. Quoted by Rabbi Nina Beth Cardin, *The Tapestry of Jewish Time: A Spiritual Guide to Holidays and Life-Cycle Events* (Springfield, NJ: Behrman House, 2000), 35.

17. Cardin, 38.

18. Cardin, 258.

19. Quoted by Cardin, 35.

20. Cardin, 40.

21. Though this quotation does not appear in Saint Teresa of Avila's collected works, it is widely attributed to her.

# CONCLUSION

Watch 365 sunrises. This was my New Year's Resolution.

My students always look at me in disbelief when I tell them this story. The idea of being awake when the sun rises is, for many if not most college students, almost unfathomable.

For me, this was a lesson in change, even though I expected to be anchored by the constancy of seeing the sunrise each day (and I was). But it was also a lesson in surprise. The American Catholic Benedictine monk David Steindl-Rast, OSB, writes, "Humdrum equals deadness; surprise equals life. In fact, my favorite name for the One I worship in wonder—the only name that does not limit God—is Surprise."[1]

For one thing, I learned how much the timing and position of the sunrise changes as I watched it rise at 5:43 on June 21, and after 7:30 in late October. I watched it rise in the summer on my back porch facing northeast, coffee in hand as the hummingbirds drank from their feeder and the blue jays bathed in the birdbath. (And from my hometown in south central Alaska, where the summer sun rises over the glacier very early indeed.) I watched it rise in autumn and winter while facing southeast from my "sunrise spot" in the living room, occasionally dashing outside in my slippers to take pictures.

I learned that to see the most stunning color, you need to start watching about 30 minutes before the sun actually rises. But about 50 minutes before sunrise, the first light appears, and that gentle sapphire sky is pretty stunning, too. I learned that every sunrise is different, as my daily journal attests: "Ribbons of lavender, pink, blue, yellow-peach." "The sky looks like a marble this morning—streaks of white against blue, and orange just starting on the horizon at 7 am." "A watercolor spectrum sky out the window this morning, trees silhouetted against it: yellow, blue, peach, orange, pink, then purple."

I learned that sometimes you cannot see the sunrise at all because of cloud cover; it just gets light. But other times, I could not contain my excitement: I flew into my children's bedrooms, pulling open the curtains of their east-facing windows. My son—a fellow early riser—jumped up, proclaiming the beauty, while my daughters rubbed their eyes and smiled sleepily as I pointed to the bands of yellow, peach, pink, and lavender stretching across the sky. (Another lesson: sunrises are better when shared with people you love.)

The poet Mary Oliver used to begin every morning standing outside her door, with her pen in hand and notebook open. She is someone who was always up for Surprise. I have a close friend who loves to watch the sunrise, too, and sometimes she texts me early in the morning with one word: "Sky." This is my cue to get to a window and take a look. The writer Jan Richardson says, "I cannot tell you how the light comes, but that it does, . . . though it may seem long ages in coming or arrive in a shape you did not foresee."[2] I can attest to what she says: I watched the light arrive 365 times in one year.

And how true it is that so very often, the light arrives in a form we were not expecting. Religious texts frequently document this. In the *Bhagavad Gita*, Arjuna hardly expects a vision of Krishna's totality—"the light of a thousand suns"—to appear the day he trudges into battle in tears. The Biblical story of the birth of Isaac to Abraham and Sarah in their old age is such a surprise that Sarah laughs (and they name him Isaac, derived from the Hebrew term for laughter). The Gospel of Matthew tells us about kings or magi who followed a star to Bethlehem to visit the infant Jesus at the request of the brutal King Herod, who asked them to report back. But it was not at all what they expected. They were "overwhelmed with joy" when the star stopped over Bethlehem, and "on entering the house, they saw the child with Mary his mother, and they knelt down and paid him homage. Then, opening their treasure chests, they offered him gifts of gold, frankincense, and myrrh. And having been warned in a dream not to return to Herod, they left for their own country by another road" (Matthew 2:1–12). The last line of this passage might be the most important part of the story. As the Reverend Sharlande Sledge puts it,

> The kings, high atop camels, their velvet robes gilded with desert sand, were impressive in their grandeur, knowledge, and exotic travels. Little did they know that their search for a Child would become legendary; their quest, a journey in which all our journeys echo; their worship, a model of humbleness; their commitment to their pilgrimage so true that every wobbly camel step through the desert to their place of arrival mattered more than anything else they could have been doing in their old kingdoms. . . . Matthew says "they went home by another road way." No doubt, they confounded Herod by taking a different geographical route. But the different way they went home was likely a way of the heart as well.[3]

As we have seen throughout this book, religious narratives contain layer upon layer of meaning. They often tell of journeys that have different shapes and routes. And these journeys usually do not end the way we anticipate. As we know, life often sends us in unexpected directions, and many times, we find ourselves going home by another way.

From the journeys of their own lives, religions, and cultures, the authors whose thoughts we have explored in this book have guided us in our exploration of the Problem of God, including different challenges to faith, religion, and spirituality.[4] Some tell about wandering with no end in sight as they have looked for God. This was certainly true for Augustine, in his long journey toward God. The sense that we are wandering with no end in sight frequently characterizes the search for God in the midst of pain and suffering, as we grapple with the Problem of Evil and consider the responses of different theodicies. Other journeys are as circuitous as a labyrinth, such as the quests to demonstrate God's existence by Anselm, Aquinas, and the members of the Nyaya tradition, and the critical responses to their proofs by interlocutors like Gaunilo, Kant, and Rowe. Some let us in on how spiritual friends have been their companions on the way, such as Arjuna, who finds that he is not alone on the battlefield with Krishna by his side, and Derek Black, who was welcomed to the Shabbat table by friends.

Others, such as the early Daoists, understood the journey as one of overcoming the confusions and hollow ways of the world, in order to return by another way to their original home with the Dao. Still others offer arguments and raise questions to push and pull us along to new places along the road—something we saw in Pascal's wager, and in Hick's discussion of religious inclusivism and pluralism. Some, like Ignatius, tell of travels that involved risk, imagination, or change in direction, or of stopping points along the way, where critics of religious faith prompted them to think more carefully about what and why they believe. Other traditions, like Confucianism, focus on how we come to find not just any other way, but *the* Way, revealed to past sages by a more ultimate yet mysterious entity that has a plan for us. All the different religious traditions and thinkers whose works we have explored offer stories of how goodness and love found them as they sought another way home.

I began this book with the story of a young soldier who, on Christmas Eve, at the height of World War I, led his fellow soldiers on the Western Front in an unofficial ceasefire. They all sought to go home by a different way. I hope that you, too, as a result of the texts, traditions, and stories you have encountered in this book, will journey home by another way. In other words, I hope the ideas, experiences, and people you have read about will leave you changed in some way—whether it is a deeper understanding of your own commitments and values or a new appreciation for the remarkable range of religious and spiritual journeys in this world. But I have a further, experiential hope for you, as well.

The year I watched 365 sunrises, my astrophysicist brother was keen to remind me that the sun does not *actually* rise; it only appears to rise and set because of the Earth's rotation. In other words: *we* are the ones who are rotating, while the sun remains in place at the center of our solar system. It is a lesson in perspective, but it is the theological and philosophical dimensions of our perspective—as opposed to the astronomical ones—that intrigue me most. Perhaps the most challenging Problem of God is that in our finitude, our perspective on the infinite is always profoundly limited. We do not always perceive the infinite, and when we do, we often catch only fleeting glimmers of it, like sunlight reflected on water. My greatest hope is that readers of this book will be more open to, and more aware of, the possibility of Surprise. I hope you will linger longer over the things that inspire a sense of awe that takes your breath away, and I hope you will stop to dwell on the experiences that bring you a peace that surpasses understanding—be it the colors in the sunrise, the ocean's vastness, a love that surprises you with joy and gratitude, or the light that shines in the darkness and is not overcome by it.

## Notes

1. David Steindl-Rast, "Giving Thanks for All the Little (and Big) Things in Life," *Spirituality and Health*, Winter 2002: 34, https://grateful.org/resource/giving-thanks-big-little/.
2. Jan Richardson, "How the Light Comes," in *Circle of Grace* (Orlando: Wanton Gospeller Press, 2015), 60.
3. Sharlande Sledge, "Introduction," in "Home By Another Way," Advent Meditation Book, manuscript, Lake Shore Baptist Church, Waco, Texas, 2022.
4. Sledge. I am indebted to the Reverend Sharlande Sledge for her description of different kinds of pilgrimages, which I incorporate into this paragraph.

# Guide to Further Reading


### William Paley, the Teleological Argument, and Science and Religion

William Paley, "The Teleological Argument," in *Ten Essential Texts in the Philosophy of Religion*, ed. Steven M. Cahn (New York: Oxford University Press, 2004).

———, *Natural Theology*, ed. Matthew D. Eddy and David Knight (New York: Oxford University Press, 2008).

F. C. Copleston, "Aquinas' Five Proofs," in *Ten Essential Texts in the Philosophy of Religion*, ed. Steven M. Cahn (New York: Oxford University Press, 2004).

Guy Consolmagno, SJ, *When Science Goes Wrong: The Desire and Search for Truth* (Mahwah, NJ: Paulist Press, 2023).

———, *God's Mechanics: How Scientists and Engineers Make Sense of Religion* (New York: Jossey-Bass, 2007).

Kenneth Miller, *Finding Darwin's God: A Scientist's Search for Common Ground Between God and Evolution* (New York: Harper Perennial, 2007).

### Aquinas and the Cosmological Argument

Thomas Aquinas, "*Summa Theologiae* (I, 1, 2)," in *Ten Essential Texts in the Philosophy of Religion*, ed. Steven M. Cahn (New York: Oxford University Press, 2004).

Denys Turner, *Thomas Aquinas: A Portrait* (New Haven, CT: Yale University Press, 2013).

Richard Taylor, "The Cosmological Argument: A Defense," in *Ten Essential Texts in the Philosophy of Religion*, ed. Steven M. Cahn (New York: Oxford University Press, 2004).

William Rowe, *The Cosmological Argument* (New York: Fordham University Press, 1998).

———, "The Cosmological Argument: A Critique," in *Ten Essential Texts in the Philosophy of Religion*, ed. Steven M. Cahn (New York: Oxford University Press, 2004).

William Lane Craig, *The Kalam Cosmological Argument* (Eugene, OR: Wipf and Stock, 2000).

———, *How Do We Know God Exists?* (Bellingham, WA: Lexham Press, 2022).

### Anselm and the Ontological Argument

Anselm, *Monologion and Proslogion: With the Replies of Gaunilo and Anselm* (Indianapolis: Hackett, 1996).

Richard W. Southern, *St. Anselm: A Portrait in a Landscape* (Cambridge: Cambridge University Press, 2002).

Immanuel Kant, "The Impossibility of an Ontological Proof of the Existence of God," in *Ten Essential Texts in the Philosophy of Religion*, ed. Steven M. Cahn (New York: Oxford University Press, 2004).

William L. Rowe, "The Ontological Argument," in *Ten Essential Texts in the Philosophy of Religion*, ed. Steven M. Cahn (New York: Oxford University Press, 2004).

### Nyaya Proofs for God's Existence, *The Bhagavad Gita*, Hinduism, and Buddhism

Matthew Dasti and Stephen Phillips, trans., *The Nyaya-sutra: Selections with Early Commentaries* (Indianapolis: Hackett, 2017).

Patrick Bresnan, *Awakening: An Introduction to the History of Eastern Thought* (New York: Routledge, 2021).

Juan Mascaro, trans., *The Upanishads* (New York: Penguin Classics, 1965).

Barbara Stoler Miller, trans., *The Bhagavad-Gita: Krishna's Counsel in Time of War* (New York: Bantam Classic, 2004).

Francis X. Clooney, SJ, *Hindu Wisdom for All God's Children* (Eugene, OR: Wipf and Stock, 2005).

Stephen P. Huyler. *Meeting God: Elements of Hindu Devotion* (New Haven, CT: Yale University Press, 2002).

Walpola Rahula, *What the Buddha Taught* (New York: Grove Press, 1974).

### Confucianism and Daoism

Edward G. Slingerland, trans., *Analects of Confucius: With Selections from Traditional Commentaries* (Indianapolis: Hackett, 2003).

Erin M. Cline, *The Analects: A Guide* (New York: Oxford University Press, 2021).

———, *Little Sprouts and the Dao of Parenting: Ancient Chinese Philosophy and the Art of Raising Mindful, Resilient, and Compassionate Kids* (New York: W. W. Norton, 2020).

Philip J. Ivanhoe, *Confucian Reflections: Ancient Wisdom for Modern Times* (New York: Routledge, 2013).

———, trans., *The Daodejing of Laozi* (Indianapolis: Hackett, 2003).

Bryan W. Van Norden, *Introduction to Classical Chinese Philosophy* (Indianapolis: Hackett, 2011).

### Augustine

John K. Ryan, trans., *The Confessions of Saint Augustine* (New York: Image, 1960).

Garry Wills, *Saint Augustine* (New York: Penguin, 1999).

Carl G. Vaught, *The Journey toward God in Augustine's Confessions (Books I–VI)*, *Encounters with God in Augustine's Confessions (Books VII–IX)*, and *Access to God in Augustine's Confessions (Books X–XIII)* (Albany: State University of New York Press, 2003, 2004, and 2005).

### The Problem of Evil, Atheism, and God's Omnipotence

John Hick, "The Problem of Evil," in *Ten Essential Texts in the Philosophy of Religion*, ed. Steven M. Cahn (New York: Oxford University Press, 2004).

———, *Evil and the God of Love* (New York: Palgrave Macmillan, 2010).

Salih Sayilgan, *God, Evil, and Suffering in Islam* (New York: Cambridge University Press, 2023).

Harry G. Frankfurt, "The Logic of Omnipotence," in *Ten Essential Texts in the Philosophy of Religion*, ed. Steven M. Cahn (New York: Oxford University Press, 2004).

George Mavrodes, "Some Puzzles Concerning Omnipotence," in *Ten Essential Texts in the Philosophy of Religion*, ed. Steven M. Cahn (New York: Oxford University Press, 2004).

Wiliam Rowe, "The Problem of Evil and Some Varieties of Atheism," in *Ten Essential Texts in the Philosophy of Religion* (New York: Oxford University Press, 2005), 301–11.

Anne Lamott, *Almost Everything: Notes on Hope* (New York: Riverhead, 2018).

### Pascal's Wager

Blaise Pascal, "The Wager," in *Ten Essential Texts in the Philosophy of Religion*, ed. Steven M. Cahn (New York: Oxford University Press, 2004).

———, *Pensées and Other Writings*, trans. Honor Levi (New York: Oxford University Press, 1995).

Marvin R. O'Connell, *Blaise Pascal: Reasons of the Heart* (Grand Rapids: Eerdmans, 1997).

Simon Blackburn, "Pascal's Wager: A Critique," in *Ten Essential Texts in the Philosophy of Religion*, ed. Steven M. Cahn (New York: Oxford University Press, 2004).

### Religious Pluralism

John Hick, "Religious Pluralism and Salvation," in *Ten Essential Texts in the Philosophy of Religion*, ed. Steven M. Cahn (New York: Oxford University Press, 2004).

———, *An Interpretation of Religion: Human Responses to the Transcendent, Second Edition* (New Haven, CT: Yale University Press, 2005).

———, *The Fifth Dimension: An Exploration of the Spiritual Realm* (New York: Oneworld, 2013).

Karl Rahner, *Encounters with Silence*, 2nd edition (South Bend, IN: St. Augustine's Press, 1999).

Karen Kilby, *A Brief Introduction to Karl Rahner* (Durham, NC: Publishdrive, 2007).

### Ignatius of Loyola, Conversion, and Faith

Joseph Tylenda, SJ, *A Pilgrim's Journey: The Autobiography of Ignatius of Loyola* (San Francisco: Ignatius Press, 2009).

Kevin O'Brien, SJ, *The Ignatian Adventure: Experiencing the Spiritual Exercises of St. Ignatius in Daily Life* (Chicago: Loyola Press, 2011).

Erin M. Cline, *A World on Fire: Sharing the Ignatian Spiritual Exercises with Other Religions* (Washington, DC: Catholic University of America Press, 2018).

Frederick Buechner, *Now and Then: A Memoir of Vocation* (New York: HarperOne, 1991).

Amy Butler, *Beautiful and Terrible Things: Faith, Doubt, and Discovering a Way Back to Each Other* (New York: The Dial Press, 2023).

Mike McHargue, *Finding God in the Waves: How I Lost My Faith and Found It Again Through Science* (New York: Convergent Books, 2017).

Anne Lamott, *Traveling Mercies: Some Thoughts on Faith* (New York: Anchor, 2000).

Eli Saslow, *Rising Out of Hatred: The Awakening of a Former White Nationalist* (New York: Anchor, 2019).

# Index